REFORMING AMERICA
1815–1860

A NORTON D

REFORMING AMERICA 1815–1860

A NORTON DOCUMENTS READER

Joshua D. Rothman

W. W. NORTON & COMPANY

New York / London

W. W. Norton & Company has been independent since its founding in 1923, when William Warder Norton and Mary D. Herter Norton first published lectures delivered at the People's Institute, the adult education division of New York City's Cooper Union. The Norton's soon expanded their program beyond the Institute, publishing books by celebrated academics from America and abroad. By mid-century, the two major pillars of Norton's publishing program—trade books and college texts—were firmly established. In the 1950s, the Norton family transferred control of the company to its employees, and today—with a staff of four hundred and a comparable number of trade, college, and professional titles published each year—W. W. Norton & Company stands as the largest and oldest publishing house owned wholly by its employees.

Manufacturing by the Courier Companies—Westford division
Book design by Jo Anne Metsch
Production manager: Eric Pier-Hocking

Library of Congress Cataloging-in-Publication Data

Rothman, Joshua D.
    Reforming America, 1815–1860 : a Norton documents reader / Joshua D. Rothman.
        — 1st ed.
    p. cm. — (Norton documents reader series)
    Includes bibliographical references and index.

ISBN 978-0-393-93226-3 (pbk.)

    1. Social problems—United States—History—19th century. 2. Social movements—
United States—History—19th century. 3. Social reformers—United States—History—
19th century. 4. United States—Social conditions—19th century. I. Title.
HN64.R8845 2010
303.48′4097309034—dc22

                                                                        2009028412

W. W. Norton & Company, Inc., 500 Fifth Avenue, New York, N.Y. 10110
www.wwnorton.com

W. W. Norton & Company Ltd., Castle House, 75/76 Wells Street, London W1T 3QT
1 2 3 4 5 6 7 8 9 0

CONTENTS

ACKNOWLEDGMENTS

I would like to thank my friend and colleague Margaret Abruzzo for reading and offering suggestions on what was originally a much longer version of the introduction. Thanks as well to Karl Bakeman, who first encouraged me to put together the proposal for this book, and to Jon Durbin and Jason Spears, who guided it through the production process.

INTRODUCTION

In the decades before the Civil War, movements to reform American lives swept the United States. Reformers endeavored to stamp out what they perceived as sin and vice, to contain the worst excesses and consequences of capitalism, to improve conditions for the less fortunate, to broaden the meaning of freedom, and to make American society not just better, but perfect. They reconsidered their personal identities, brought new approaches to family and community life, and looked to make themselves physically healthy and spiritually vibrant people primed for the rigors of the modern world. Antebellum reformers believed they lived in an especially challenging and fast-moving age, but also that a better nation would emerge from their grappling with its demands and possibilities.

Reform activities reflected the antebellum era's characteristic blend of optimism and anxiety. In the first half of the nineteenth century the nation became more politically democratic and militarily powerful, and its physical expansion dovetailed with technological innovations to offer exciting economic prospects for a large, diverse, and mobile population. These trends made Americans tremendously confident in themselves and the country, and many imagined a future of limitless progress and prosperity. But reformers also saw obstacles and pitfalls littering the path to national greatness. For some, America's vaunted embrace of individual liberty seemed hopelessly compromised by the growth of slavery, extensive restrictions on the rights of women, and cruel treatment of the mentally ill. Others realized that while economic and territorial growth created wealth and opportunity it also yielded widespread instability, massive class disparities, and unabashed greed and materialism, suggesting the need to reconstitute or shore up familiar social arrangements, behavioral norms, cultural institutions, and religious morality. Reformers were a varied lot with wide-ranging ideas, strategies, and goals. But they generally shared the belief that a bright future depended on the American people finding moral integrity, lifting limitations on human potential, and maintaining social cohesion amid tumultuous change. Examining their efforts offers insight to central components of antebellum American culture. Moreover, as technology and the forces of globalization make uncertain our own moorings and futures, it provides invaluable lessons about how previous generations struggled with a world in flux and boldly imagined a better one.

Making the Age of Reform

The reform impulse in American life was inextricable from demographic, territorial, and economic changes so rapid and dramatic that by the outbreak of the Civil War the United States only vaguely resembled what it had looked like at the end of the colonial period. Instead of a seaboard nation threatened by European and Native American enemies, by 1860 the United States had become a continental power, its geographic reach extending from less than one million square miles to more than three million and its population growing from less than four million people to more than thirty million, nearly half of whom lived west of the Appalachian Mountains. As the nation's land claims grew larger, meanwhile, the country also became an economic dynamo by building an infrastructure comprising thousands of miles of roads and canals and railroads, developing more sophisticated financial and legal systems, and capitalizing on technologies ranging from the cotton gin and the mechanical reaper to the steam engine and the telegraph. Many historians have referred to these transformations as a "market revolution" for the way they made the country over from an economy rooted in local networks of farmers, artisans, and home manufacturers to an integrated commercial economy operating on a national scale. Whatever term is used to describe what transpired, one thing was unmistakable. Between the cotton, corn, wheat, and other farm products of its countryside and the textiles and other consumer goods made in its growing number of mills and factories, by mid-century the United States was among the leading economic producers in the world.[1]

These economic changes, in turn, were intimately linked to the growth of cities. As connection points for America's growing transportation system, as locations that gathered countryside agricultural products for market sale, and as population centers that provided labor forces for employers, cities were crucial to the country's development. In 1800, around 6 percent of the American population lived in cities, defined at the time as places with over 2,500 residents. Just two cities, New York and Philadelphia, had more than 50,000 inhabitants, and five of America's ten largest cities had fewer than 15,000 people. By 1860, though, nearly 20 percent of the population lived in urban areas, and in the northeast almost a third did. By 1860, over a dozen cities were bigger than the biggest city had been in 1800, and more than forty cities housed over 20,000 people. New York City's population alone grew from just over 60,000 in 1800 to more than 800,000 in 1860.

Older eastern cities like Boston, New York, Philadelphia, and Baltimore grew by combining the advantages of being ports, canal destinations, road and rail hubs, and manufacturing centers. The invention of the steamboat, meanwhile, made it possible to move people and goods efficiently both with and against river currents, turning western places like St. Louis, Pittsburgh, Louisville, and Cincinnati from villages and trade outposts into bustling commercial cities. The Erie Canal, running more than 360 miles across New York State, connected the Hudson River to Lake Erie and helped make New York the largest and most important city in America. But it also led to the rise of Great Lake cities like Buffalo, Cleveland, Detroit, Milwaukee, and Chicago, and prompted along its route the development of cities like Rochester, Syracuse, and Utica. Even below the level of large cities, urbanization was noticeable. Dozens of places that had been sleepy hamlets of hundreds early in the nineteenth century transformed into thriving small cit-

---

[1] The strongest statement of the "market revolution" thesis remains Charles Sellers, *The Market Revolution: Jacksonian America, 1815–1846* (New York, 1991). For a somewhat different take on the changes of the era, see Daniel Walker Howe, *What Hath God Wrought: The Transformation of America, 1815–1848* (New York, 2007).

ies of thousands. In 1800, for example, just around twenty-five places could claim between 2,500 and 10,000 inhabitants. By 1860, more than 300 could.

It was a heady time to be an American, and many found it thrilling. A thriving and expanding United States yielded a burgeoning sense of pride and nationalism. Markets, railroads, and newspapers connected Americans to goods and people in far-flung places, enabling them to imagine themselves parts of large economic, cultural, and political networks. Moreover, it seemed anyone could grab a piece of American prosperity through nothing but hard work, determination, and a little luck. If your birthplace frustrated your ambitions, you could simply pick up and move to a flourishing western frontier or a booming city. The era ultimately produced an ethos grounded in the notions that the United States had boundless national prospects and that its individual citizens could rise above their origins, make new lives for themselves, and achieve anything they imagined. This was the age when the self-made man emerged as a vital cultural archetype, exemplified by people as different in politics and temperament as backwoods wastrel turned plantation owner Andrew Jackson and self-educated frontiersman turned corporate lawyer Abraham Lincoln.

Yet the very changes and possibilities that excited so many could be profoundly disconcerting. Territorial expansion made for confidence. But confidence lent itself to arrogance and to fervor for warfare whenever the nation's imperial designs faced resistance from people whose lands white Americans craved. Migrating to frontiers and cities offered second chances. But large-scale migration created upheaval that threatened social cohesiveness and undid traditional sources of authority like the family, the church, and the community. An integrated national economy brought prosperity and gave Americans the sense they could direct their own fates and make their own fortunes. But it engaged them in economic relations with people they had neither met nor seen, and left them vulnerable to forces they neither controlled nor fully understood—a reality made frighteningly clear during crippling depressions that occurred three different times in the antebellum era. Industrial, commercial, and urban development offered new kinds of economic opportunities. But human relationships in industrial, commercial, and urban society seemed coarse, insincere, amoral, hyper-individualistic, and inherently combative, the ruthless quest for profits among throngs of strangers running roughshod over concerns for one's spiritual life, one's fellow man, or the public good.

Perhaps most disturbing and disorienting, urbanization and industrialization fundamentally altered how millions organized their domestic lives. Before the nineteenth century, most American households were organized around economic production, with men, women, and even children working together toward a family's survival. Men generally worked in the fields or a small shop while women raised children, minded small livestock, and produced household goods like cloth and soap. But despite a gendered division of labor, family economies were inescapably collective enterprises in which every person had an important role he or she was expected to fill.

As the nineteenth century progressed, however, the understanding of households and families as self-sufficient economic units went into some decline. It hardly disappeared, of course, and most Americans remained farmers. But as the commercial economy penetrated even previously isolated rural areas many were tempted to abandon the household production model and become commercial farmers instead—growing grain, cultivating produce and dairy products, or raising livestock on a large scale primarily for market sale, and purchasing at stores goods previously made at home.

Changes in household economies were even more pronounced for Americans in cities and towns. There, the very nature of making a living changed, as workplace and home increasingly became distinct places. Instead of working on or near their own property and trading goods and services with neighbors, men started going to work—leaving their homes in the morning, working a predetermined number of hours, and returning in the evenings with cash wages. And larger numbers of those men began making money in new ways offered by the urban economy. Instead of working in small craft shops, they could run stores selling groceries or consumer goods. They might enter the swelling professional ranks and become doctors, lawyers, ministers, or teachers. Younger men in particular started following career paths that had hardly existed when their fathers were growing up but that in the antebellum era seemed promising and exciting, working in offices as accountants, bookkeepers, clerks, insurance salesmen, and managers of factories and other businesses.

In the families of such men, meanwhile, domestic labor traditionally performed by women became less necessary and often less cost effective. Servants could be hired to do much of the housework, and given the spread of cheap, quality consumer items accompanying expanding markets and factory production, it made more sense to use cash that men earned at work to buy household items at the store than to make them at home. All in all, where families in the eighteenth century had been held together by mutual responsibilities for economic survival, in the nineteenth century men were more likely to meet that responsibility by themselves. Where women had filled their days and nights with domestic tasks, as time passed they had less to do in the home and, especially for married women, very few opportunities to work outside it.

These sorts of shifts threatened to become a crisis in American family life. They raised questions about what would hold families together if not a common economic purpose and about what roles women would fulfill if men alone were going to provide for their families' material welfare. They provoked concerns about how the young would be prepared for the challenges of a rapidly changing world if not by the discipline and moral training imparted while learning and laboring among a tightly knit, well-ordered family and community. Amid the antebellum era's unsettling instabilities, it seemed that customary understandings of family life were just one more thing thrown into turmoil and imperiled with incoherence.

In the face of such anxieties, a new understanding of domestic life emerged in the United States, in which home and work became as distinct in culture as they were becoming in practice. Instead of seeing the home primarily as a site of production and the place where one engaged and participated in the economic world, antebellum Americans increasingly viewed it as precisely the opposite. They came to imagine the home as a refuge and hiding place from the world, a shelter where family life provided love, companionship, and comfort while aggressive, impersonal, and competitive forces

of moneymaking swirled outside the front door. In lieu of cooperative economic production, these less tangible but equally real bonds
of emotion and sentiment would hold American families together
while they steeled themselves to meet the demands of the
marketplace.

This rethinking of family life also entailed rethinking the roles
and responsibilities of men and women more broadly, with the
worlds of work and home acquiring gender-specific meanings.
More and more, Americans described men and women as rightly
inhabiting discrete "spheres" of influence appropriate to their sex.
Men, understood to be innately aggressive, carnal, rational, and
competitive, were to find the highest expressions of their nature in
the public realms of politics and the marketplace, working and
providing materially for their families. Women, by contrast, understood to be innately passive, emotional, chaste, moral, and religious,
found the highest expressions of their nature in the private domestic realm, becoming mothers and establishing a loving and secure
abode for their husbands and children.

Obviously, these divisions of space and character did not objec-
tively describe how men and women "really" were, what their lives
were like, or even what they necessarily wanted. On the contrary,
such norms were consciously crafted ideological creations. In
magazines, newspapers, etiquette guides, religious tracts, and other
inexpensive popular literature that proliferated in the antebellum
era, American men and women received recommendations about
proper and improper ways to behave, dress, eat, deal in business,
speak to acquaintances, find a spouse, regulate their sex lives, maintain a home, raise children, and countless other facets of life. Books
like *The Young Man's Guide* and *A Treatise on Domestic Economy*, and
periodicals like *Godey's Lady's Book* were essential reading materials,
and prominent authors like William Alcott and Catherine Beecher
became household names valued for the lessons they had to offer
and the wisdom they had to convey.

Given their uneasiness about impersonality becoming more
prevalent in society, it might seem peculiar for Americans to take
advice about such important and intimate matters from strangers.
But the prescriptive mores and values forwarded by these authors

provided a model of stability and order to people hungry for one. They promised individuals not only the ability to assert control over what was happening to and around them in a confusing age but also that they could succeed amid those changes. If men were hard-working, frugal, and self-disciplined, and if they avoided the temptations of sin and vice; if women were selfless, pious, affectionate, and morally upstanding; if each found a spouse with complementary virtues who understood and accepted his or her proper familial and social roles; and if as a couple they passed such values on to their children within the nurturing confines of a loving home, they would find happiness, domestic harmony, and economic prosperity. Moreover, collectively they would provide a sound foundation for the United States and keep it from devolving from tumult into chaos. As one popular author suggested in the 1840s, "even if we cannot reform the world in a moment, we can begin the work by reforming ourselves and our households."[2]

It is crucial to recognize that while the advocates of these values believed them to be universally appropriate, the values came out of and spoke to a particular kind of experience. The idealized sentimental home where women could devote their energies to light domestic chores and raising honest and industrious children bore little resemblance to the lives of most working-class, poor, and enslaved families, in which women were more likely to be servants than to hire them and nearly everyone had to work long hours to survive. Rather, the new values of home and family resonated especially with members of the growing middle class concentrated in burgeoning northeastern cities and towns. Not simply "middling" individuals who were neither rich nor poor, these were the men employed in offices and stores who earned enough to furnish comfortable homes for their families, and the women who had time to maintain those homes and act as moral guides for their offspring. Relatively new in American life, the middle class was primarily responsible for articulating this new worldview, in which everyone ought to aspire to "respectability."

[2] T. S. Arthur, *The Lady at Home* (Philadelphia, 1847), cited in Barbara Welter, "The Cult of True Womanhood, 1820–1860," *American Quarterly* 18, no. 2, part 1 (Summer 1966): 162–163.

But if this worldview grew especially out of a regional class experience, it had extensive power and influence. Members of the middle class lived all across the United States, and they were hardly the only Americans worried about the breakdown of a familiar socioeconomic order and how to raise children in an unfamiliar one. The mores of the middle class, in fact, arguably became the most culturally powerful mores in antebellum America. Middle-class men and women wrote most of the newspaper articles and books advocating a new morality, and those articles and books were not read within their class alone. As members of the middle class became teachers and educational leaders, meanwhile, they spread their values to children of varying backgrounds in emerging public school systems. And middle-class Americans would provide much of the energy for antebellum reform movements, as they determined that their values held the key to widespread individual and social improvement.

Hardly all members of the middle class became reformers, and hardly all reformers came from the middle class. Indeed, some people were driven to engage in reform by the sense that middle-class values, which allowed Americans to adjust to and embrace socioeconomic change, were precisely the problem with the United States, and that the country needed to head down a different path altogether. Nonetheless, the domestic ideology of the middle class became central to antebellum social and cultural life. Whether reformers hoped to further that ideology or convince Americans to reject it, it was a framework for thinking and talking about where the nation and its people ought to be headed within which nearly all of them worked.

The Call to Action

Remaining to be explained is the reformers' sense of mission, their conviction that changing others and the nation as they had changed themselves was not merely possible but their obligation. A widespread secular belief in human progress provided some of the intellectual urgency for reform. As heirs of the Enlightenment, whose philosophers stressed mankind's ability to comprehend the world's workings and improve the human condition through reason, many nineteenth-century Americans had a fundamentally optimistic view of human nature. Reformers tended to believe people were basically good and possessed roughly equal moral capacities, that they could accomplish great things if given genuine opportunities to do so, that failure to fulfill their potential was due more to unfavorable social environments than to innate or fixed personality flaws, and that it was possible to create environments in which all people could thrive.

If ideas derived broadly from the Enlightenment gave reformers the sense that no human condition was unchangeable, the specific context of pre–Civil War America only enhanced that sense. Just as Americans generally believed people could make their own destinies and fortunes through hard work and determination, reformers in particular believed they could make the nation as a whole even better than it was by eradicating limitations on human achievement, thus unleashing the best the human spirit had to offer. Reformers had misgivings about their changing world, but they did not lack confidence to address matters that concerned them. On the contrary, they felt that precisely because they lived in the United States, they had the ability and the responsibility to do so. In fact, as legatees of the Revolution as well as the Enlightenment, many reformers envisioned their activities as attempts to realize the ideals of virtue, freedom, and equality enshrined in the Declaration of Independence.

One influential strain of thought fusing belief in unlimited human potential with the sense that antebellum America was a time and place of enormous possibility was transcendentalism. Essayist and orator Ralph Waldo Emerson was probably the most famous and significant transcendentalist. But Emerson was just one among a cluster of authors, journalists, poets, and intellectuals, mostly based in New England, who insisted that Americans need only have courage, passion, and confidence in themselves to find spiritual fulfillment. Transcendentalists argued that materialism, traditional belief systems, and social institutions stifled individuality, but also that those brave enough to use their intuition, to discover for themselves what was genuinely true, and to live by that truth regardless of what others said and believed could liberate themselves from those influences, escape conformity, and find lives of integrity and meaning.

In some ways transcendentalists advocated an exaggerated version of the era's individualism that seems contrary to the spirit of reform. But transcendentalism was not necessarily so self-centered a creed as it might appear. Transcendentalists believed every person had to find truth for himself or herself, but they also stressed the importance of acting upon that truth. Ultimately, transcendentalism called for engagement with the world, for showing what a principled life looked like, and for attacking institutions and breaking down barriers that prevented social progress by denying people the freedom to become self-directed. As Emerson argued in 1837, the thinking person's responsibility was "to cheer, to raise, and to guide men by showing them facts amidst appearances."[3] Accordingly, many individuals inspired by transcendentalism became reformers, especially in the antislavery and women's rights movements, driven by the idea that all persons possessed the absolute right to live as free and equal human beings.

Part metaphysical philosophy and part ethical code for living, transcendentalism was spiritual without being religious in any conventional sense, and even individuals who considered themselves freethinkers or atheists could be quite energetic reformers. Industrialist Robert Owen, for example, did not believe in God yet helped pioneer the creation of socialist utopian communities and was active in labor and education reform. Most reformers, however, were motivated at least partially by a religious imperative. Some were drawn to reform by rationalist Protestant theologies like Unitarianism and Universalism, both of which stressed the need for Christians to do good and moral works in pursuit of universal human brotherhood and salvation. Downplaying God's wrath and mankind's innate sinfulness, Unitarians and Universalists emphasized instead God's boundless love and the possibilities for improving the world by using reason when reading Scripture and acting upon the teachings of Jesus.

Unitarianism appealed especially to wealthy and educated individuals, which gave the denomination influence beyond its numbers. But in the grand scheme of antebellum religious life,

[3] Ralph Waldo Emerson, *Essays and Lectures* (New York, 1983), 63.

Unitarians and Universalists attracted relatively few converts, their strengths centering primarily in New England. To some extent, both spoke theologically to the spirit of the times by rejecting the hopelessness of the human condition. In accentuating calm rationalism and an intellectual rather than an emotional approach to faith, however, both lacked an experiential intensity that many Americans sought. Fearing the nation was headed toward disorder, secularism, and materialism, thousands wanted faith that offered not just a model for living but a transformation of their souls, a total reawakening and rebirth. They wanted religion that provided a simple but powerful connection to the divine, and religion that gave them a palpable sense that redemption from sin would restore order to their lives and reinvigorate their communities. What they wanted, and what they got, was the sacred drama, the spiritual immediacy, and the emotional release of evangelical revivalism.

From the 1790s through the 1850s, wave after wave of revivals swept the United States, a phenomenon known as the Second Great Awakening. Outdoors in the woods, huddled inside tents, and gathered in meeting halls, Americans by the thousands heard evangelical ministers tell them the Second Coming of Christ was near and that the time had come to repent for their sins. But in an important departure from America's religious past, when attendees at revivals were told mostly of God's anger, their worthlessness, and the likelihood of eternal punishment, Second Great Awakening preachers both warned and rallied their audiences, energizing them with the promise that Jesus would save them from damnation if they would acknowledge their sinfulness, atone, and be reborn.

The response to this message was astonishing. It was not uncommon to hear reports from revivals of individuals moved so powerfully that they cried, shrieked, groaned, fainted, or danced uncontrollably. More significantly, multitudes of Americans converted and joined churches, with reported church membership more than doubling between 1800 and 1830 alone. All denominations grew, but the major evangelical denominations of Baptism, Methodism, and Presbyterianism exploded in size. There were just fifty Methodist congregations in the United States in 1780, for example. But there were roughly 20,000 by 1860, at which point

Methodism was the nation's largest Protestant denomination, with over one million adherents.

The revivals of the Second Great Awakening began along southern and western frontiers, but by the 1820s and 1830s they were most furious in the northeast, especially in places like western New York, western Pennsylvania, and northeastern Ohio. This was no coincidence. Projects like the Erie Canal were producing booming canal towns in the area, attracting new people in search of new economic opportunities, and rapidly transforming the lives of Americans accustomed to a region of farms and villages. These circumstances made for excitement and high expectations, but also for discontent and anxiety, an environment perfect for revivalists to spread their message. The heat of revival fires repeatedly surged with such ferocity through towns, cities, and the countryside surrounding the Erie Canal, in fact, that western New York came to be known as the "Burned-Over District."

No one harnessed this spiritual energy better than Charles Grandison Finney. Though he began his career as a lawyer, Finney became a Presbyterian minister after having a conversion experience in the early 1820s, and he began leading revivals in towns throughout the northeast. By the time he achieved his greatest success in the winter of 1830–1831, leading a revival in the canal city of Rochester that lasted nearly six months, Finney was perhaps the most famous clergyman in the United States. In part, Finney owed his success to a plain and colloquial rhetorical style, a booming voice, and the showmanship he brought to his sermons. But it was his message that persuaded audiences most, and at its core it was relatively simple: every person was responsible for his or her own sinfulness and every person could achieve salvation. Rejecting the notion that human beings were naturally inclined to sin, Finney argued that sin was a choice that individuals could will themselves not to make, ultimately freeing themselves from sin altogether. At a time when Americans celebrated the self-made man and felt the nation could overcome any obstacle, Finneyite perfectionism—the assertion that people could make themselves whatever they chose in religion—was theologically controversial but many found it both appealing and plausible.

Finney and other revivalists, though, not only encouraged people to embrace religion and remake themselves, they told converts to bring the word of God to others and remake society by performing holy works. As Finney told an audience in the 1840s, those who had been born again wanted to advance anything that promised moral righteousness and the consequent improvement of mankind. They therefore had to be committed to "the universal reformation of the world." Indeed, he argued, it was for that purpose that "they live and move and have their being."[4] It was here that the evangelical theology of the Second Great Awakening connected directly to the reform impulse, providing a more powerful source of that impulse than rationalist religion ever would—because to Finney and other revivalists, the point of stamping out sin in society was about as profound as it could get for Christians. Advocates of a theological doctrine known as millennialism, which held that Jesus would return after a thousand years of peace and prosperity, ministers like Finney claimed that if the world could be freed from sin, human beings could build God's kingdom on earth and play an active role in bringing about Christ's Second Coming.

Advancing the millennium was a universal charge, and the message of revivalism appealed to people of various regional, racial, and class backgrounds. In some ways, however, it was especially attractive to middle-class Americans. Ministers often described moral Christian behavior in terms of middle-class values like industriousness and self-discipline. For members of the middle class who cultivated those values but who also wanted to demonstrate that they were not lost in materialism and indifferent to society, revivalism simultaneously sanctioned their economic behavior and prompted them to encourage others to act similarly. Women were particularly drawn to revivals, in keeping with the idea that they were naturally religious. And even though the era's domestic ideology said pious women ought to act in the private realm, it also said they were the country's moral guardians, a notion many would use to move beyond their homes and into the wider world of reform.

No matter their class or gender, reformers moved by evangelical religion understood matters like sin and evil not as abstract con-

---

[4] Charles G. Finney, *Lectures on Systematic Theology* (New York, 1846), 550.

cepts but as real, present, and tangible things. You could see them, and once you saw them you had to act to eliminate them. To some, sin was drinking alcohol. To others, it was prostitution, or war, or poverty, or slavery. Given that making a sacred world meant trying to make a perfect world, reformers not uncommonly got involved in multiple crusades. Whatever their chosen cause or causes, however, many were guided by the mindset that only the dissemination of Christian principles could save individual souls and improve mankind. Frequently working outside the regular political system through voluntary associations that became a popular way for antebellum Americans to forge connections with like-minded people in pursuit of common interests, many reformers sought to hasten the world's salvation by fulfilling what they saw as America's national destiny.

Assessing Antebellum Reform

Though influential and significant, reformers were not universally admired. Indeed, nearly every antebellum reform effort met some resistance and provoked some measure of antagonism. Opposition to women's rights and abolitionism was especially intense, but reformers of varying stripes were accused of being self-righteous, elitist, condescending, and hopelessly naïve. They were resented for mixing private morals and public affairs, opposed by religious conservatives skeptical of revivalism's influences, and sometimes simply ridiculed for ideas and plans that many thought blasphemous or downright bizarre.

Historians have been no more successful at reaching consensus on antebellum reformers than were their contemporaries, and scholarly interpretations have changed significantly over time. Early in the twentieth century, the most influential scholars paid little attention to the reform impulse, contending that it was primarily a by-product of changing economic conditions. Such arguments were not meritless, but they were also gross oversimplifications. By the 1930s and 1940s, numerous historians began giving reform greater consideration, challenging materialist approaches with arguments that reformers were courageous humanitarians and noble idealists whose religious faith, commitment to social progress, and dedication to democratic individualism drove them to tackle the seemingly intractable ills of their time. Such admiration for reformers' efforts nearly always came with some measure of skepticism about their wide-eyed optimism, and in the years after World War II that skepticism lent itself to new scholarly arguments that reformers were extremists, neurotics, and fanatics responding irrationally to socioeconomic changes that they were psychologically ill-equipped to handle.

By the 1950s, meanwhile, an equally critical and more thoroughly revisionist reading of reform began emerging from the work of historians who questioned reformers' motives altogether, making the case that in their hunger for order reformers sought mostly to impose the economic and religious values of the Protestant middle class on American society. Variations on this "social control" thesis were commonplace into the 1980s, and its influence can still be seen in the works of many authors, particularly those in which class imperatives take center stage. While analytically apposite for some reforms and reformers, arguments for social control often betray more than a hint of conspiracy, and they frequently neglect to consider the extent to which people of varying backgrounds actively embraced and made meaning out of the reform impulse. Historians of gender in particular have repeatedly noted that such arguments usually focus so heavily on the efforts of male reformers that they fail to account for how reform activism enabled a transformation of both women's collective consciousness and their understanding of their roles in American society.

Given the array of reforms and reformers, in fact, no single model seems likely ever to describe them all aptly. Their politics, morals, and worldviews do not fit neatly into modern categories, and anyone examining their efforts is likely to see different concerns and motivations as particularly salient. Assessing whether reformers ultimately succeeded or failed, meanwhile, depends on the movement and how one defines success and failure. The Civil War, for example, ended slavery and thus fulfilled the wishes of abolitionists, but it resulted in hundreds of thousands of battlefield casualties and nearly destroyed the country in the process. Moreover, for most reformers the death and destruction wrought by the war profoundly challenged their optimism, their faith in the capacity of human beings to perfect the world, and their belief that the millennium was at hand. The war eviscerated a spirit of reform that would not be invigorated again in the United States for more than a generation after it ended, returning in a significantly different guise during the Progressive Era of the late nineteenth and early twentieth centuries. That the focus of those reformers returned to poverty, women's rights, racial justice, the consumption of alcohol, and many of the other issues identified by their antebellum predecessors suggests just how much remained undone in 1865. That Americans to this day find it acceptable and even admirable to ask how their society and country might be made better points toward antebellum reformers' finest legacy.

CHRONOLOGY: ANTEBELLUM REFORM

1810: American Board of Commissioners for Foreign Missions founded

1815: War of 1812 ends

1819: Auburn Prison, one of the earliest jails to implement a penitentiary system, opens in upstate New York; Panic of 1819 touches off economic depression lasting for four years

1825: Erie Canal completed; American Tract Society founded; Robert Owen founds New Harmony community in Indiana; first House of Refuge opens as a juvenile reformatory in New York City; Lyman Beecher delivers his *Six Sermons on Intemperance*

1826: American Temperance Society founded

1828: Fanny Wright delivers her *Course of Popular Lectures*

1829: New York Working Men's Party founded; David Walker publishes his *Appeal . . . to the Colored Citizens of the World*

1830: Book of Mormon published

1830–1831: Charles Grandison Finney leads revival in the canal city of Rochester, New York

1833: American Anti-Slavery Society founded; slavery abolished in the British Empire

1834: New York Female Moral Reform Society founded

1837: Panic of 1837 touches off economic depression lasting nearly six years; *American Phrenological Journal* begins publication; Horace Mann of Massachusetts becomes first state secretary of education; abolitionists Sarah and Angelina Grimké give controversial lecture series

1838: New England Non-Resistance Society founded

1839: Sylvester Graham publishes *Lectures on the Science of Human Life,* the most thorough exposition of the "Graham System"

1840: Abolitionist movement splits; Liberty Party founded; Washington Temperance Society founded; Elizabeth Cady Stanton and Lucretia Mott meet in London at the World's Anti-Slavery Convention

1843: Dorothea Dix brings conditions of the insane to the attention of Massachusetts legislature

1844: Order of United Americans, one of many antebellum nativist organizations, founded in New York City

1848: First women's rights convention held in Seneca Falls, New York; Oneida Community founded in upstate New York

1851: American Hydropathic Institute, first hydropathic medical school, opens; Maine becomes the first state to ban the manufacture and sale of alcoholic beverages

1857: Panic of 1857 touches off economic depression lasting about three years

1860: Nearly 20 percent of Americans live in cities, more than tripling the figure from 1800

1861: Civil War begins

The Origins of Reform

Forging the Character of America's Men

Many early nineteenth-century Americans feared the institutions traditionally holding society together were faltering among an increasingly mobile population in an increasingly urban world. Numerous writers responded to this sense of social and cultural crisis with advice manuals for young people. Designed to instill new sets of morals, manners, and other behavior deemed appropriate and advantageous for the modern age, the advice on offer did not necessarily translate to any particular kind of reform activism. But authors frequently told readers that Americans were capable of tackling any task in their personal, professional, or civic lives and of making great changes in the world. Represented in the following selection from an advice manual for young men written by William Alcott (himself a medical doctor and a health and education reformer), this optimistic and patriotic outlook helped propel antebellum reform. Such was especially the case among members of the burgeoning middle class to whom authors like Alcott geared their suggestions and who contributed the bulk of the membership and financing of most reform organizations.

William Alcott, Importance of Having a High Standard of Action (1833)

I am now prepared to give the following general direction; *Fix upon a high standard of character.* Or, as it has sometimes been expressed,

Determine to be somebody in *the world*. To be *thought* something is not sufficient: the point you are to aim at, is, to *be* so.

As a motive to this, let me urge in the first place, a regard to *your own happiness*. To this you are by no means indifferent at present. Nay, the attainment of happiness is your primary object. You seek it in every desire, word, and action. But you sometimes mistake the road that leads to it, either for the want of a friendly hand to guide you, or because you refuse to be guided. Or what is most common, you grasp at a smaller good, which is near, and apparently certain; and in so doing cut yourselves off from the enjoyment of a good which is almost infinitely larger, though more remote.

Let me urge, in the second place, a regard for the family to which you belong. It is true you can never fully know, unless the bitterness of ingratitude should teach you, the extent of the duty you owe to your relatives; and especially to your parents. You *cannot* know—at least till you are parents yourselves,—how their hearts are bound up in yours. But if you do not *in some measure know it*, till this late period, you are not fit to be parents. Hence, then, one evidence of the need in which you stand of the lessons of experience.

In the third place, it is due to society, particularly to the neighborhood or sphere in which you move, and to the *associations* to which you may belong, that you strive to attain a very great elevation of character. Here, too, I am well aware that it is impossible, at your age, to perceive fully, how much you have it in your power to contribute, if you will, to the happiness of those around you; and here again let me refer you to the advice and guidance of aged friends.

But, fourthly, it is due to the nation and age to which you belong, that you fix upon a high standard of character. This work is intended for American youth. *American!* did I say? This word, alone, ought to call forth all your energies, and if there be a slumbering faculty within you, arouse it to action. Never, since the creation, were the youth of any age or country so imperiously called upon to exert themselves, as those whom I now address. Never before were there so many important interests at stake. Never were such immense results depending upon a generation of men as upon that which is now approaching the stage of action. These rising millions are destined, according to all human probability, to form the greatest nation that ever constituted an entire community of freemen, since the world began. To form the character of these millions involves a greater amount of responsibility, individual and collective, than any work to which humanity has ever been called. And the reasons are, it seems to me, obvious.

Now it is for you, my young friends, to determine whether these weighty responsibilities shall be fulfilled. It is for you to decide whether this *greatest* of free nations shall, at the same time, be the *best*. And as every nation is made up of individuals, you are each, in reality, called upon daily, to settle this question: "Shall the United States, possessing the most ample means of instruction brought within the reach of all her citizens, the happiest government, the healthiest of climates, the greatest abundance of the best and most wholesome nutriment, with every other possible means for developing all the powers of human nature, be peopled with the most vigorous, powerful, and happy race of human beings which the world has ever known?"

There is another motive to which I beg leave, for one moment, to direct your attention. You are bound to fix on a high standard of action from the desire of obeying the will of God. *He* it is who has cast your lot in a country which—all things considered—is the happiest below the sun. *He* it is who has given you such a wonderful capacity for happiness, and instituted the delightful relations of parent and child, and brother and sister, and friend and neighbor. I might add, *He* it is, too, who has given you the name *American*,—a name which alone furnishes a passport to many civilized lands, and like a good countenance, or a becoming dress, prepossesses every body in your favor. So that all the foregoing motives unite in one to swell the appeal to your feelings, and increase the weight of your responsibility.

Some may think there is danger of setting *too high* a standard of action. I have heard teachers contend that a child will learn to write much faster by having an *inferior copy*, than by imitating one which is comparatively perfect; "because," say they, "a pupil is liable to be discouraged if you give him a *perfect* copy; but if it is only a little in advance of his own, he will take courage from the belief that he shall soon be able to equal it." I am fully convinced, however, that this is not so. The *more* perfect the copy you place before the child, provided it be *written,* and not *engraved,* the better. For it must always be *possible* in the nature of things, for the child to imitate it; and what is not absolutely impossible, every child may reasonably be expected to aspire after, on the principle, that whatever man *has done,* man may *do.*

So in human conduct, generally; whatever is possible should be aimed at. Did my limits permit, I might show that it is part of the divine economy to place before his rational creatures a perfect standard of action, and to make it their duty to come up to it.

He who only aims at *little,* will *accomplish* but little. *Expect* great things, and *attempt* great things. A neglect of this rule produces more of the difference in the character, conduct, and success of men, than is commonly supposed. Some start in life without any leading object at all; some with a low one; and some aim high:— and just in proportion to the elevation at which they aim, will be their progress and success. It is an old proverb that he who aims at the sun, will not reach it, to be sure; but his arrow will fly higher than if he aims at an object on a level with himself. Exactly so is it, in the formation of character.

The Young Man's Guide (Boston, 1833), 21–25.

STUDY QUESTIONS
1. What sorts of goals did Alcott urge young men to pursue?
2. What responsibilities did Alcott believe young men had to themselves, and what responsibilities did they have to others?

Invoking the Influence of American Women

Central to behavioral models offered by writers like Alcott were gender norms designed to be foundations for a well-ordered family life. Authors therefore geared advice manuals toward young women in addition to young men. Catherine Beecher's Treatise on Domestic Economy, *from which the excerpt below is taken, was primarily a comprehensive guide to housekeeping and child rearing, but it was more broadly a handbook for how women might act as domestic moral counterbalances to men and the treacherous working world. Beecher did not believe in full political rights for women. But she was a powerful advocate for women's education, and her insistence that women had a responsibility to instill Christian morality in American life helped pull them from the private sphere of the home toward the public sphere of reform activism.*

Catherine Beecher, Peculiar Responsibilities of American Women (1842)

There is a day advancing, "by seers predicted, and by poets sung," when the curse of selfishness shall be removed; when "scenes surpassing fable, and yet true," shall be realized; when all nations shall rejoice and be made blessed, under those benevolent influences, which the Messiah came to establish on earth.

And this is the Country, which the Disposer of events designs shall go forth as the cynosure of nations, to guide them to the light and blessedness of that day. To us is committed the grand, the responsible privilege, of exhibiting to the world, the beneficent influences of Christianity, when carried into every social, civil, and political institution; and, though we have, as yet, made such imperfect advances, already the light is streaming into the dark prison-house of despotic lands, while startled kings and sages, philosophers and statesmen, are watching us with that interest, which a career so illustrious, and so involving their own destiny, is calculated to excite. They are studying our institutions, scrutinizing our experience, and watching for our mistakes, that they may learn whether "a social revolution, so irresistible, be advantageous or prejudicial to mankind."

There are persons, who regard these interesting truths merely as food for national vanity; but every reflecting and Christian mind, must consider it as an occasion for solemn and anxious reflection. Are we, then, a spectacle to the world? Has the Eternal Lawgiver appointed us to work out a problem, involving the destiny of the whole earth? Are such momentous interests to be advanced or retarded, just in proportion as we are faithful to our high trust?

"What manner of persons, then, ought we to be," in attempting to sustain so solemn, so glorious a responsibility?

But the part to be enacted by American women, in this great moral enterprise, is the point to which special attention should here be directed.

The success of democratic institutions, as is conceded by all, depends upon the intellectual and moral character of the mass of the people. If they are intelligent and virtuous, democracy is a blessing; but if they are ignorant and wicked, it is only a curse, and as much more dreadful than any other form of civil government, as a thousand tyrants are more to be dreaded than one. It is equally conceded, that the formation of the moral and intellectual character of the young is committed mainly to the female hand. The mother forms the character of the future man; the sister bends the fibres that are hereafter to be the forest tree; the wife sways the heart, whose energies may turn for good or for evil the destinies of a nation. Let the women of a country be made virtuous and intelligent, and the men will certainly be the same. The proper education of a man decides the welfare of an individual; but educate a woman, and the interests of a whole family are secured.

If this be so, as none will deny, then to American women, more than to any others on earth, is committed the exalted privilege of extending over the world those blessed influences, which are to renovate degraded man, and "clothe all climes with beauty."

No American woman, then, has any occasion for feeling that hers is an humble or insignificant lot. The value of what an individual accomplishes, is to be estimated by the importance of the enterprise achieved, and not by the particular position of the laborer. The drops of heaven which freshen the earth, are each of equal value, whether they fall in the lowland meadow, or the princely parterre. The builders of a temple are of equal importance, whether they labor on the foundations, or toil upon the dome.

Thus, also, with the labors which are to be made effectual in the regeneration of the Earth. And it is by forming a habit of regarding the apparently insignificant efforts of each isolated laborer, in a comprehensive manner, as indispensable portions of a grand result, that the minds of all, however humble their sphere of service, can be invigorated and cheered. The woman, who is rearing a family of children; the woman, who labors in the schoolroom; the woman, who, in her retired chamber, earns with her needle, the mite, which contributes to the intellectual and moral elevation of her Country; even the humble domestic, whose example and influence may be moulding and forming young minds, while her faithful services sustain a prosperous domestic state;—each and all may be animated by the consciousness, that they are agents in accomplishing the greatest work that ever was committed to human responsibility. It is the building of a glorious temple, whose base shall be coextensive with the bounds of the earth, whose summit shall pierce the skies, whose splendor shall beam on all lands; and those who hew the lowliest stone, as much as those who carve the highest capital, will be equally honored, when its top-stone shall be laid, with new rejoicings of the morning stars, and shoutings of the sons of God.

A Treatise on Domestic Economy (Boston, 1842), 35–38.

STUDY QUESTIONS

1. According to Beecher, what roles should women play in American life? How important were those roles?
2. What did Beecher mean when she suggested that the United States was a "spectacle to the world"?

The Duties of Christian Churches

As Catherine Beecher's writings suggest, reform activity often was rooted explicitly in an evangelical Christian impulse to prepare the world for the second coming of Christ. Evangelical revivalism thrived in antebellum America, and no revivalist minister was more significant than Charles Grandison Finney. A powerful and inspirational orator, Finney called on Christians to do good works in society and free the world from sin. A supporter himself of numerous reforms,

Finney here acknowledges the roles played by individual Christians in reform organizations but exhorts American churches to lend their full institutional muscle, leadership, and moral clout to the day's major causes.

Charles Grandison Finney, The Pernicious Attitude of the Church on the Reforms of the Age (1846)

There is one subject upon which I must remark further, and yet I fear it will be impossible to do it justice without giving offence. One of the most serious impediments that have been thrown in the way of revivals of religion and one that has no doubt deeply grieved the Spirit of God is the fact that the church to a very great extent has lost sight of its own appropriate work and has actually left it in a great measure to be conducted by those who are for the most part illy prepared for the work. The work to which I allude is the reformation of mankind.

It is melancholy and amazing to see to what an extent the church treats the different branches of reform either with indifference, or with direct opposition. There is not, I venture to say upon the whole earth an inconsistency more monstrous, more God-dishonoring, and I must say more manifestly insane than the attitude which many of the churches take in respect to nearly every branch of reform which is needed among mankind.

To such an extent is this true that scarcely a church can be found in the land which as a body will have any thing to do with reform. Hence the only way in which Christians in the churches who would do any thing towards reforming mankind can make their influence felt is by forming societies, composed often partly of Christians and partly of those who profess no religion. These unite together to concentrate their influence against some form of iniquity that is cursing mankind.

Now the great business of the church is to reform the world—to put away every kind of sin. The church of Christ was originally organized to be a body of reformers. The very profession of christianity implies the profession and virtually an oath to do all that can be done for the universal reformation of the world. The Christian church was designed to make aggressive movements in every direction—to lift up her voice and put forth her energies against iniquity in high and low places—to reform individuals, communities, and governments, and never rest until the kingdom and the greatness of the kingdom under the whole heaven shall be given to the people of the saints of the most High God—until every form of iniquity shall be driven from the earth.

Now when we consider the appropriate business of the church— the very end for which she is organized and for which every Christian vows eternal consecration, and then behold her appalling inconsistencies every where apparent, I do not wonder that so many persons are led to avow the solemn conviction that the nominal church is apostate from God.

* * *

Believe me, dear brethren, it grieves me greatly to feel constrained to speak thus. Is it not a shame; are we not ashamed and shall we not blush to see the Church of God not only turn back from reforming the world—refusing to lead in reform as she ought to do, and then turn round and oppose others who are compelled to lead for want of the help and countenance of those who ought to go forward in these enterprises? If doctors of divinity—if ecclesiastical bodies, theological seminaries and colleges would but lead on in these enterprises, God forbid that they should not have their place. If they would but go forward the Church would follow them, and many who are now compelled to lead because these refuse, would rejoice to fall in behind and sustain them with all their might.

* * *

My brethren, let us all come forward and show ourselves to be reformers—put our heads and hearts together to promote every branch of reform and also revivals of religion, and then we shall hold a position in which we can successfully oppose and correct the errors of the day either in revivals or reforms.

Oberlin Evangelist (January 21, 1846) 11, 12.

STUDY QUESTIONS
1. According to Finney, what role should churches play in American life?
2. How did Finney feel churches were failing in their missions?

Religious Rationalism and Reform

Religious inspiration for reform did not come from evangelical Christianity alone. Unitarians, for example, argued for a more liberal, more rationalist, and less emotional approach to faith and the Bible than revivalists like Finney, but their convictions about human goodness and potential inspired many to look beyond their own lives and participate in reform activities. Indeed, William Ellery Channing, a prominent Boston minister and the intellectual leader of American Unitarianism, argued that the very essence of Christianity was God's desire for all human beings to achieve moral perfection and liberation from sin.

William Ellery Channing, The Essence of the Christian Religion (1831)

I believe that Christianity has one great principle, which is *central*, around which its truths gather, and which constitutes it the glorious gospel of the blessed God. I believe that no truth is so worthy of acceptance and so quickening as this. In proportion as we penetrate into it, and are penetrated by it, we comprehend our religion, and attain to a living faith. This great principle can be briefly expressed. It is the doctrine that "God purposes, in his unbounded fatherly love, to perfect the human soul; to purify it from all sin; to create it after his own image; to fill it with his own spirit; to unfold it for ever; to raise it to life and immortality in heaven,—that is, to communicate to it from himself a life of celestial power, virtue, and joy." The elevation of men above the imperfections, temptations, sins, sufferings, of the present state, to a diviner being,—this is the great purpose of God, revealed and accomplished by Jesus Christ; that it is that constitutes the religion of Jesus Christ,—glad tidings to all people: for it is a religion suited to fulfil the wants of every human being.

* * *

When I look into man's nature, I see that moral perfection is his only true and enduring good; and consequently the promise of this must be the highest truth which any religion can contain. The loftiest endowment of our nature is the moral power,—the power of perceiving and practising virtue, of discerning and seeking goodness. Having this as our essential principle, we can have but one happiness as our end. There is a guide to felicity fixed by God in the very *centre* of our being, and no other can take its place. Whoever obeys faithfully this principle of duty has peace with himself and with all beings. Whoever silences or withstands this is at war with himself and with all.

* * *

How can this truth, without which we are so poor, be called into energetic life, and become a bright reality to us? It must become so, through our own resolute grasp,—by effort, by reflection, by prayer, by resistance of the body, the senses, and the outward world, by descending into our own minds, by listening to experience, as it daily teaches that there is no true good which has not its spring in the improvement of our highest nature.

* * *

I have hope in the present struggle of the world, because it seems to me more spiritual, more moral, in its origin and tendencies, than any which have preceded it. It differs much from the revolts of former times, when an oppressed populace or peasantry broke forth into frantic opposition to government, under the goading pressure of famine and misery. Men are now moved, not merely by physical wants and sufferings, but by ideas, by principles, by the conception of a better state of society, under which the rights of human nature will be recognized, and greater justice be done to the mind in all classes of the community. There is then an element—

spiritual, moral, and tending towards perfection—in the present movement; and this is my great hope.

_____

The Works of William Ellery Channing (Boston, 1891), 1001, 1002, 1005.

STUDY QUESTIONS
1. What did Channing believe was the "one great principle" of Christianity?
2. What did Channing think would result from humans embracing that principle?

The Transcendentalist Impulse

_____

Inspiration for reform did not necessarily originate in an explicitly Christian religious worldview at all. With their beliefs in the transformative power of individualism and the significance of individuals' ability to discover their own truths beyond established religious doctrine, adherents to transcendentalist teachings like those of Ralph Waldo Emerson often tried to put their personal, ethical, and moral codes into social action through reform activities. Emerson's absolute dedication to individualism made him personally ambivalent about associating with formal groups or organizations, but as the lecture excerpted below suggests, he clearly felt individuals ought not to be afraid to challenge any and every customary socioeconomic arrangement in American life.

_____

Ralph Waldo Emerson, Man the Reformer (1841)

In the history of the world the doctrine of Reform had never such scope as at the present hour. Lutherans, Hernhutters, Jesuits, Monks, Quakers, Knox, Wesley, Swedenborg, Bentham, in their accusations of society, all respected something,—church or state, literature or history, domestic usages, the market town, the dinner table, coined money. But now all these and all things else hear the trumpet, and must rush to judgment,—Christianity, the laws, commerce, schools, the farm, the laboratory; and not a kingdom, town, statute, rite, calling, man, or woman, but is threatened by the new spirit.

What if some of the objections whereby our institutions are assailed are extreme and speculative, and the reformers tend to idealism; that only shows the extravagance of the abuses which have driven the mind into the opposite extreme. It is when your facts and persons grow unreal and fantastic by too much falsehood, that the scholar flies for refuge to the world of ideas, and aims to recruit and replenish nature from that source. Let ideas establish their legitimate sway again in society, let life be fair and poetic, and the scholars will gladly be lovers, citizens, and philanthropists.

It will afford no security from the new ideas, that the old nations, the laws of centuries, the property and institutions of a hundred cities, are built on other foundations. The demon of reform has a secret door into the heart of every lawmaker, of every inhabitant of every city. The fact, that a new thought and hope have dawned in your breast, should apprize you that in the same hour a new light broke in upon a thousand private hearts. That secret which you would fain keep,—as soon as you go abroad, lo! there is one standing on the doorstep, to tell you the same.

* * *

I do not wish to be absurd and pedantic in reform. I do not wish to push my criticism on the state of things around me to that extravagant mark, that shall compel me to suicide, or to an absolute isolation from the advantages of civil society. If we suddenly plant our foot, and say,—I will neither eat nor drink nor wear nor touch any food or fabric which I do not know to be innocent, or deal with any person whose whole manner of life is not clear and rational, we shall stand still. Whose is so? Not mine; not thine; not his. But I think we must clear ourselves each one by the interrogation, whether we have earned our bread to-day by the hearty contribution of our energies to the common benefit? and we must not cease to *tend* to the correction of these flagrant wrongs, by laying one stone aright every day.

But the idea which now begins to agitate society has a wider scope than our daily employments, our households, and the institutions of property. We are to revise the whole of our social structure, the state, the school, religion, marriage, trade, science, and explore their foundations in our own nature; we are to see that the world not only fitted the former men, but fits us, and to clear ourselves of every usage which has not its roots in our own mind. What is a man born for but to be a Reformer, a Re-maker of what man has made; a renouncer of lies; a restorer of truth and good, imitating that great Nature which embosoms us all, and which sleeps no moment on an old past, but every hour repairs herself, yielding us every morning a new day, and with every pulsation a new life? Let him renounce everything which is not true to him, and put all his practices back on their first thoughts, and do nothing for which he has not the whole world for his reason. If there are inconveniences, and what is called ruin in the way, because we have so enervated and maimed ourselves, yet it would be like dying of perfumes to sink in the effort to reattach the deeds of every day to the holy and mysterious recesses of life.

* * *

Let us begin by habitual imparting. Let us understand that the equitable rule is, that no one should take more than his share, let him be ever so rich. Let me feel that I am to be a lover. I am to see to it that the world is the better for me, and to find my reward in the act. Love would put a new face on this weary old world in which we dwell as pagans and enemies too long, and it would warm the heart to see how fast the vain diplomacy of statesmen, the impotence of armies, and navies, and lines of defence, would be superseded by this unarmed child. Love will creep where it cannot go, will accomplish that by imperceptible methods,—being its own lever, fulcrum, and power,—which force could never achieve. * * * The virtue of this principle in human society in application to great interests is obsolete and forgotten. Once or twice in history it has been tried in illustrious instances, with signal success. This great, overgrown, dead Christendom of ours still keeps alive at least the name of a lover of mankind. But one day all men will be lovers; and every calamity will be dissolved in the universal sunshine.

Ralph Waldo Emerson: Essays and Lectures (New York, 1983), 135–136, 145–146, 149.

STUDY QUESTIONS
1. What did Emerson see as the purpose of reform?
2. To what extent were Emerson's notions of reform similar to or different from those of Channing or Finney?

One Reformer Calls for a "World's Convention"

Industrialist and utopian socialist Robert Owen was Welsh by birth, but he spent several years in the United States, where his notions about the ideal social order were extremely influential. Owen opposed the received wisdom of organized religion even more radically than Emerson, and he stressed a communitarian worldview rather than transcendentalist individualism. Nonetheless, like many reformers of both religious and individualist bents, Owen had faith that the American people could demonstrate possibilities for eliminating the seemingly intractable human woes plaguing modern society. The "World's Convention" that Owen proposed in the following speech did meet, but its promise disintegrated amid the competing agendas of those gathered. A proposal was adopted for an annual convention, but no such meeting was ever held again.

Robert Owen, Address on Leaving the United States for Europe (1845)

I have seen in my travels through New England and the middle States, and presume the same has occurred in the south and west, a great increase to your cities—to your population, and in the extended cultivation of the soil. I have also ascertained that your means to increase wealth and power, for good or evil, are illimitable for many hundreds or thousands of years, and you could now beneficially absorb into your Union the present population of Europe.

You have also progressed in a most extraordinary manner in new discoveries in science, and in mechanical inventions, to render manual labor of diminished value, and to open the path to a new state of things, which will make labor of little or no commercial value, or unsaleable, for the rightful support of the industrious.

In proportion as your scientific power to create wealth has increased, individual competition has increased ignorant selfishness, vice, crime and misery among the masses, so as to make all parties blind to their present position of high capabilities and to their interests as individuals and members of society.

Your statesmen are occupied in unprofitable and nationally injurious politics.

Your politicians in petty local party contests, useless for the attainment of great results.

Your capitalists and extensive merchants are overwhelmed in speculations, hazardous to themselves, and of little comparative benefit to their country or to the world. There is no foresight, wisdom, or order—no permanent, prosperous future in any of their proceedings.

Your traders, wholesale and retail, are wasting, most injuriously, much of the capital, talent and industry of your country, and at the same time keeping the mind and morals of the Union upon a low level, most disadvantageous to every class.

Your most industrious classes are kept unnecessarily in toil, ignorance, and consequent degradation.

Senseless superstitions pervade the land without a particle of real charity being created between any of the classes, sects or parties, possessing any one of these monster obstacles to human progress, for any who have been made to differ from them; and religion is perverted to worldly purposes.

Your prisons and punishments increase, and the necessity for more, while the present state of things continues, will daily become stronger.

You have already, to a great extent, throughout the Union, ignorance, poverty, division, and misery. And yet, as the *causes* of these evils have been discovered, they may be now easily removed.

* * *

But how can this change be speedily effected?

* * *

The answer is obvious.

All great improvements commence with one or a few, and these, by judicious measures, interest more and more, until a sufficient number unite to accomplish the object.

There is an admirable spirit abroad anxiously looking out for the right commencement of this change and bold truths announced in the pure spirit of charity will now accomplish that object.

Let then the proper measures to create this public opinion be now adopted, and let all good men of every class, sect, party and state unite for this Godlike purpose.

To this end let a Convention be called of delegates from every State and territory in the Union, to consider what practical measures can be immediately carried into execution to apply the enormous means to secure prosperity for all the people of these States, that they may become an example to the world of what, with sound judgment, in peace, with order and with the least injury and the most benefit to every one, from the highest to the lowest, may be done.

But what is every one's business is no one's in particular, and is too often neglected by all. I, therefore, feeling a deep interest in the immediate improvement of our race, recommend such Convention to be called the "World's Convention," to consider what measures of a practical character can be adopted to ensure the immediate benefit of every class, without violence, contest or competition, and especially what can be done to well educate and employ the uneducated and unemployed, to fit them for the superior state of society, to create which, for all the means are now so superabundant, not only in these States, but wherever men need to live; or it may be called "The World's Convention" to emancipate the human race from ignorance, poverty, division, sin and misery.

* * *

It will be found, on full investigation, that there is but one interest amongst all of the human race, and that is, that each one should be the best taught from birth, the best employed through life, and that the inferior circumstances of man's creation should be replaced from around all by those only of a superior and permanent character, whether animate or inanimate, for as these are, so will man become.

These measures have no individual interest or object in view; it is, therefore, earnestly requested, for the good of humanity, that the press will advocate the call and object of this Convention, and prepare the minds of the public for the great and glorious results which may, by these measures, be speedily obtained for all of every class in every country.

New York Herald, May 26, 1845.

STUDY QUESTIONS
1. What "evils" did Owen see in American society?
2. What did he believe his "World's Convention" could accomplish?

The Significance of Voluntary Associations

Whatever their ideological origins and motivations, critical to many reform movements were groups of ordinary American men and women who formed organizations dedicated to addressing what they identified as social problems. Especially common in towns and cities, whose residents experienced most intensely the rapid changes of the antebellum era, voluntary associations provided much of the energy and financing that kept numerous reform movements active and vibrant. When French government emissary Alexis de Toqueville visited the United States in 1831, he marveled at the wide variety of voluntary associations and what he saw as their crucial roles in American democracy.

Alexis de Tocqueville,
Democracy in America (1835)

Americans of all ages, all conditions, and all dispositions, constantly form associations. They have not only commercial and manufacturing companies, in which all take part, but associations of a thousand other kinds—religious, moral, serious, futile, general or restricted, enormous or diminutive. The Americans make associations to give entertainments, to found establishments for education, to build inns, to construct churches, to diffuse books, to send missionaries to the antipodes; and in this manner they found hospitals, prisons, and schools. If it be proposed to advance some truth, or to foster some feeling by the encouragement of a great example, they form a society. Wherever, at the head of some new undertaking, you see the Government in France, or a man of rank in England, in the United States you will be sure to find an association. I met with several kinds of associations in America, of which I confess I had no previous notion; and I have often admired the extreme skill with which the inhabitants of the United States succeed in proposing a common object to the exertions of a great many men, and in getting them voluntarily to pursue it. I have since travelled over England, whence the Americans have taken some of their laws and many of their customs; and it seemed to me that the principle of association was by no means so constantly or so adroitly used in that country. The English often perform great things singly; whereas the Americans form associations for the smallest undertakings. It is evident that the former people consider association as a powerful means of action, but the latter seem to regard it as the only means they have of acting.

Thus the most democratic country on the face of the earth is that in which men have in our time carried to the highest perfection the art of pursuing in common the object of their common desires, and have applied this new science to the greatest number of purposes. Is this the result of accident? Or is there in reality any necessary connection between the principle of association and that of equality? Aristocratic communities always contain, among a multitude of persons who by themselves are powerless, a small number of powerful and wealthy citizens, each of whom can achieve great undertakings single-handed. In aristocratic societies men do not need to combine in order to act, because they are strongly held together. Every wealthy and powerful citizen constitutes the head of a permanent and compulsory association, composed of all those who are dependent upon him, or whom he makes subservient to the execution of his designs. Among democratic nations, on the contrary, all the citizens are independent and feeble; they can do hardly anything by themselves, and none of them can oblige his fellow-men to lend him their assistance. They all, therefore, fall into a state of incapacity, if they do not learn voluntarily to help one another. If men living in democratic countries had no right and no inclination to associate for political purposes, their independence would be in great jeopardy; but they might long preserve their wealth and their cultivation: whereas if they never acquired the habit of forming associations in ordinary life, civilization itself would be endangered. A people among whom individuals should lose the power of achieving great things single-handed, without acquiring the means of producing them by united exertions, would soon relapse into barbarism.

* * *

As soon as several of the inhabitants of the United States have taken up an opinion or a feeling that they wish to promote in the world, they look out for mutual assistance; and as soon as they have found each other out, they combine. From that moment they are no longer isolated men, but a power seen from afar, whose actions serve for an example, and whose language is listened to.

* * *

Nothing, in my opinion, is more deserving of our attention than the intellectual and moral associations of America. The political and industrial associations of that country strike us forcibly; but the others elude our observation, or if we discover them, we understand them imperfectly, because we have hardly ever seen anything of the kind. It must, however, be acknowledged that they are as necessary to the American people as the former, and perhaps more so. In democratic countries the science of association is the mother of science; the progress of all the rest depends upon the progress it has made.

Democracy in America, translated by Henry Reeve (New York, 1904), vol. 2, 593–595, 597, 598.

STUDY QUESTIONS

1. Why did Tocqueville believe voluntary associations were especially popular and necessary in democratic societies?
2. Does Tocqueville's characterization of American democracy still seem to hold true?

Christian Reform

The Missionary Crusade

Given the importance of evangelical Christianity to antebellum reform, it seems appropriate that many of the earliest national reform organizations were explicitly Christian in inspiration and intent. Among the more significant was the American Board of Commissioners for Foreign Missions. Missionary work was nothing new in the nineteenth century, but the Board, founded in 1810 and interdenominational in spirit, was the largest missionary society in the United States before the Civil War. With tens of thousands of dollars at its annual disposal, the Board translated the Bible into multiple languages, opened schools, and sponsored hundreds of missionaries who evangelized among Indians in North America and non-Christians around the world. In 1831, a contributor to a religious periodical reflected on the Board's progress and its impact both domestically and abroad.

Twenty Years of the American Board of Commissioners for Foreign Missions (1831)

The American Board of Commissioners for Foreign Missions has now been in existence twenty years, having been organized in the year 1810. The history of its origin is well known. Four members of the Theological Seminary in Andover, having devoted their lives to the propagation of the gospel among the heathen, sought advice of their fathers in the ministry, convened in an ecclesiastical body, as to the best mode of accomplishing their design. This occasioned the appointment of the Board. But it will scarcely be believed, twenty years hence, that not one leading minister in our churches appears then to have conceived the possibility of obtaining funds enough in this country, to warrant the sending of these four young men to the heathen, without some foreign guarantee! One of the first measures, therefore, after the formation of the Board, was the deputing of one of the young men to England, to ascertain, among other things, whether he and his brethren could be supported for a time, if necessary, by the London Missionary Society.

Meanwhile an effort was made to raise funds in this country, which succeeded beyond expectation; and five missionaries embarked in 1812 for India, at the expense of the American churches.—These have since been followed into the heathen world by not less than EIGHTY preachers of the gospel, sent forth by the same Board; of whom about sixty are now in the field. The number of persons sent out as physicians, printers, schoolmasters, etc. besides females, is at least equal to that of the preachers. The whole number of missionaries, and of assistant missionaries male and female, now in foreign service, and dependent on funds placed at the disposal of the Board for their support and means of usefulness, is *two hundred and thirty four.*

* * *

What these missionaries have accomplished among the heathen, what they have written about the heathen, and what they have suffered for Christ, have been sending, all the while, an invaluable influence through our land. It is capable of being shown with certainty, that our churches are better supplied with ministers, that there are more candidates for the ministry, and more persons preparing for the sacred office, than there would have been, if we had kept all our ministers at home.

* * *

Regarding only our own religious welfare, and the success of those institutions which are designed chiefly for our own benefit, the Providence of God evidently calls upon us to extend our foreign operations. The more we export of our religion, the more we shall have at home. * * * The more missionaries we send abroad, the more ministers we shall have at home. Our domestic missionaries will keep pace with our foreign missions. The gospel will rise in our estimation with our efforts to send it to all nations, and our disposition will increase to make efforts and submit to self-denials to sustain it among ourselves. And as no command in the decalogue is plainer, or more binding, than that to publish the gospel to the heathen; as none comes to us with a higher sanction, and none (I had almost said) with such affecting motives to obedience;—we may well regard the duty and the interest of churches and individual Christians as eminently harmonising in missions to the heathen.

* * *

We now pass to the *direct influence of the missions of the Board upon the heathen world.*

A moment's reflection will teach us, that but a part, and probably a small part, of this influence is open to distinct human observation. Who can look into the thousands of minds and hearts, to which our missionaries have access? Who can observe the happy changes and modifications in the thousands of family circles, effected by their conversations, preaching, and publications, and by the sight or report of their holy lives? Who can relate the particular histories of all their tracts, and of all the portions of God's word, which they have put in circulation? Some of the more obvious facts are these:

Fifteen distinct missions have been established, some antipodes to others.

Fifty missionary stations have been formed, at each of which the gospel is regularly preached.

Three languages, before unwritten, have been reduced to writing by persons in the employment of the Board.

The New Testament, and parts of the Old Testament, have been translated into three languages;—that of the Sandwich Islanders, after reducing the language to writing; that spoken by the great body of the Armenians; and that used by the 12,000,000 of the Mahratta people.

One of the Gospels has been translated into each of three Indian languages in North America.

* * *

Numerous other works have been prepared in *eleven* different languages—four spoken chiefly in Asia, one in Europe and Asia equally, one in Europe, one in Polynesia, and four in the forests of North America.

A printing establishment, with two presses, has been set up in the Sandwich Islands; another, with three presses, in the Mediterranean; a third, with two presses, in India; and a fourth is about being sent to China.

More than ten millions of pages have been printed at Bombay; a greater number at Malta; and a still greater number at the Sandwich Islands. The whole number of pages in the eleven languages, filled with matter prepared chiefly by our own missionaries, and printed at the expense of the Board, is nearly *forty millions,* most of them stored with divine truth.

Full 70,000 learners have enjoyed the benefit of our mission schools; and now, there are at least 50,000, the greater part adults.

* * *

[T]aking the whole field again into view, we count more than *twelve hundred* converts from heathenism, in consequence of our missions, coming up every communion day, to the Lord's Table, glad with the hopes of heaven.

A great and indispensible *work of preparation* has been accomplished. Much land was to be possessed, and most of it was unexplored when the Board was instituted. Large tracts have since been arrayed, and some forests cleared, much ground broken, much good seed sown. In several, the time of harvest is not yet come; but here and there, over hill and dale and plain, the harvest waves.

Religious Intelligencer, containing the principal transactions of the various Bible and Missionary Societies, with Particular Accounts of Revivals of Religion, April 2 and 9, 1831.

STUDY QUESTIONS

1. Why did this author believe foreign missionary work would increase religiosity and improve spiritual life within the United States as well?

2. What were some of the various activities of the Board?

Forging Connections and Spreading the Word

Christian reform societies pioneered many of the strategies and organizational structures used by various antebellum reformers. They were among the first, for example, to capitalize on cheap printing technologies to mass produce literature and to implement a system in which members of local and state auxiliaries raised money and distributed movement materials under a national society's auspices. Particularly successful were groups like the American Bible Society, founded in 1816, and the American Tract Society (ATS), founded in 1825, which between them circulated millions of Bibles and other religious texts in the hope of sparking moral improvement among their readers. The following article, describing the merger of several preexisting tract societies into the ATS, speaks to some of the practical challenges of getting activists to unite behind a national banner and work together across denominational lines.

The Formation of the American Tract Society (1825)

At a large and respectable meeting of the citizens of New-York, and the vicinity, from various religious denominations, held at the City Hotel, on Friday evening, March 11, Col. Richard Varick was called to the Chair, and Mr. William A. Hallock, appointed Secretary. The meeting was opened with prayer by the Rev. Dr. M'Aulay. Zechariah Lewis, Esq. President of the New-York Religious Tract Society, then proceeded to state the object of the meeting. The Board of Managers of that Society, he said, had, some months since, in view of the great facilities afforded by the city of New York, for circulating Religious Tracts, and the importance of uniting the efforts of the friends of Tracts throughout the country in one National Institution, resolved to take measures to form such a Society in this city, in May next, on the plan of the American Bible Society. There being, however, at Boston, a Religious Tract Society, which had already assumed the name, and much of the character of a National Institution, it was thought proper, previous to the adoption of other measures, to address that Society, and propose a removal of the seat of its operations to New-York. This measure the Society at Boston did not think consistent with the prosperity of the Tract Cause in New-England; and as that Society had already become so far National in its character, they proposed still to continue their operations at Boston, and that the New York Religious Tract Society should become a Branch. To this proposition the Board of the New-York Society felt that they could not give their assent, believing that the local advantages of this city, united with the liberality and Christian enterprise of its inhabitants, leave no room to question that it is the most favorable location for the National Institution.

In these circumstances, the Committee of the Society at Boston proposed to unite with the Society at New-York in forming the plan of a National Institution, distinct from both, to be located in New-York and from which, should it prosper, the Society at Boston may receive its supplies of Tracts. And the negotiation had been happily concluded in a manner calculated, it was believed, to give universal satisfaction. Such a procedure on the part of the Society at Boston, immediately suggested the necessity of erecting a house in this city, in which the National Society may enjoy every facility for conducting its operations. In order to accomplish this object, it was thought advisable to call the present meeting, for the purpose of organizing the Society, and adopting measures to obtain the requisite funds; that the people of New-York may thus give to the Society at Boston, and other Tract Societies and friends, who may be invited to unite in the National Society in May next, as assurance that the Society shall here be furnished with every accommodation; and that, by the grace of God, there is here a spirit of Christian benevolence and zeal which, it may be believed, will never permit the Society to languish.

The following Constitution was then read and unanimously adopted.

Constitution.

Art. 1. This Society shall be denominated, *The American Tract Society*; the object of which shall be to diffuse a knowledge of our Lord

Jesus Christ as the Redeemer of sinners, and to promote the interests of vital godliness and sound morality, by the circulation of Religious Tracts, calculated to receive the approbation of evangelical Christians of all denominations.

Art. 2. Each subscriber of two dollars annually, shall be a member; and each subscriber of twenty dollars at one time, shall be a member for life. Each subscriber of five dollars annually shall be a Director; and each subscriber of fifty dollars at one time, or who shall, by one additional payment, increase his original subscription to fifty dollars, shall be a Director for Life.

Art. 3. Members of the Society shall be entitled to Tracts, annually, to the value of one dollar, and Directors, to the value of two dollars; or, if preferred, they may receive Tracts at any one time, to the value of half the sum given.

Art. 4. The Society shall meet annually on the Wednesday immediately preceding the second Thursday in May, when the proceedings of the foregoing year shall be reported, and a Board, consisting of a President, Vice Presidents, a Corresponding Secretary, a Recording Secretary, a Treasurer, and thirty-six Directors shall be chosen.

* * *

Art. 6. To secure the interests of the various denominations of Christians who may co-operate in this Society, its officers and directors shall be elected from all those denominations; the Publishing Committee shall contain no two members from the same denomination; and no Tract shall be published to which any member of that Committee shall object.

Art. 7. Any Tract Society contributing one fourth part or more of its annual receipts to the Treasury of this Society, shall be considered an Auxiliary, and be entitled to purchase Tracts at the most reduced prices. And any Agent or Treasurer of such Auxiliary, annually transmitting five dollars to the Treasury of this Society, shall be entitled to vote at all meetings of the Board of Directors; and the Officers of any Auxiliary annually contributing ten dollars, shall be entitled to the same privilege.

* * *

Art. 10. That the benefits of the Society may be enjoyed no less in distant places than near the seat of its operations, the prices of its Tracts shall be, as far as practicable, the same in all parts of the United States.

Religious Intelligencer, April 2, 1825.

STUDY QUESTIONS

1. What were some of the obstacles to creating a unified national tract society, and how were those obstacles overcome?
2. Why did the leaders of the American Tract Society think their organization was so important? Do you think distributing religious tracts was an effective activity?

Creating "Nurseries of Piety"

Missionary societies sent people around the world to teach the gospel and encourage conversion, and Bible and tract societies sought to spread Christian morals through religious texts. Sunday school movement activists combined these strategies. First created in England in the 1780s and established in several eastern American cities in the 1790s, Sunday schools initially focused on teaching poor children to read and write while stressing Christian faith and "orderly" behavior. The schools became increasingly popular in the early nineteenth century, and by the time the American Sunday-School Union (ASSU) was created as a national organization in 1824 it could already claim over 700 schools, 7,000 teachers, and nearly 50,000 students. It also no longer aimed to educate poor urban children exclusively but rather to bring Christian teachings to American children more broadly. Though it continued programs in towns and cities, the ASSU focused on rural and frontier regions, where reformers feared morality would crumble amid the scarcity of religious institutions. The ASSU published cheap tracts and magazines for classrooms, distributed curricular guides for teachers, and sent missionaries to organize local schools. Below, a contributor to the American Sunday School Magazine *explains the value of Sunday school education even for the children of already devout parents.*

Influence of Sunday Schools upon Family Religion (1824)

The object of Sunday schools, as stated in our last number, "is to teach, on the Lord's-day, *all classes* of persons who may avail themselves of the privilege, to read and understand the Bible; and to invite them to the practice of its precepts." There is a class of persons who speak approvingly of Sunday schools, but refuse their assent to this position; and would limit the attendants upon our Sabbath teaching to the children of immoral and grossly wicked parents, whose dispositions and habits unfit them for the religious instruction of their offspring. They affirm of Sunday schools that they detach the young from the case of their natural guardians, and interrupt, or overthrow family religion; that they tend to displace the far better, and more beautiful system in which the father rears the family altar, becomes the Sabbath teacher of his own offspring, guides them into the ways of holy obedience, and renders his own dwelling a mansion of domestic piety.

* * *

It is not true that family religion is superseded by these schools, so as to make Christianity less the topic of mutual exercise and conversation between parents and children, than before the period of their institution. Instead of banishing this topic from families, they have been known, in very many instances, to have first introduced it into dwelling-places where before it was utterly unknown. The most careless of parents are found to give their ready and delighted consent to the proposal which comes to them from the Sabbath teacher, for the attendance of their children. And the children, instead of carrying off from their own houses an ingredient of worth which truly had no place in them, do, in fact, impart that very ingredient from the seminaries which have been branded as the great absorbents of all the family religion in the land. Parents in spite of themselves, feel an interest in that which interests and occupies their children; and through the medium of natural affection have their thoughts been caught to the subject of Christianity; and the very tasks and exercises of their children have brought a theme to their evening circle, upon which, aforetimes, not a syllable of utterance was ever heard; and still more when a small and select library is attached to the institution, has it been the means of circulating, through many a household privacy, such wisdom and such piety as were indeed new visitants upon a scene, till now untouched by any print or footstep of sacredness.

* * *

Meanwhile, we not only see that the Sabbath school system tends directly to the establishment of the household system of education, but that, even in those families where the latter is in full operation, the former does not interfere with it.

* * *

[E]ven granting the case of parents altogether religious, and granting them to be fully observant of all the ordinances, and that, in particular, their well-filled family pew holds out, Sabbath after Sabbath, the pleasing aspect of a well-conditioned and a well-disciplined household; still we do not hold a Sabbath school for the children of such parents to be at all hurtful, or even superfluous. There is time both for the household and the school exercises, during the currency of a Sabbath evening, consisting, at the very least, of four hours; and it is, on many accounts, better that this time should be so partitioned, than that it should all be spent by the children, in what they are apt to feel the weary imprisonment of their own dwelling places. It is well that there should be such a variety to keep up and enliven their attention, among religious topics. It is well that the parent should guide their preparations for the teacher; and that a judicious teacher should lead on the parent to a right track of exercise and examination, for the children. There is time, under such a system, both for the lessons and the prayers of the family; and it is further right, that there should be time for the heads of families to have their own hours of deeper sacredness, not to be interrupted even by the religious care of those who have sprung from them. The seminaries we plead for, instead of having any effect to mar, do, in fact, harmonize, at all points, with the spiritual complexion of our most decent and devoted families. Nor can we conceive any degree of piety or Christian wisdom, on the

part of parents, that should lead them to regard a well conducted Sabbath school in any other light than as a blessing and
an acquisition to their children.

American Sunday School Magazine, August 1824.

STUDY QUESTIONS

1. Why did some Christian parents resist sending their children to
   Sunday School?
2. How does the author of this essay try to counter that resistance?
   Is the argument convincing?

Making the Sabbath Holy

*Among the consequences of nineteenth-century social and economic change was
a general decline in Sunday being a publicly observed day of rest. Most colonial
laws enforcing observance fell by the wayside in the early republic, and even the
federal government, which mandated Sunday mail delivery, seemed complicit in
the trend. Many evangelicals worried that religious values would be entirely
trumped by marketplace values that made no provisions for days without commerce. Those who were most concerned forged a Sabbatarian movement that
sought to return public Sabbath observance to the rhythm of weekly life.
Sabbatarians in New York began petition campaigns, boycotted businesses that
stayed open on Sundays, and founded in 1828 the General Union for the
Promotion of the Observance of the Christian Sabbath to organize the movement. The organization had the support of some very influential ministers and
businessmen and soon had auxiliary chapters from Maine to Ohio. Ultimately,
however, Sabbatarians infuriated even many religious people, who resented their
presumption that it was appropriate to impose personal religious preferences in
the public sphere. In their failure, Sabbatarians exposed Americans' limited
tolerance for reform societies that used tactics more aggressive than moral persuasion alone, a barrier many other groups would face as well. Below, the founders
of the General Union, having recently gathered at a convention in New York*

City, try to explain to the American public the need they saw for their organiza-
tion and its approach.

Address of the Convention to the People of the United States (1828)

From statements made to this Convention, as well as from what was before notorious, it appeared that the respect of former generations for the Sabbath was in many places gone, and in all places fast failing before the inundation of business and pleasure; that commerce, on our seaboard, and rivers, and canals, and turnpikes, is putting in motion a secular enterprise, which is fast and fearfully annihilating the national conscience in respect to the Sabbath, and rolling the wave of oblivion over that sacred day.

It was the opinion of this Convention, that the time had come in which the moral energies of the Sabbath must be preserved or abandoned, and that God had devolved upon them the responsibility of acting upon a question whose decision will affect deeply and permanently the destiny of this nation and the world.

* * *

Thus alarmed, and thus cheered and animated with hope, what, Fellow-Citizens, could we do, but, relying on the favour of Heaven, and presuming on your approbation, to resolve, that we will make the attempt to preserve to the nation the invaluable blessings of the Sabbath-day? We have done it. On the ninth day of May, 1828, which we trust will hereafter be remembered as an era in our moral history, we formed an Association, to be denominated "THE GENERAL UNION FOR PROMOTING THE OBSERVANCE OF THE CHRISTIAN SABBATH," the Constitution of which will accompany this address.

It is not the object of this Union to enforce the laws of the several States in favour of the Sabbath. We have not the madness to think of coercion merely. We know that our countrymen can violate the Sabbath if they will; and our only hope is, that, by the blessing of God, we shall be able to persuade them not to do it. It is by the calling up of a general attention to the subject—by the

extension of information—by the power of example—by reno-
vated vigilance in families and among the ministers of Christ and
the professors of his religion—and by withdrawing our capital and
patronage, as fast as may be, from all participation in the violation
of the Sabbath—that we hope to convince the understandings of
our countrymen, and awaken their consciences, and gain their
hearts to abstain voluntarily and entirely from the violation of that
day which God has given to us as the token of his love, and upon
which he has suspended all our hopes for time and eternity.

* * *

The plea of coercion, as resulting from the distribution of patronage, with reference to moral results, is without foundation. We
cannot fear that the common sense of this nation will decide, that
we may not wield the influence of property in such a manner as will
array powerful motives on the side of well doing, and against doing
evil; for if this be wrong, the government of God would be the
height of compulsion and injustice.

Were it even true, however, that powerful persuasion is unlawful
force, what must be said of the array of motives, so constantly
pressed upon the friends of the Sabbath, to lend the influence of
their capital and patronage to perpetuate the violation of that day?
Is it unlawful to employ powerful motives for the preservation of
the day; and at the same time, lawful to urge by powerful motives,
its continued and hopeless profanation? We disclaim coercion in
any proper sense of the term; but we avow our purpose, to employ
all lawful motives to persuade our fellow citizens to "cease to do
evil, and learn to do well" on the Sabbath day. We have come to the
conclusion, to withdraw our capital and patronage from the prostration of the Sabbath, because no alternative remains but this, or
the ruin of our republic. * * * BY THE GRACE OF GOD, THE
MEMBERS OF THIS UNION WILL EXERCISE THEIR
RIGHTS OF PROPERTY, FOR THE PRESERVATION OF
THE SABBATH, OF THEIR FAMILIES AND THEIR
BELOVED COUNTRY, UNANGERED AND UNAWED.

And now we look for co-operation to the government of this nation, the representatives of freemen, to aid us by their conspicuous
and powerful example, by their cogent arguments in the cabinet
and halls of legislation, and by their manifestation of a sacred re-

gard for the Sabbath in all the arrangements of business at the seat of government, in the army and the navy, and upon the highways of our land. We trust that those whom we have clothed with power by our suffrage "to see to it that the commonwealth receive no detriment," while they guide the destinies of this great nation, will not stop their ears against the supplication, nor disappoint the hopes of millions.

To the entire class of our fellow-citizens who inconsiderately, for amusement or gain, violate the Sabbath, we would say, Alas, brethren, why do you this evil thing? Do not imagine that we shall engage with you in angry controversy of words or deeds, or that we are insensible to the difficulties which by some of you must be encountered, to retrace steps which should never have been taken, and to withdraw yourselves from alliances that ought never to have been formed. But the emergency is tremendous. The liberties of your country, the welfare of the world are at stake. If this nation fails in her vast experiment, the world's last hope expires;—and without the moral energies of the Sabbath it will fail. You might as well put out the sun, and think to enlighten the world with tapers— destroy the attraction of gravity, and think to wield the universe by human powers, as to extinguish the moral illumination of the Sabbath, and break this glorious mainspring of the moral government of God.

Christian Watchman, May 30, 1828.

STUDY QUESTIONS

1. Why did Sabbatarians believe observing the Christian Sabbath was so important? What did they fear would be the consequences of neglecting that observance?

2. How did they justify economically boycotting businesses that opened on Sundays? Why did their critics claim that such activities constituted "coercion"? Were they right?

Religious Alternatives and Utopian Communities

The Appeal of the Latter-Day Saints

Evangelical denominations predominating among antebellum Protestants pro-
vided much energy for reform movements. But hundreds of thousands of
Americans failed to find spiritual fulfillment or a framework for confronting
changes in their lives in mainstream evangelicalism, which enabled new religious
sects to draw adherents as well. The most controversial antebellum religious
venture was the Church of Jesus Christ of Latter-Day Saints. Founded in
1830 by Joseph Smith and colloquially known as the Mormon Church, it was
ultimately also the most successful. Mormon beliefs that Smith was a prophet,
that the Book of Mormon he published constituted a new divine revelation, and
that his was the one true church to reestablish God's earthly kingdom antago-
nized many Americans, who believed both Smith and his teachings frauds. So
did the power of church leaders, who had significant influence over members'
economic and political lives. In the early 1840s, Smith alienated even some fel-
low Mormons who felt he was exercising authoritarian control over the church
and who were uncomfortable with his assertion that God had sanctioned the
practice of polygamy. Mormonism's appeal to believers, however, was powerful,
as evidenced by the experience of Sarah DeArmon Rich. Born in 1814, Sarah
grew up on the Illinois frontier, and Mormon missionaries converted her and
several family members in 1835. The family moved shortly thereafter to
Missouri, where Smith and most Mormons were then living, and where Sarah
married her husband Charles, who would later take four additional wives. In

the following portion of her recollections, written in 1891, Sarah describes set-tling in Nauvoo, Illinois, a place she and many other Mormons temporarily found peace after fleeing violence in Missouri. Though inspired by faith, Sarah's commitment was clearly strengthened by the experience of persecution she shared with fellow Mormons, all of whom found in the religion a belief system and lifestyle that spoke to them as nothing else in antebellum America did. So deep was Sarah's commitment that after Joseph Smith and his brother were murdered by an Illinois mob in 1844, she and her family determined to relocate with thousands of other church members to Utah. Reflecting decades later, she con-ceded the trip was dangerous, but claimed the Mormons found courage in their conviction that they "were preparing to help lay the foundation for the building up of the kingdom of our Heavenly Father on this earth."

Autobiography of Sarah DeArmon Pea Rich (1814–1893)

I can assure you my friends, it was a happy time for us to once more feel at home among the Saints of God, and to be where we could hear word of comfort from the mouth of our Prophet Joseph Smith. For we were now where we could attend meeting every Sunday; also where we could visit with our dear brothers and sisters who, like ourselves had been driven and robbed; and they like us, were glad of a resting place out of the reach of those that had sought our lives and the lives of our Prophet and all our leaders who had been delivered from prison by the hand of our Heavenly Father. We were truly a thankful and humble people.

Our new home consisted of a comfortable log house with a lot of an acre and a quarter of ground, covered with beautiful large trees, which furnished us plenty of wood for a long while, and our nearest neighbor on the west was Brother Heber C. Kimball, only a few rods from us; and our next neighbor on the south was Brother Charles Hubbard, now a resident of Wilford City, Utah. God bless him and his dear wife, Mary Ann, for their many kindnesses to us in the days of the first settling of Nauvoo; also Sister Vilate Kimball, whose husband, Heber C. was then on a mission to Great Britain. She, like us, was a new settler in Nauvoo, and Brother

Kimball being on a mission caused us to take great interest in her welfare. So we soon became strong friends to each other, and we felt for each other's interest. She truly was a noble sister, and one full of faith in the work of God. And we took solid comfort together, and were thrown together in many trying circumstances. And if my husband and I had any nice thing to eat that she did not have we shared it with her, and she did the same by us.

She opened the door for the brethren to hold meetings in her house; and many was the time that the Lord poured out His Spirit upon us in our meetings that caused us to rejoice together, and many were the blessings we enjoyed together; also with Brother and Sister Hubbard, for they too, were good Latter-day Saints, and were faithful to help administer to the wants of Sister Vilate Kimball and family in the absence of her husband.

Thus we passed the winter and summer together; and the Prophet Joseph would also call on us from time to time. He would also inquire after the wants of dear Sister Kimball, as he took great interest in the welfare of the families of those that were off on missions, to see that they did not want for the comforts of life. We then, as a people were united and were more like family than like strangers. And as there were many sick there the Prophet Joseph Smith would to go from house to house with others of the brethren and administer to the sick, and see that they had the necessary comforts that the sick needed, and many were healed and raised up from a bed of sickness, looking as though they were nigh unto death.

Thus we as a people struggled through poverty and sickness in trying to make another new home for ourselves after being robbed and driven from the state of Missouri. The people of Illinois seemed to open their hearts toward us and treated us kindly for a season; and thus the Lord opened the way for us as when we were cast as exiles in a strange land, as it were, we were protected and blessed so that the work of the Lord continued to prosper and gain ground, and we began to prosper and gather means by hard labor until we were again beginning to be more comfortable.

Original in Harold B. Lee Library, Brigham Young University, Salt Lake City, Utah.

STUDY QUESTIONS

1. What benefits did Sarah DeArmon Rich see in living surrounded by fellow Mormons?

2. In what capacities did Sarah see Joseph Smith acting among his followers? How do you think those activities strengthened allegiances of the Mormons to his leadership?

Communal Life among the "Shakers"

As Sarah DeArmon Rich's narrative suggests, Mormonism's appeal lay not only in its theology but also in its communalism. Wherever they went, among fellow believers Mormons elevated cooperation and service to the church over economic competition, and they often drew in people displaced by the commercial economy or who were repelled by the individualism it encouraged. The creation of separate communities to pursue beliefs most Americans found unusual, in fact, was a widespread impulse in the decades before the Civil War, as scores of experimental utopian communities came into being. Not entirely unlike those who followed preachers such as Charles Grandison Finney, inhabitants of utopian communities thought it possible to eliminate the sins and social evils of the world. But while evangelical perfectionists mostly sought to repair the consequences of the emerging socioeconomic order, those in utopian communities felt that order's basic organizational principles hindered human progress. If the world were to become perfect, they believed human beings needed to liberate themselves completely from oppressive and immoral customs, structures, and institutions. Americans who were not members of them often found utopian communities eccentric if not outright strange, and communitarians could find themselves subjects of misconception and ridicule. This was especially so when their lives were rooted in religious doctrine departing from the Protestant mainstream, like the Mormons and like those belonging to the United Society of Believers in Christ's Second Appearing. Commonly referred to as the Shakers, the most distinctive feature of their communities was that their members practiced celibacy in the belief that carnality was the root of all sin. More abstractly, celibacy was about denying the self of worldly pleasures in pursuit of pure, holy, orderly, and egalitarian communities as Shakers believed early Christians had inhabited.

*Accordingly, Shakers lived very simple material lives and held property in com-
mon, the restrained rhythms and strict discipline of their existence breaking only
at worship. There, Shakers unleashed themselves in ecstatic and enthusiastic
dances, whirling, moaning, convulsing, and, of course, shaking. The Shakers
established roughly two dozen settlements, and while many who visited them still
found the Shakers quite odd, they also discovered much to admire.*

Visiting a Shaker Community, Niskayuna, New York (1829)

We approach the settlement from the southeast; the road runs directly through the landed property of the United Society, which
consists of about two thousand acres. There are four villages or
families—one on the left of the road, and three on the right; and
the distance between each of these settlements is generally from
one-fourth to half a mile. We turned short to the right, and entered
the first village—the very emblem of neatness and good arrangement. * * * We rode to the trustee's house, found no one present to
answer our inquiries, and proceeded onward until we came to an
enclosure, beyond which stood three or four large dwellings. At the
door of one of them we saluted a venerable man and benevolent
looking woman; we inquired for an early friend who was now a
member of this community; an answer was given in tones of kindness. With a look of great tranquility and sweetness the woman
added—"dost thou know him?" He was further on, in a village past
the grove, on the left hand side of the road. It was a beautiful ride
to the place. We could not help observing the neat appearance of
the fields and the grove on our left. Every unsightly, or decaying
tree had been carefully converted into fuel, and nothing remained
but the vigorous and healthful. We soon saw the desired village, and
took our friend of other days by the hand.

It is impossible to describe the air of tranquility and comfort that
diffuses itself over a Shaker settlement. It is no matter what the
enemies of such peaceful, unoffending communities may say about
them. The acute observer of human manners will testify for them
that they do not live after the manner of the world.

* * *

[With the Shakers] the two sexes together bear the burden, if burden it may be, of celibacy; they enliven its dullness by the amenity of their intercourse with each other. And this intercourse is, indeed, much less restricted than is generally supposed. A stranger may not intermeddle with those affectionate friendships and pure platonic enjoyments that may spring up under what the world, perhaps, falsely, calls an overwhelming obstacle to earthly happiness. The union of these people, their uniform kindness to each other, and the singularly benevolent and tender expression of their countenances, speak a stronger language than their professions.

* * *

From a cursory examination of their dwellings, gardens and modes of life, we are prepared to speak decidedly favorable to their plans of worldly management and thrift. They have steam engines to aid in the mechanical trades, and the cutting of their fuel, which is done by a circular saw attached to a wheel, revolving by the power of steam, and they have numerous contrivances to lessen the weight of manual labor, that might be profitably copied by farmers and mechanics.

An inquiry in regard to their religious belief was answered in the following words—"we are impressed with the misery and wickedness of living after the manner of the world; we have departed from this way, and, although we regard ourselves as in an infant state, we have already realized great temporal and spiritual blessings."

We took leave of our friend, whose words at parting were—"be, as you appear to be; this is one of the most heavenly precepts."

The quiet and many comforts of these people suggested ideas of melancholy interest as we rode away. The people, comparatively, know of no change. No one of them rides above the other on a sudden surge of prosperity and then is broken on a hidden rock and his spoils scattered, far and near, over the seething billows. The storm of war may rage all around them—but they are not men of battle; they lend no energy to the Moloch of ambition. Through the plainness of their dress and living, and the community of their labors they will ever have a plenty and ever be on the increase.

Niles' Weekly Register, September 19, 1829.

Witnessing Shaker Worship, New Lebanon, New York (1828)

We next repaired to the meeting house, which is a spacious but plain frame building. The whole floor, which appears never to have been wet, was as clean as a dining table, and without any incumbrance of pews or other fixtures, excepting a narrow galley upon one side, for the accommodation of visitors, to whom they are very attentive, and of whom, as the morning was fine, a large number attended. After waiting some time, the brethren and sisters began to assemble, and took their seats upon moveable benches, at opposite ends of the room. Their attire in perfectly in character with that neatness which appears to be the *sine qua non* of their religion: the women wear white dresses of a peculiar cut, white neck and pocket handkerchiefs, tab caps which obscure the face, except from a front view, and high heeled buckskin shoes. The dress of the brethren is generally of domestic manufacture, but not so uniform as that of the females. Many of them wore no coats, and had their shirt sleeves confined to the arms by green ferret. Their shoes were light; and their hats * * * are broad rimmed and low crowned. These, as well as the plain bonnets of the women, were laid off on entering the meeting house. * * * When about two hundred of the Society were assembled, at a silent signal given, they arose, removed their seats to the further ends of the room, and formed themselves in opposite ranks. The meeting was opened by a short address from an Elder, expressive of gratitude for their preservation through the week, and for the present opportunity for worship, with a hope that it might prove profitable to them. The spectators were then exhorted to conduct themselves with becoming seriousness and decorum; with an undisguised warning, that in case of their misconduct or levity, the right of government belonging to the Society would be exercised freely, and the offender disposed of. This was followed by singing two or three hymns to lively music but rendered monotonous by its admitting of no *rests* or intermissions in the whole course of a hymn; the singing was accompanied with a slight bodily tremour on the part of a few of the performers. After this the brethren and sisters were requested to resume their seats, and give room for public speaking. This having been done, a shrewd looking elderly man advanced towards the visitors and notified them of his intention of addressing them, and of grounding his remarks upon "the strangeness of Christianity, and the consequent strangeness of the Shakers," whom he regarded as the only people who adhered strictly to the principles and practices of Christianity.

In the course of his illustrations, he made several pointed allusions to what he considered the mal-practices of professing christians, particularly those of war of every description, and all *sexual intercourse.* Many of his arguments were forcible and logical, a proportion of them truly ridiculous, and some of them calculated to call up the blush of modesty. * * * After speaking nearly three quarters of an hour, he concluded his harangue, and the benches having been again removed, we learned that they should next proceed to "go forth to worship God in the *dance* and in the exercise." To describe the manoeuvres which succeeded, in an intelligible and accurate manner, can hardly be expected from one who has had but a single opportunity of witnessing them. I should, however, compare their dances to a drill of marches and countermarches of two companies of well disciplined soldiers, performed on tip-toe, and on a kind of half trot, substituting the vociferous singing of a selected band, with powerful lungs, sometimes with words and sometimes without, for the martial drum and fife. These evolutions were performed with a regularity as pleasing as it was surprising, each one seeming to know their part and to act it with the exactness of veteran practitioners. In these dances, however, the sexes never intermingle. This was carried on for about twenty minutes without intermission, when the singers took the centre of the floor, while the rest, males and females, formed themselves into a circle around them, four abreast, and commenced the exercise or travelling around the room (symbolical, as they say, of their travelling to Heaven,) at a rapid and uneasy gait, also on tip-toe, singing as they went, and occasionally clapping their hands with a tremendous noise. This truly fatiguing exercise was continued for nearly half an hour, with occasional short intermissions, when we were informed that the meeting had been protracted to the full time usually occupied in worship, and that it would now be dismissed. No prayer was offered, nor was any invitation given to the spectators to unite in any part of their devotions. Thanks were however returned to them for their orderly conduct, followed by a wish for our future welfare, and that we might be enabled to discover the true light of the gospel and live accordingly. The whole meeting then retired in an orderly manner. Candour demands the remark, that however the narrative I have given may excite the risibility of the reader, I can say with truth that except at some dry remarks made in the course of the address, I felt no disposition to laugh or even to smile at any part of their singular mode of worship. There certainly was an air of solemnity pervading the meeting, and which seemed to extend even to the spectators, whose conduct throughout was strictly decorous. The sincerity of the greater part of the worshippers, we could have no reason to question, and upon the just principle of "rendering to all their due," it is but fair to award credit to those singular people for their hospitality, cleanliness, honesty and apparent piety.

Saturday Evening Post, March 1, 1828.

STUDY QUESTIONS

1. What words would you use to characterize the Shakers and life in their villages? How would you say their values differed from those of mainstream Americans?
2. What did visitors find appealing and admirable about the Shakers? What did they find peculiar?

The Perfectionists at Oneida

No other antebellum religious movement provoked the violence that the Mormons did. But the Oneida community in upstate New York, founded by John Humphrey Noyes in the late 1840s, rivaled Joseph Smith's church in outraging mainstream American mores. Like the Mormons and the Shakers, Noyes envisioned a sacred order that reconceived customary understandings of the relationship among sex, gender roles, family, individualism, and materialism, and like members of those religious alternatives he concluded that a collective economy was holier and more conducive to fellowship and harmony than competitive capitalism. What set Noyes and the Oneidans apart was their fusion of a communal economic plan to extreme theological perfectionism and a radical critique of American family life, as they concluded that among perfect Christians all things, including husbands and wives, ought to be shared in the interests of unity and love. Accordingly, at Oneida monogamous marriage was replaced with "complex marriage" in which any man and any woman could have sexual intercourse. The community monitored intimacy to prevent the formation of exclusive attachments, and no couples were supposed to reproduce without communal approval. Critics nonetheless accused Oneidans of participating in "free love," and between the indignation of outsiders and the jealousies "complex marriage" likely fostered (not to mention engagement in the ritual of "free criticism" where community members publicly discussed each other's flaws), we might reasonably suspect Oneida rested on shaky foundations. In fact, Oneida attracted hundreds of members and thrived for thirty years, making it one of the most successful nineteenth-century experimental communities. Below, an imaginary Oneida spokesman named "Mr. Freechurch" explains some of the community's basic theories and practices.

Bible Communism; A Compilation from the Annual Reports and Other Publications of the Oneida Association and Its Branches (1853)

The Reader. * * * I have heard of the Oneida Association as a body of Communists living in the State of New York. Can you give me information about them?

Mr. F[reechurch].—I am well acquainted with the society you speak of—being in fact a member myself; and shall be happy to answer your questions, and to assist you as far as possible to a correct knowledge of their views and position.

* * *

Reader.—What is the number of members?

Mr. F.—About 150; of whom one third are men, one third women, and one third children.

Reader.—Do these all live in one house, and eat at one table?

Mr. F.—* * * The main building is sixty feet long, thirty-five feet wide, three stories high, with a habitable garret. The basement is divided into three equal rooms, each thirty-five feet long, (the width of the house,) and twenty feet wide. The first, (in front,) is the dining room, where all eat together. The second is the kitchen. The third, (which runs into the offset on which the house is situated,) is the cellar. Over the dining room is a parlor of the same size, for general gatherings.—The rest of the house is divided into sleeping rooms; which, with those in the children's house and out-buildings, accommodate the whole family.

* * *

Reader.—What are your most important articles of faith?

Mr. F.—We believe in the Bible as the text-book of the Spirit of truth; in Jesus Christ as the eternal Son of God; in the Apostles and Primitive church, as the exponents of the everlasting gospel. We believe that the Second Advent of Christ took place at the period of the destruction of Jerusalem; that at that time there was a primary resurrection and judgment in the spiritual world; that the final kingdom of God then began in the heavens; that the manifestation of that kingdom in the visible world is now approaching; that its approach is ushering in the second and final resurrection and judgment; that a church on earth is now rising to meet the approaching kingdom in the heavens, and to become its duplicate and representative; that inspiration, or open communication with God and the heavens, involving perfect holiness, is the element of connection between the church on earth and the church in the heavens, and the power by which the kingdom of God is to be established and reign in the world.

* * *

Reader.—What are your means of religious influence?

Mr. F.—We have meetings every evening, and they are generally devoted to religious conversation and reading; though business and other topics are not excluded. Then there is a religious meeting on Sunday, open to the public. The Bible is the daily study of men, women, and children.

Reader.—Explain, if you please, what you mean by Free Criticism.

Mr. F.—It is a system of telling each other plainly and kindly our thoughts of each other, on all suitable occasions. We have introduced a fashion of judgment and truth-telling, which gives voice and power to the golden rule—"Whatsoever ye would that men should do unto you, do ye even so to them." Selfishness and disorder inevitably annoy the circle around them; and the circle thus annoyed, in our Association, has the liberty and the means of speaking the truth to the offender. All are trained to criticise freely, and to be criticised, without offense. Evil, in character or conduct, is sure to meet with effectual rebuke from individuals, from platoons, and from the whole Association. Sometimes criticism is given by the whole circle in a general meeting: at other times it is given more privately, by committees, or individuals. In some cases, criticism is directed to general character, and in others to specific faults and offenses. It is also exercised in the discovery and commendation of value in character, as well as in the exposure of defects. Generally, criticism is invited by the subject of it, and is regarded as a privilege. It is well understood that the moral health of the Association depends on the freest circulation of this plainness of speech; and all are ambitious to balance accounts in this way as often as possible. Here is the whole secret of government among us. Our government is Democratic, inasmuch as the privilege of criticism is distributed through the whole body, and the power which it gives is accessible to any one who will take pains to attain good judgment. It is Aristocratic, inasmuch as the best critics have the most power. It is Theocratic, inasmuch as the Spirit of Truth alone can give the power of genuine criticism.

* * *

Reader.—Do you hold to community of property?

Mr. F.—* * * We hold—1, That all the systems of property-getting in vogue in the world, are forms of what is vulgarly called the "grab-game," i.e., the game in which the prizes are not distributed by any rules of wisdom and justice, but are seized by the strongest and craftiest; and that the laws of the world simply give rules, more or less civilized, for the conduct of this game.

2. That the whole system thus defined, is based on the false assumption that the lands and goods of the world, previously to their possession by man, have no owner; and rightfully become the property of any one who first gets possession; which assumption denies the original

title of the Creator, excludes him from his right of distribution, and makes the "grab-game," in one form or another, inevitable.

3. That God the Creator has the first and firmest title to all property whatsoever; that he therefore has the right of distribution; that no way of escape from the miseries of the "grab-game" will ever be found, till *his* title and right of distribution are practically acknowledged; that in the approaching reign of inspiration, he will assert his ownership, be acknowledged and installed as distributor, and thus the reign of covetousness, competition and violence, will come to an end.

4. That God never so makes over property to man, as to divest himself of his own title; and of course that man can never in reality have absolute and exclusive ownership of lands, goods, or even of himself, or his productions, but only subordinate, joint-ownership with God.

* * *

It will be seen from this statement of principles, that the Oneida Association cannot properly be said to stand on any ordinary platform of Communism. Their doctrine is that of community, not merely or chiefly with each other, but with God; and for the security of individual rights they look, not to constitutions or compacts with each other, but to the wisdom and goodness of the Spirit of truth, which is above all. The idea of their system, stated in its simplest form, is, that all believers constitute the family of God; that all valuables, whether persons or things, are family property; and that all the labors of the family are directed, judged and rewarded in the distribution of enjoyments, by the Father.

* * *

Reader.—Do you carry out these principles, and apply them to social rights, i.e., property in wives and children?

Mr. F.—Certainly. * * * We apply these principles, not only to property and social rights, but to our ownership of ourselves.

Reader.—Do you separate husbands and wives?

Mr. F.—No; but we teach them the law of love: "Thou shalt love [not merely thy wife and children, but] thy *neighbor* as thyself;" and when they have got that lesson by heart, they *separate themselves* far enough to let in their neighbor.

Reader.—Do parents take care of their own children?

Mr. F.—Yes, if they please. But members, as fast as they become intelligent, come to regard the whole Association as one family, and all children as the children of the family.—Their special relation to their own children, though it is not extirpated or despised, is reduced to subordination to the general family relation. The care of the children, after the period of nursing, is committed to those who have the best talent and most taste for the business, and so the parents are made free for other avocations.

Reader.—What are your regulations about labor?

Mr. F.—Labor in the Association is free; and we find that "free labor" is more profitable than "slave labor." By this I mean, that labor among us is for the most part redeemed from the base motive of *necessity*, and is placed on higher grounds. The common anxiety about "getting a living"—that curse of the apostasy—and the overseer system that exacts so many hours of labor, whether there is a spirit for it or not, are totally discarded; and in their place we depend on a free, inspired appetite. The men and women organize themselves, or are organized by the general managers, into groups, under chiefs, for the various departments of work. These groups are frequently changed, and constant rotation goes on, so that all have variety of occupations, and opportunity to find out what each one is best adapted to. The practice of doing work "by storm," or in what is more commonly called "a bee," in which the men, women and children engage, has been found very popular and effective. It may be employed in a great variety of operations, especially of out-door business, and always contributes to enliven and animate the most uninteresting details of work.

Bible Communism; A Compilation from the Annual Reports and Other Publications of the Oneida Association and Its Branches (Brooklyn, N.Y., 1853), 5–6, 7, 9–11, 12–13.

STUDY QUESTIONS

1. What was the ritual of "free criticism," and how did Oneidans believe it helped bind their community together?
2. Why did Oneidans believe in the communal ownership of all property rather than in individualized ownership? What, in their understanding, constituted "property"?

Owenism in Theory and Practice

The search for utopia did not need to be grounded on any religious foundation. Like the Mormons, Shakers, and Oneidans, secular utopians also sought alternatives to the prevailing competitive and individualistic economic environment, and like them they hoped their lifestyles would inspire imitation by a broader public. But secular utopians were more interested in this world than in eternity, and they rarely set themselves so dramatically apart from society with controversial theologies or unconventional sexual and family practices. Guiding them instead was the idea that modern social and economic arrangements forced human beings into unsatisfying lives of frustrated isolation. What people needed instead was a socioeconomic plan that encouraged cooperation and personal fulfillment without sacrificing the prosperity modernity made possible. One popular secular idea for utopian community life came from Robert Owen. Disturbed by the consequences of the industrial age for workers' lives at the Scottish cotton mills he managed, Owen concluded that human beings were almost entirely the product of their surroundings and that it was possible to craft the perfect environment for fostering individual happiness. He purchased 20,000 acres of land in Indiana as a sort of laboratory for creating that environment, which he believed depended on equality of condition, freedom of conscience, and the practical abolition of private property. The village established at New Harmony only survived for three years after its founding in 1825, but Americans looking for an alternative to competitive individualism created more than a dozen Owenite communities before the Civil War.

Robert Owen, Address at the Founding of New Harmony (1825)

I am come to this country, to introduce an entire new state of society; to change it from the ignorant, selfish system, to an enlightened, social system, which shall gradually unite all interests into one, and remove all cause for contest between individuals.

The individual system has heretofore universally prevailed; and while it continues, the great mass of mankind must remain, as they comparatively are at present, ignorant, poor, oppressed, and, consequently, vicious, and miserable; and though it should last for numberless ages, virtue and happiness cannot be attained, nor can man, strictly speaking, become a rational being.

Until the individual system shall be entirely abandoned, it will be useless to expect any substantial, permanent improvement in the condition of the human race; for this system ever has been, and must ever remain, directly opposed to universal charity, benevolence and kindness; and until the means were discovered, and can be brought into practice, by which universal charity, benevolence, and kindness, can be made to pervade the heart and mind of every human being, a state of society in which "peace on earth and good will to man" shall exist, must remain unknown and unenjoyed by mankind.

These invaluable blessings can be obtained only under a social system; a system derived from an accurate knowledge of human nature, and of the circumstances by which it is, or may be, governed.

This knowledge has been, until now, hidden from man; he therefore knew not how to put the social system into practice; for without this knowledge, the social system is utterly impracticable. The slight attempts which have been made, in ancient and modern times, to procure some of the innumerable advantages, with which the social system abounds, have not proceeded from this knowledge, but have been founded on some artificial or unnatural view of our nature, and in consequence, only partial and temporary benefits have been obtained.

The knowledge of our nature, and of the circumstances which govern the character and conduct of man, are to be acquired only by attending to the facts which exist around us, and to the past history of the human species.

These facts and this history demonstrate, that all men are formed by a creative power, and by the circumstances which are permitted to surround them from birth; and that no man has ever had any will, or power, or control, in creating himself, nor in forming the circumstances which exist around him at birth, in his childhood, in youth, or in manhood. He is a being, then, whose general nature,

whose individual, or personal nature, and whose artificial acquirements, or character, have been formed for him. He cannot, therefore, become a proper subject for praise or blame, nor for artificial
reward or punishment, or artificial accountability; but he becomes
a being capable of being formed into the extremes of good or bad,
and to experience the extremes of happiness or misery, by, and
through the circumstances which shall exist around him at birth, in
childhood, in youth, and in manhood; he cannot, therefore, become a rational object for anger or displeasure of any kind; but in
whatever deplorable circumstances he may be found, and whatever
may be the character which nature and these circumstances may
have formed for him, he is a being who justly claims our compas-
sion, care, attention and kindness, in proportion to the extent of the
evil and misery which he has been made to experience; and to this
rule there can be no exception.

These fundamental principles being understood, and the real
nature of man being thus laid open to us, the proceedings requisite
to produce good instead of evil, and happiness instead of misery,
become obvious and easy to practice.

I have bought this property, and have now come here to introduce this practice, and to render it familiar to all the inhabitants of
this country.

From the Articles of Union and Cooperation, New Harmony (1826)

WE, the undersigned, form ourselves and our children into a
Society and Community of Equality, for the benefit of ourselves
and our children and of the human race; and do agree to the
following:

Article I.

The Society shall be called "The New-Harmony Community of
Equality."

Article II.

SEC. 1. All the members of the Community shall be considered as one family, and no one shall be held in higher or lower estimation on account of occupation.

SEC. 2. There shall be similar food, clothing and education, as near as can be, furnished for all, according to their ages; and, as soon as practicable, all shall live in similar houses, and in all respects be accommodated alike.

SEC. 3. Every member shall render his or her best services for the good of the whole, according to the Rules and Regulations, that may be hereafter adopted by the Community.

Article III.

It shall always remain a primary object of the Community to give the best physical, moral and intellectual education to all its members.

Article IV.

SEC. 1. The power of making laws shall be vested in the Assembly.

SEC. 2. The Assembly shall consist of all the resident members of the Community above the age of twenty one years, one sixth of whom shall be necessary to form a quorum for the transaction of business.

Article V.

SEC. 1. The Executive power of the Community shall be vested in a Council, to consist of the Secretary, Treasurer, and Commisary of the Community, and four Superintendents of Departments, to be chosen as hereinafter provided.

SEC. 2. The Secretary, Treasurer, and Commisary shall be elected by the Assembly.

SEC. 3. The Community shall be divided into six Departments:
   Of Agriculture,
   Of Manufactures and Mechanics,
   Of Literature, Science, and Education,
   Of Domestic Economy,
   Of General Economy, and
   Of Commerce;
And these Departments shall be subdivided into Occupations.

* * *

Article VI.

No person shall hereafter be admitted a member of this Community without the consent of a majority of all the members of the Assembly; and no person shall be dismissed from the Community, but by a vote of two thirds of all the members of the Assembly; and in neither instance, until the subject shall have been discussed at two successive weekly meetings.

Article VII.

The Real Estate of the Community shall be held in perpetual trust for ever for the use of the Community, and all its members, for the time being;

* * *

Article XI.

Every member shall enjoy the most perfect freedom on all subjects of knowledge and opinion; especially on the subject of religion.

* * *

Article XIII.

All misunderstandings that may arise between members of the Community, shall be adjusted WITHIN the Community.

Article XIV.

As this system is directly opposed to secrecy and exclusion of any kind, every practical facility shall be given to strangers, to enable them to become acquainted with the regulations of the Community, and to examine the results which these have produced in practice; and an unreserved explanation of the views and proceedings of the Community shall be communicated to the government of the country.

New Harmony Gazette, October 1, 1825, and February 15, 1826.

STUDY QUESTIONS

1. According to Robert Owen, what were the differences between the "individual system" and the "social system," and which was more in keeping with human nature? Do you agree?
2. What were the guiding principles of the New Harmony community, and how did its rules help to advance a "social system"?

American Fourierism

―――――――――――――――

Enthusiasm for Owenite utopianism waned somewhat during the 1830s, but the economic depression that began in 1837 revived Americans' interest in communal alternatives to capitalism, and during the 1840s experiments based on the ideas of French author Charles Fourier became even more popular than those modeled on Owen's theories. Owen and Fourier similarly argued that a cooperative society was superior to an individualistic one, and each believed his plan for the ideal socioeconomic order rested on a scientific understanding of human nature. Fourier's program, however, depended not on total equality of material conditions but on creating carefully organized communities known as "phalanxes" that would facilitate individual happiness, social harmony, and efficient productivity by allowing men and women alike to labor at tasks they found personally fulfilling. An American named Albert Brisbane popularized Fourier's complicated theories in the United States, inspiring the creation of more than fifty American phalanxes. The selection below, from Brisbane's 1843 work, Concise Exposition of the Doctrine of Association, *describes the flaws Fourierists saw in how America functioned and some of the exacting specifications their alternative called for.*

Albert Brisbane, *Concise Exposition of the Doctrine of Association* (1843)

Society, as at present constituted, is based upon principles which in their operation misemploy, misdirect and pervert the faculties and passions of man, and defeat all the ends and hopes of life. It is based upon the principle of isolation, of separation of man from his fellow-man, upon individual effort, and envious strife and anarchical competition, upon selfishness, distrust, antagonism, overreaching, fraud and injustice, upon the conflict of all interests, and upon universal duplicity of action. There is no combination or Unity; no harmony of action, of interests, or of feeling; no connection or association. Every family has, for example, a separate house, a separate interest, separate hopes, and a separate welfare to attain; it is in conflict with most of the families around it, eager to detract from their prosperity to add to its own, instead of seeking to unite with them to advance by their combined effort their mutual welfare and happiness.

A Social Order, governed by such principles, must, it is evident, be opposed to Reason, to Justice and to Truth, and should be reformed.

We advocate a Social Order based upon the principle of Association—of Union between Man and his fellow-man—upon Unity and Harmony of Interests—upon generous Devotion, Confidence and Love—upon Kindness and Justice—and upon perfect Liberty and Independence, with Law and Order.

We believe the broad and comprehensive principle of Association to be the Divine Law for the government of Human Societies, and that a Social Order, based upon this principle, is the true and natural System of Society.

* * *

The System of Society propounded by CHARLES FOURIER, and which we are now laboring to realize in practice, is based upon those laws of Order and Harmony which govern the Universe— the divine laws of Attraction and Repulsion, the universality of which, and their application to the Moral government of Man, as well as the Mechanical movement of Material things, were first discovered by that profound genius. This new Social Order will form a new plane on which the highest Truth can securely rest, and upon which Christianity can be fully and truly developed. Man will there be surrounded by influences that will refine and elevate him to a high standard of excellence, and direct him rightly in his earthly career. There he will fulfill his destiny, and accomplish the grand objects of his creation.

* * *

The proper number of persons for an Association is about Eighteen Hundred, or, if we suppose six persons on average to a family, three hundred families. This number is not chosen arbitrarily, but is based upon the number of distinct Characters which we find in Man, and which compose the full scale of human Character. It is only in large Associations of eighteen hundred persons, that all varieties of talents and capacities, as well as the proper capital, skill and knowledge, can be combined, which are necessary to secure a perfect prosecution of Industry, and the Arts and Sciences.

If the members of an Association are of different degrees of fortune, of different characters, tastes and talents, and possess varied theoretical and practical acquirements, the easier it will be to associate and harmonize them. Diversity in these respects will, in a true system of Association, be a source of Concord, Union and Harmony.

* * *

For a large Association, a tract of land containing about six thousand acres, or three miles square, will be necessary. * * * The surface of the soil should be undulating and adapted to a varied cultivation, and a small stream of water should, if possible, flow through it. * * * In the centre of the Domain, the Association would erect a commodious and elegant Edifice, capable of accommodating comfortably the members, with spacious and convenient suites of apartments, separated by division walls, and at different prices, to suit the fortunes of the inhabitants, and storehouses, granaries and other necessary outhouses in the vicinity. The Edifice, rising in the midst of the finely cultivated fields and gardens of the Domain, would present a beautiful spectacle of architectural Unity, in comparison with which our present little and isolated constructions would appear most insignificant and discordant.

* * *

Would not eighteen hundred persons, united in an Association, prosecuting with order and economy all their industrial and business operations, and dividing equitably the product of their Labor and Talent—each receiving a share according to the part which he or she has taken in creating it—live much more in accordance with the dictates of wisdom, than if they were divided into three hundred families, inhabiting as many isolated little tenements, as lonely in general as they are inconvenient, with poor farms and workshops, poor flocks, tools, implements and machinery, and without the charm of varied social relations,—without Art, Science and other intellectual enjoyments, which give to human existence its elevation, and constitute the true life of Man? We leave the reader to answer the question himself.

To furnish more data for forming an opinion, let us contrast more minutely the manner in which three hundred families now live, and the manner in which they would live in Association. The contrast will show us the immense superiority of Association, as regards Economy, and Unity of action and interests over the present System.

Three hundred families require at present three hundred separate houses, three hundred kitchens, three hundred kitchen fires, three hundred sets of cooking utensils, three hundred women to do the cooking—and if they are farming families—three hundred little farms, three hundred barns and sheds, three hundred teams, innumerable walls and fences, and every thing else equally as complicated and uselessly wasteful.

All the cares and labor attendant upon providing for the wants of a family, such as cooking, washing, marketing and keeping up fires, must be gone through with three hundred times daily by the three hundred families, and with the same detail as for an assemblage of eighteen hundred persons, except the difference of scale.

Association will avoid this monstrous complication and waste; instead of three hundred little kitchens and three hundred fires, it will have four or five large and convenient kitchen[s], with as many fires by means of which, not only the cooking can be done, but the entire Edifice warmed; instead of three hundred little fire-places and cooking-stoves, and as many sets of cooking utensils, it will have its extensive kitchen ranges, its large boilers and ovens, and machinery on the largest scale and the best that can be invented for facilitating culinary operations; instead of three hundred women to do the cooking, it will have a few experienced cooks, engaged by turns every other day; instead of three hundred poor teams, half the time idle, it will have merely the requisite number, and of the best quality; instead of the immense number of walls and hedges now required, it will have a few extensive hedges; and instead of making all its sales and purchases at retail, paying in profits to traders one-half the product of its labor, it will make them at wholesale, and in the most economical manner.

To what immense Economies would Association give rise! What a source of Riches it would be! We live in an Age, the all-absorbing desire of which is wealth. If men would but add sentiments of justice and philanthropy to their greedy strife after money, they would see, that it is only in Association that their wishes can be satisfied, and that all can attain prosperity.

If people would associate, economize and apply their talents and energies in a judicious manner, they could produce wealth in abundance, and escape want and anxiety; whereas in striving to wrest from each other by fraud, over-reaching and other unjust means the little that is produced under the present false and repugnant system of Labor, ninety-nine out of a hundred live amidst cares and perplexities, and die in poverty and destitution.

* * *

Any plans of reform—any measures or efforts which have for their aim the social elevation and the happiness of Mankind, and *which are not based upon a Reform in the system of Isolated Households and the present repugnant system of Industry*, will prove in practice abortive and useless.

Politicians and Reformers in all spheres have yet to comprehend—for they seem not to be aware of the fact—that so long as disunion, anarchy, strife, conflict of interests, fraud and injustice, exist in the *foundation of Society*—that is, in the household System and in Industry, disunion, anarchy and conflict will exist also in the other departments of Society—in politics, religion and social relations. A reform in Industry and in the system of Isolated Households is the practical commencement of a true social Reform. The moral and intellectual development of Mankind and their spiritual regeneration cannot be effected so long as their interests, efforts and aims are not associated and harmonized, and Industry, which is the means by which they secure to themselves temporal prosperity, and by which they subdue material Nature, is not rendered pleasing, attractive and honorable.

They who wish to introduce justice, equality, liberty, order and morality into society and who endeavor to do so by operating on the political power or government, or by recommending merely good precepts, may be compared to men who are striving to build the roof of a house, before having laid the foundation. If we wish to introduce those great principles into the social existence of Mankind, we must first organize the foundation of society rightly— that is, the industrial and domestic systems. Until this be done the higher aims of the enlightened statesman, the conscientious reformer and the philanthropist, cannot be attained.

Concise Exposition of the Doctrine of Association (New York, 1843), 2, 15, 16–17, 18–19.

STUDY QUESTIONS

1. As Brisbane described it, what was Fourier's "principle of Association," and how did it differ from the principles on which he felt society generally operated?
2. What advantages did Brisbane see in replacing a system of "Isolated Households" with a one grounded in Fourierist "Associations"? How exactly would an Association work?

Bodily Reform and Self-Improvement

Fortifying the Body

Where utopians like Owen and Fourier aimed to create ideal societies, other reformers concerned themselves instead with the personal well-being of individuals. They advocated new ideas about health and disease, talked in new ways about the importance of what people ate and drank, and advised people to develop their personalities, modify their characters, and exploit their innate talents. Various in their techniques and suggestions, body and health reformers got Americans' attention because they promised that proper management of the physical self protected an individual from the dangers of a disorderly world, cultivated the discipline and self-mastery necessary to thrive in it, and enabled personal triumphs over illness and appetites that would lay the groundwork for widespread social progress. The best-known antebellum health reformer was Sylvester Graham. Initially trained as a minister, Graham never dismissed the popular notion that perfecting the world meant overcoming sin. But he became famous for his "Science of Human Life," a complex and sweeping program that called upon Americans to change their dietary and hygiene practices in pursuit of physical self-improvement. Presented in basic terms below in the Graham Journal of Health and Longevity, *the "Graham System" might superficially seem to reject the antebellum urban lifestyle, with its questionable diet, lack of bathing, and fast-paced yet very sedentary routine. Grahamism, however, also demanded regimentation and self-discipline that were commercially advantageous, and testimonials from the system's adherents suggest they believed it equipped them to master themselves and the world around them while insulating themselves from its perils.*

The Graham System. What Is It? (1837)

This question has been asked by some of our subscribers already, but they must not expect too much; we wish to give them facts, and as many of the principles as our limits will permit;—here follows a mere sketch or outline of the system, as relates to diet.

Although man can adapt himself to almost any and every kind of aliment, there are certain kinds which are best suited to his real physical wants, to health and long life.

So far as man deviates from that course to which his Creator has adapted his physical constitution, he becomes more liable to disease, short life, &c.

The best manner of living in civic life is as follows:—

The chief food should be vegetables and fruit, to be eaten in as near their natural state as possible.

Bread made of unbolted wheat (that being its natural state) is the best, although if made of rye, or indian, it is good, if unbolted. Rice, sago, &c are very wholesome, if plainly cooked.

Good cream may be used instead of butter. Milk and honey are substances somewhat of the nature between animal and vegetable, and are allowed if desired.

Care should be taken to make use of the teeth and masticate the food thoroughly.

Eat slow.

Flesh-meat and fish in all their forms had better be omitted.

No fat or gravies of any kind are allowed.

None of the common condiments, such as pepper, mustard, oil, vinegar, &c. are allowed.

All stimulants, of every sort and kind, as tea, coffee, wine, tobacco, (in all its forms,) cider, beer, &c., are prohibited.

No drink except pure soft water, is proper at meals or at any other time.

All liquid foods, as soups, broth, &c. should be avoided.

Only three meals should be taken and they should be as near six hours apart as possible; the last meal of the day should be light and three or four hours before going to bed—*not a particle of food should be taken except at meals*—every little luxury, like nuts, apples, &c. should constitute a part of a meal. Children may be allowed a very light luncheon of fruit or bread. The sick should not sip anything which requires digestion, as gruels, &c., but should have regular times of taking nourishment, as a well person would.

Care should be taken not to eat too much; if such a circumstance should sometimes happen, or if you are deprived of your meal at the usual time, the next meal should be lighter than usual.

Abstinence should always be preferred to taking medicine—it is a benefit to lose a meal occasionally.

About 7 hours should be the average time of sleeping, say from 10 P.M. to 5 A.M. After dinner naps are highly injurious and should never be indulged in.

Sleeping apartments should be properly ventilated, but no current of air should come direct upon the bed.

No tight clothing should ever be worn, all bed clothes should be well aired   all clothes worn through the day should be taken off on going to bed.

Bathing in warm or cold water is highly recommended, particularly with a sponge and cold water daily in the morning, taking care to wipe dry, and immediately after rub well with a coarse towel or flesh brush.

The usual clothing should not be too warm.

Exercise in the open air is very necessary; walking, or riding on horseback are two of the best modes.

It is a wrong notion that aged people require wine and other stimulants, because they are least able to bear them: all stimulants, narcotics, &c. are offensive to the human system, particularly to the nerves; and instead of exciting to healthy action, only force the organs (to their injury,) to use great exertion to repel the offending substances.

No pastry should be used—pies can be made with unbolted wheat and cream; avoid cakes of all kind in which butter or fat is used; they can be made of unbolted wheat with little sweetening, bread must not be eaten till 12 to 24 hours old.

Feather beds are highly injurious and do not possess a single redeeming quality and are of course proscribed—Mattresses are good made of curled palm leaf, straw, corn husks, rowen, &c., no matter if hard.

Testimonials from Followers of the Graham System (1837)

Henry Douglass: Before I was 21 years of age, I was afflicted much with the sick-headache and dizziness, so as to be often obliged to stop my work for some time; my nerves were much affected, which I concluded was caused by drinking strong tea, I therefore abandoned that for a number of years; I was also troubled with a weakness in my stomach, my food distressed me very much soon after eating, and left me faint and exhausted before the time for another meal arrived. I was in the frequent use of physic to obtain relief from my dizziness and sick-headache; but I concluded it was an unavoidable evil, and that there was no other course but to seek for the best remedies. * * * When I first attended the lectures of Mr. Graham, in 1833, I must say that I became particularly interested in the great principles laid down and illustrated by him.

The study of my own physical nature had never particularly engaged my attention before; but when I began to study myself, a new world opened to my view; I found I had been a stranger to myself, wandering in a strange region of perplexity and uncertainty, without the knowledge of any certain *law* to guide me to happiness; but when I returned to myself and studied myself and became acquainted with myself, I found I had not to ascend nor to descend to bring it nigh, for it was within me a true light to lead to the fountain of healthfulness. The more I studied nature, the more I became convinced that all her laws were wisely adapted to produce the happiest results. * * * When I became convinced of the truth, I desire[d] to be honest enough to obey its dictates, and although I had received some unfavorable impressions in relation to Mr. Graham's principles before I heard him, when they commended themselves so forcibly to my judgment that I could not resist the conviction of their truth, as an honest man I was determined to give them a fair trial. I commenced this course three or four weeks before I said much about it, but I soon began to experience a benefit from it, and I made up my mind to pursue it faithfully. My bread was made of the unbolted flour, my drink was the pure element unmixed, together with healthy vegetables and a plenty of good ripe fruit. This made up my wholesome repast. My feather bed was exchanged for straw,—a part of my burden of bedclothes were dispensed with; I retired at seasonable hours and awoke at a regular time with my body and my mind refreshed as I had never experienced before. I arose when the lark and robin began their joyful melodies—I went forth with joy, and the trees clapped their hands before me; all nature with her ten thousand tongues burst forth into singing; and all within me and around me, united in sweet harmony to move in obedience to the great laws of life and of happiness.

I bathed in cold water at least once a week in winter, and oftener during summer, always careful to put on my clothes when the skin was in a warm flush. My mind was clear and cheerful, which was the greatest luxury of all. I had no symptom of sick head-ache or dizziness for more than a year and a half, and had not enjoyed so good health for more than fifteen years.

Simeon Collins: I am now in the fifty-first year of my age. I have been extensively engaged in mercantile business, from 1813 down to 1835. For several years previous to 1833, I had been much afflicted with a severe cough, and viewed myself as bordering upon the consumption; could get no sleep except by the aid of anodynes. In the summer of 1833, I saw frequent extracts from Dr. G[raham]'s lectures in the New York papers, and being satisfied that the doctrines which he was teaching were rational, I determined in some way to avail myself of the advantages of a course of his lectures. * * * After attending strictly to his instructions I determined to make a thorough trial of what is now called Grahamism, but it is in fact Biblism. I immediately discontinued the use of flesh meat, fish, fowl, butter, gravy, tea, and coffee, and made use of a plain vegetable diet. My bread is made of the unbolted wheat meal, my drink is pure cold water, my bed for winter and summer is made of the everlasting flower, my health is and ever has been perfect since I got fairly cleansed from the filthiness of flesh meat and other pernicious articles of diet in common use.

Since I entered upon my present course of living, my happiness and activity have been greatly increased. For two years after entering upon this system, I did all the business that had before required three men to perform, my present business requires a great degree of activity, and I can truly say that I am a stranger to weariness or languor. At the time of entering upon this system I had a wife and five children, the youngest eight years of age, they all soon entered upon the same course of living with myself, and soon were all benefited in health. * * * Previous to the time of our adopting the present system of living my expenses for medicine and physician's bill would range from twenty to thirty dollars per year, and for the four last years it has been nothing worth naming.

Graham Journal of Health and Longevity, April 4, April 18, and June 6, 1837.

STUDY QUESTIONS
1. What were the basic provisions of the Graham System? Does it seem to you to be the "best manner of living in civic life"?
2. Why did those who testified on behalf of the Graham System find it so beneficial? Do their claims seem believable?

The Hydropathic Promise

Although Sylvester Graham attracted ridicule as a crackpot and elicited accusations from physicians that following his plan could be fatal, he attracted legions of followers. Graham also influenced other reformers, including advocates of the water cure, or hydropathy, which was one of the most popular health reforms of the late antebellum period. Made fashionable in Europe by a farmer named Vincent Preissnitz, hydropathy promised to cure nearly any disease or physical ailment primarily through water, generally administered internally by enema or externally by different wet wraps or baths. Hydropathy's growth came at a moment when medical authority was less firmly established than it is today, and when conventional (or allopathic) medicine entailed painful procedures like bloodletting or the use of drugs that often seemed to do more harm than good. The movement also called for a dietary and hygienic regimen similar to Grahamism, and supporters like Dr. Thomas Nichols maintained that mass adherence to natural and clean living exemplified by the water cure would bring about broad social improvement. The water cure particularly appealed to women, whose health was so badly misunderstood by conventionally trained doctors that pregnancy itself was treated as a pathological condition. In 1851, at the opening of the American Hydropathic Institute Mary Gove Nichols founded with her husband the first training facility for water-cure physicians. She denounced the health care women generally received in the United States, arguing that hydropathically trained women would be able to take control of their own well-being and that of other women better than any man. Popular into the late nineteenth century, by the middle of the 1850s there were already more than sixty facilities scattered across the United States where people might take the cure under the guidance of hydropathic physicians, and the movement's most significant educational tool for laypersons, a periodical entitled The Water-Cure Journal, *had over 100,000 subscribers at its peak.*

T. L. Nichols, M.D., The Future Results of Water-Cure (1852)

It is vain to expect purity of conduct, virtue, morality, religion, or any good thing, until the soul have a firm basis in the health and purity of its bodily organs. We, who earnestly desire to reform the world, must do with it, as we would with some poor, wretched, ragged, filthy individual. The first step is to make it clean, and surround it with healthy conditions. It is thus that the Health Reform is the basis of all reforms.

* * *

One result of the spread of Water-Cure principles and literature will be, in due time, the universal knowledge of the laws and conditions of health. From this knowledge must grow up a conscience, public and private, in regard to all sins against natural laws. Health will be regarded, not as a "blessing," as it is now called, but a right, which it is our duty to secure. The first object of every person will be to secure for himself healthy conditions; and public health, or the means of its preservation, will be the first object of every government and society. We shall have then no stifling, unventilated steamboats, railroad cars, theatres, or churches; no crowded buildings, filled with filthy and diseased beings, pouring out their deadly miasmata; no stagnant marshes, exhaling malaria; no pestiferous piggeries, distilleries, and slaughter-houses. Every one will enjoy the conditions of pure air, pure food, cleanliness, and a healthy occupation, as the first necessities of life.

Another result will be the general abandonment and avoidance of all the causes of disease. We shall not send our hundreds of ships to China for tea, to poison us into nervous diseases. We shall not waste the products of our industry, in importing coffee from St. Domingo, Java, or Arabia. We shall not convert the blessings of a bounteous nature into deadly curses, by turning wheat, rye, corn, and potatoes into whisky, and its various sophistications, which are sold, and drunk, as gin, rum, and brandy. We shall not blast millions of acres of our fair land, by cultivating that pest and nuisance, which civilization has borrowed from the savage; that meanest of all diseasing abominations—tobacco. We shall refrain, I trust, from the bad economy and loathsomeness of converting good corn into scrofulous pork, when we lose three-fourths of the nutritious matter, and get disease in its stead.

Another result will be the universal abstinence from drugs, as medicines. The well will avoid them that they may keep well—the sick, that they may have some reasonable chance to get well. Fifty millions of dollars is a moderate estimate of the annual expenditure in this country for drug poisons, or useless nostrums. The waste of wealth is nothing, compared with the waste of health. War has never cost us one-tenth part, in money or lives, that we have sacrificed to medicine. Even the lancet has slain more than the sword. Water-Cure will put a stop to all this.

Another fast-coming result, which every day draws nearer, and the terrific sign of which is written on the walls of our medical colleges, is the utter downfall of the medical profession. It is doomed; and its doom is just. It deserves its fate, for it has never done its duty, even with the light it had. Instead of enlightening the people, as it might have done to a great extent, in the laws of health, it has kept them in darkness. It has never made any great and generous effort to prevent disease. It has not given its earnest testimony against the violations of health laws. With a few honorable exceptions, the great mass of the medical profession has been bigoted in its errors, mercenary in its motives, and utterly faithless to its true function. Diseases, drugs, and doctors must all be swept off together. Instead of them, we must have a new and noble profession of teachers and healers. A vast field of missionary effort is now opened, and a few strong-hearted pioneers are already at work; but hundreds more are needed. Let the friends of Water-Cure see that they lack not for material aid.

* * *

And now let us see the final result of this progress and triumph of Water-Cure. No tea, coffee, rum, pork, or tobacco, and all the millions these are annually costing us saved for education, for improvements, for comfort, for beauty everywhere. No drugs, or drug doctors; and all these millions saved for good purposes; and all this intellectual wealth turned to some good account. None of the diseases there are everywhere producing; and here will be not only a saving of unutterable suffering, but of the time, and labor, and comfort of the sick, and those who are called from other duties to take care of them. Everybody washed clean, so we can move about among our brethren without the offence of their filthiness. Everybody fresh, and strong, and healthy, so that we shall not have our pity constantly excited by the spectacle of human misery.

What a glorious spectacle is here presented! A country full of health, and purity, and beauty; without deformity, or disease, or crime. A country abounding in power and wealth; strong enough, rich enough, and generous enough to govern and save the world. A country freed from all nastiness and nuisances. A country beautified with the highest cultivation, the noblest architecture, and the divinest art. A country where every citizen will have better opportunities for education, than wealth can now purchase for the richest. A country where all the faculties of man will be so harmoniously developed, and have such free exercise and full employment, that there shall be no bar to human progress, and no hindrance to human happiness.

These, my friends, are the natural, legitimate, and inevitable results of Water-Cure.

Mrs. M. S. Gove Nichols,
Woman the Physician (1851)

Bad men can more deeply outrage and abuse woman in the medical profession than in any other. Many men, under the name of doctor, are amassing fortune, and corrupting the weak and ignorant multitude of women; therefore I demand that woman be educated and qualified to protect herself and her sex. I can bear honorable testimony to the moral worth and good intention of a majority of the medical profession, though I consider their practice bad and poisonous in the extreme. But there are numbers of men who shield themselves under the title of doctor, for whose deeds murder is too mild a name, and for whose punishment a new penal code might be needful, for the death penalty would be wholly inadequate.

I cannot trust myself to speak much on this subject. It is too fraught with horror, with all that is revolting to benevolence and purity. Men whose victims are the last to understand or complain, are insured fortune, and safety from the prison or the gallows by the fatal disease, and still the more fatal ignorance of woman. There is neither hope nor help for this, but in educating woman to be physician of her sex. Year after year have I labored to rescue woman from her degrading bondage to quackery. Abuses are constantly coming to my knowledge. Men are practising in large numbers, who have neither learning, honor, nor common decency; but others who pretend to all these, are probably more mischievous. Abuses, deception, and outrage have been communicated to me by my patients, till my whole being has been aroused almost to madness, and I had wished I had the power to curse and wither from the earth those who could deliberately do such foul wrong.

* * *

[I]t is time that God and man should say, *Let there be light!* Educate woman, and you give her the first and most indispensible condition of salvation. So long as she is helpless from disease and ignorance, she is the prey of bad men. Give her knowledge, let her know the causes of disease, and the methods of cure; let her know herself better than the best and wisest man *can* know her. Do this, and the hour of her redemption has come. And woman will not be redeemed alone. She is the mother of man. If she is degraded, her offspring is degraded. If she is elevated, man is correspondingly elevated.

* * *

We want truer and more elevated ideas of womanhood. We must have free, noble, healthy mothers, before we can have men. The cramped waist, the crushed vitals, the loaded spine, the trailing skirts, the fettered limbs, the feeble, fearful being, who has no rights but to be maintained, protected, and doctored, can train us no Washingtons, Franklins, or Jeffersons, no wise or great men, and no women worthier the name than their mothers. We want women who can break the bonds of custom, who are great enough to be emancipated from all that weakens, degrades, and destroys, and who will teach others the holy lessons of a true freedom, not to be independent of man, but that man and woman should be mutually dependent.

In the life-struggle of a wise humanity, men and women must be united, and strive together for the highest good. There are brave women in our land—women who dare to work for God and their brethren—who are ready to devote themselves religiously to their own elevation, and that of their fellows. In these, and for these, there is hope. We want a band of devoted physicians, who shall be the teachers and the healers. Woman must enter upon this work, with her whole being possessed and informed by a devotion, deep as the fountains of her existence, and broad as life, with all its duties and developments.

Water-Cure Journal, December 1852 and October 1851.

STUDY QUESTIONS

1. What did Thomas Gove Nichols mean when he claimed that "the Health Reform is the basis of all reforms"? How did he see the water cure changing American society more generally?

2. According to Mary Gove Nichols, why were women so poorly served by male physicians? Would improvement in women's health care help women alone? Is it surprising that supporters of women's rights often supported hydropathy as well?

The Phrenological Path to Self-Mastery

The publishing firm of Fowlers and Wells, founded by brothers Orson and Lorenzo Fowler, became a sort of clearinghouse for antebellum health reform literature. This made sense, given the affinity among reforms like Grahamism, hydropathy, and the cause that made the Fowlers famous—phrenology. Literally meaning "science of the mind," phrenology's basic premise was that the brain was divided into several dozen "faculties," each roughly corresponding to a personality trait, and that by measuring and feeling the contours of a person's skull a properly trained phrenologist could assess those faculties and thus "read" a person's character. Phrenology achieved semi-respectability among some medical professionals in the early nineteenth century, but men like the Fowlers turned it into a national phenomenon by making it "practical." Just as other health reformers promised individual and social improvement through proper management and manipulation of the body's natural propensities, the Fowlers told Americans that phrenological readings could be used to guide everything from career paths and marriage partners to child rearing and choosing political candidates. Phrenology was nearly bankrupt in terms of actual science, and many Americans saw it as little more than an entertaining diversion. But it was no fad. Indeed, the movement's leading periodical, the American Phrenological Journal, *published for more than seventy years. Ultimately, phrenology owed its popularity to the fact that it offered both the orderly society and the possibility of personal perfection that reform-minded Americans craved. Below is a map of the head the Fowlers published in a home guide to phrenology, and essays from the Fowler brothers describing phrenology's usefulness and value.*

Symbolical Head, from *The Illustrated Self-Instructor* (illustration, 1857)

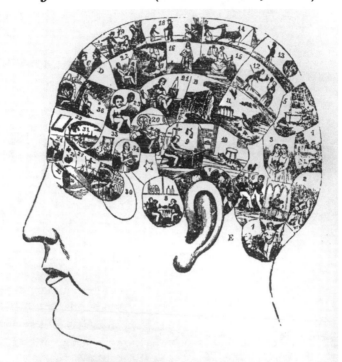

NUMBERING AND DEFINITION OF THE ORGANS.

1. AMATIVENESS, Sexual and connubial love.
2. PHILOPROGENITIVENESS, Parental love.
3. ADHESIVENESS, Friendship—sociability.
4. UNION FOR LIFE, Love of one only.
5. INHABITIVENESS, Love of home.
6. CONTINUITY, One thing at a time.
7. COMBATIVENESS, Resistance—defence.
8. DESTRUCTIVENESS, Executiveness-force.
9. ALIMENTIVENESS, Appetite, hunger.
10. ACQUISITIVENESS, Accumulation.
11. SECRETIVENESS, Policy—management.
12. CAUTIOUSNESS, Prudence, provision.
13. APPROBATIVENESS, Ambition—display.
14. SELF-ESTEEM, Self-respect—dignity.
15. FIRMNESS, Decision—perseverance.
16. CONSCIENTIOUSNESS, Justice—equity
17. HOPE, Expectation—enterprise.
18. SPIRITUALITY, Intuition–spiritual revery
19. VENERATION, Devotion—respect.
20. BENEVOLENCE, Kindness—goodness.
21. CONSTRUCTIVENESS, Mechanical ingenuity

21. IDEALITY, Refinement—taste—purity
B. SUBLIMITY, Love of grandeur.
22. IMITATION, Copying—patterning.
23. MIRTHFULNESS, Jocoseness—wit—fun.
24. INDIVIDUALITY, Observation.
25. FORM, Recollection of shape.
26. SIZE, Measuring by the eye.
27. WEIGHT, Balancing—climbing.
28. COLOR, Judgment of colors.
29. ORDER, Method—system—arrangement
30. CALCULATION, Mental arithmetic.
31. LOCALITY. Recollection of places.
32. EVENTUALITY, Memory of facts.
33. TIME, Cognizance of duration.
34. TUNE, Music—melody by ear.
35. LANGUAGE, Expression of ideas.
36. CAUSALITY, Applying causes to effects
37. COMPARISON, inductive reasoning.
C. HUMAN NATURE, perception of motives
D. AGREEABLENESS, Pleasantness—suavity

O. S. and L. N. Fowler, *The Illustrated Self-Instructor in Phrenology and Physiology* (New York, 1857), vi.

O. S. Fowler, Practical Utility of Phrenology (1840)

Men now worship two deities, Wealth and Fame, with more than pagan idolatry; and value things in proportion as they further these objects. But this standard of valuation is evidently erroneous. Whatever can be made to augment human happiness, or to promote morality or virtue—to diminish or alleviate human suffering, or in any way to improve man physically, or mentally, or morally, is useful in proportion as it is capable of effecting these important but difficult objects. All this phrenology is calculated to accomplish. It is therefore useful—

1. AS A STUDY. *"Knowledge is power."*
* * *

[I]t is self-evident that a knowledge of this science is the key that opens up to man all the hidden capabilities of enjoyment belonging to his nature, and will also enable him to remove, to a great extent, those causes of mental anguish and suffering which afflict either mankind in general, or individuals in particular. By fully and clearly analysing and unfolding the primary powers of the human mind, and thereby showing what is, and what is not, their natural, legitimate, and healthy function, and thus what actions and feelings are virtuous, and what sinful, phrenology will teach every one how to exercise his faculties in accordance with their primitive constitution, or in other words, how to obey the laws of his mental and moral nature, and thereby how to become the recipient of uninterrupted mental enjoyment.

2. "KNOW THYSELF" was written in golden capitals upon the splendid temple of Delphos, as the most important maxim which the wise men of Greece could hand down to unborn generations. The Scriptures require us to "search our own hearts and try ourselves"; and the entire experience of mankind bears testimony, that *self-knowledge* is the most important of *all* knowledge. A thorough

knowledge of one's own self—of his good properties, and how to make the most of them; of his defects, and how to guard against the evils growing out of them; of his predispositions to, and sources of, temptation to excess and error, and means of keeping these desires quiescent; of what he is capable of doing and of becoming, and what not; and wherein he is liable to err, either in judgment or conduct—is more intimately associated with his virtue, and happiness, and success through life than any other, than *all* other knowledge united. Before he can correct any defect, he must know precisely in what that defect consists—must know the *precise faculty* that is too strong, or too weak, or wrongly exercised.

Now this very knowledge, phrenology, if true, furnishes, and that with the certainty of *physical demonstration*. It will enable every individual to place his own fingers upon every element of his character * * * and teach men precisely what they are.

* * *

Let parents but apply the principles of phrenology to the choice of occupations adapted to their children—let the agriculturalist be located upon his farm, the mechanic in his workshop, the artist in his studio, the merchant behind his counter, the statesman in the halls of legislation, the teachers of morals and of letters in their respective places; let the orator mount the rostrum, the judge between man and man ascend the bench, the naturalist be places in the open fields of nature—let every member of society be placed in circumstances the most favourable for calling into full and delightful exercise all his talents and mental energies, and this divinely contrived machine of human society, with every wheel, every thing in its proper place, would work out an incalculable amount of happiness to mankind in general, and to individuals in particular; * * * But alas! this machine is deranged, its wheels misplaced, and its product is misery; the natural mechanic is put into the study, and the scholar upon the farm, their natures crossed, their talents lost to themselves and the world, and their happiness greatly abridged, if not exchanged for misery. Now if phrenology be true, the natural talents even of children can be discovered with certainty, and their pursuits directed accordingly; and thereby these evils be avoided, as well as these blessings secured.

3. IT WILL INCALCULABLY ADVANCE THE ARTS AND SCIENCES. Only the very threshold of science is yet entered. For every discovery thus far made, doubtless scores remain yet to be made. Future centuries, like those that are past, will unquestionably witness clusters of new sciences, as the present one has chemistry, geology, and phrenology, unfolding new truths and new worlds of facts, by means of which the knowledge and happiness of mankind will be vastly augmented. There are multitudes of minds calculated to bring to view the phenomena and laws of nature, and make scientific discoveries, which are now either wholly engrossed with other minor matters, or enter upon a literary course too late to make much progress; whereas, had their talents been early known, and their education conducted upon phrenological principles, such naturalists and mathematicians, such artists and mechanics, such statesmen and poets, such orators and divines, such philanthropists and such profound philosophers would rise upon our world as would complete eclipse every thing past and present—as would incalculably improve, adorn, and bless mankind. It would also throw out from under the wheels of science multitudes of those who now retard their progress, and clear the various professions of those drones who are now their bane and disgrace, besides being useful in making choice of our public officers.

4. IT WILL GREATLY PROMOTE MORALITY AND TRUE RELIGION. Phrenology, if true, unfolds the moral and religious nature of man. To this same moral nature of man, true religion is also adapted; so that each will confirm and strengthen the other, and both *together* do much more for man's moral elevation than either could do *alone*. Phrenology, more than any thing else, is calculated to do away with sectarian prejudices, and wear off the edge of those asperities which grow out of them, and which are a deep disgrace to the Christian world. It also teaches forbearance and forgiveness, and does away with bigotry. It will teach natural theology and natural religion more clearly and forcibly than any other department of science whatever.

5. A knowledge of phrenology will give its possessor an almost unlimited command over the minds and feelings of his fellow-men.

* * *

[P]hrenology teaches you how and when to appeal to the reason, or to the feelings, or to the particular *class* of feelings required by the occasion, and also how to avoid arraying against you large Combativeness, or Firmness, or Self-esteem, or Destructiveness, and thus how to be *always* successful, meting out to every man his portion in due season.

* * *

But all these beneficial results, capable of being derived from an application of the principles of phrenology, sink into insignificance, when compared with its application to the *modification, moulding, and formation* of the minds and characters of children, and, indeed, of every individual in reference to himself. To *state* this principle, is all that can be done here; its full elucidation would require a volume. The principle is this: every faculty has its own appropriate aliment and stimulant, by the presentation of which it is excited, and its organ thereby enlarged, and by the removal of which its action is diminished, and its size thereby reduced. By teaching us the true nature and proper aliment of every faculty, and thus how to excite and how to allay each at pleasure—by distinctly pointing out first the excess or defect, and then the remedy, phrenology directs us how to change their relative power, and thus how to produce perfect and well-balanced characters and intellects, which is the greatest of all other desiderata.

American Phrenological Journal, November 1, 1840.

American Phenological Journal for 1849

Ten years ago, this periodical spread its pages before the greatest and the best nation on earth. It was projected, not to make money nor to acquire fame, but simply to DO GOOD. It had a single eye to teaching mankind the LAWS OF THEIR BEING, and persuading them to obey them, that they might thus become virtuous and happy.

* * *

But its work is not yet done—only just begun. It is not about to retire from the field, but having become fairly warmed up in its labor of love, it is putting on new armor and preparing to redouble its exertions. * * * At first it was content to do a little good, but now, like a strong man ascending mountain peaks, as it attains one summit it sees another higher, and pushes off to gain its ascent, which gained, its ambition aspires to do still greater things.

Not that it is actuated by merely worldly ambition. It cares nought for fame or praise as such. Its aspiration is a high and holy one, namely, to stand foremost in activity and power in that array of means now working out the deliverance and regeneration of the race.

It's present desire is this—to PHRENOLOGIZE OUR NATION, for thereby it will REFORM THE WORLD. No evil exists in society but it sternly yet calmly rebukes, and points out a more excellent way. No reform, no proposed good, but it strenuously enforces. It is the very "HEAD AND FRONT" of that new and happy order of things now so rapidly superceding the old misery-inflicting institutions of society.

* * *

Pecuniary profit is NOT its object. If any one will step forward and guarantee to extend its circulation materially beyond what we can, we will surrender it—any thing to increase its USEFULNESS. But what it desires is to MOULD THE NOW FORMING CHARACTER OF OUR REPUBLIC. Ours is THE nation of the whole earth: not the most numerous, but the most influential; not the mistress of the sea, but the queen of the human MIND. Our world is just merging from the feudal bondage, and king-craft, and preist-craft, and fashion-craft, of feudal institutions into the glorious liberty of its true destiny. What mean those desperate struggles and throes of the old world? That the day of man's redemption draws nigh. Kings, while shaking on their tottering thrones, point the sword of wrath at us, and say, "You did it," and then gnash their rabid but almost powerless teeth at us. They know who gives them all this trouble. And their distresses will come faster and wax greater the longer our republic lasts, till some sudden shock overturns their man-devouring thrones and institutions, and buries every vestige of feudalism beneath the ruins. Would to God that every son and daughter of this heaven-blessed republic appreciated the responsibility of our nation, and of themselves as an integral part of it! The more perfectly we fulfill our destiny, the sooner will every nation, and kindred, and tongue, and sect, and individual, upon the whole earth, be brought out of the present kingdom of sin and suffering into that of virtue and happiness. Our nation is the world's leaven, and the better we make it the sooner will the human mass become leavened.

Now what the Journal wants to do is this—to PERFECT OUR REPUBLIC, to reform government abuses, and institute a higher and better state of private society and common usage throughout all our towns and villages. That is, it wishes to place mankind upon the true basis of our common nature, by teaching them that nature. This teaching, Phrenology, and the Journal as its exponent, does in a most effectual manner. Neither individuals nor communities can read it without clearly seeing their errors, and discovering in its teachings a more excellent way. Nor see without putting in PRACTICE. It discloses the laws of the human mind, the conditions of man's happiness, the causes of public and private suffering, and shows how to obviate them by simply following that NATURE OF MAN which it develops. Let its teachings become national, and those evils and abuses about which so much is said, will silently disappear, and humanity grow, bud, blossom, and bear the fruit of its true destiny.

American Phrenological Journal, January 1, 1849.

STUDY QUESTIONS

1. Examine the "symbolical head" published by the Fowler brothers. Does it seem to you to cover the full range of human personality? What sorts of traits does it stress as being particularly important to measure? What sorts of traits does it neglect?

2. What, according to the Fowlers, was the personal and social usefulness of phrenology, and how could it serve to "perfect our republic"?

Urban and Labor Reform

Helping the Poor

Relative to where most Americans lived, a disproportionate number of reformers resided in cities. Cities were places where people lived in close proximity, which facilitated building and sustaining reform organizations. They housed many of the publishing and printing concerns that produced and disseminated reform literature as well as businesses and companies that employed members of the middle class. Moreover, because the economic changes of the market revolution were especially marked in urban areas, many social ills exacerbated by those changes became particularly noticeable there. Thus, while many antebellum reform movements arguably responded to issues especially salient in cities, in some cases they addressed problems so particularly severe in cities that they can reasonably be classified as "urban reforms." Poverty, for example, was hardly limited to urban areas. But the material circumstances of the poor seemed increasingly dire and the number of destitute people increasingly large in cities as metropolitan populations and disparities of wealth both grew in the decades after 1820. One significant hurdle faced by those who wished to draw attention to and alleviate poverty was the widely held assumption that most poor people were poor because of their own laziness or immorality and were therefore undeserving of help. Even religious reformers working in urban missions often brought moral condescension along with financial assistance to families they tried to aid. By the 1830s, though, some who examined the issue, like Philadelphia publisher Mathew Carey, began arguing that poverty did not generally result from personal failings of the poor. Rather, they insisted that random misfortune and structural impediments in urban economies made it nearly impossible even for hard-

*working individuals of the lower classes to succeed financially and lead up-
standing lives.*

Mathew Carey, *Essays on the Public Charities of Philadelphia* (1830)

Many citizens entertain an idea that in the present state of society
in this city, every person able and willing to work, may procure
employment; that all those who are thus employed, may earn a
decent and comfortable support; and that if not the whole, at least
the chief part of the distresses of the poor, arises from idleness, dissipation, and worthlessness. Alas! nothing can be much farther
from the truth, and nothing can have a greater tendency to harden
the hearts of those who have the means to afford relief to the distressed, rendering them indifferent to the sufferings of their fellow
mortals. There cannot be a doubt that this unfeeling and un-
founded cant has produced indifference to a great extent, and para-
lyzed the hands of charity and beneficence. It is an error, therefore,
which calls loudly for refutation.

In the most prosperous times there are always some trades and
occupations that are depressed, in which there is a deficiency of
employment, and, consequently, when the earnings of former days,
laid up by the frugal and industrious, are consumed, and pinching
distress is the result. There is almost always a superabundance in
this city in some occupations, particularly clerks and shopkeepers.
At some trades, employers take too many apprentices, and dismiss
them as soon as their apprenticeships expire, when they frequently
find it difficult to procure employment. General depression, moreover, occasionally takes place, in which there is a redundance of
hands at almost all occupations. These facts, which are of public
notoriety, ought to silence the heartless, withering, and deceptious
cant, so often reiterated—that "nobody need be idle, who is willing
to work."

That among the poor there are dissipated, idle, and profligate
persons, [are there not among the rich, and perhaps, allowing for
the difference of numbers, an equal proportion?] cannot be denied.

But the proportion is small, much smaller than might be reasonably supposed, from the various disadvantages and discouragements under which that class labours. The worthless and profligate meet the public eye in our streets, on the wharves, and, occasionally, stretched in a state of intoxication on the pavements; and are brought before the mayor's court, where their profligacy is made conspicuous. The numbers are magnified tenfold by the imaginations of the spectators. Whereas the thousands and tens of thousands, who are industriously employed, early and late, to make a sorry subsistence, at a miserable pittance, pass wholly unnoticed. Who can think without sympathy for the sufferers, and regret for such a state of society, when he is informed of the appalling fact, that there are, as I have stated, thousands of seamstresses in this city, who, by the utmost industry and skill, cannot earn above a dollar, a dollar and a quarter, or a dollar and a half per week; the last very rarely, and scarcely ever! Competition has reduced the price of making soldiers' and slop-shop shirts and pantaloons to twelve and a half cents each, and in some cases to ten, and even eight! At this paltry price, whenever they are to be given out, the applications are too numerous to be supplied, and the work is sought after with as much avidity as if it afforded a liberal support At certain seasons even this sort of work is very scarce, and numbers of poor women are wholly unemployed!

A very expert, skilful woman, unburdened with family, cannot make eight, nine, or ten shirts per week, unless she works from four or five in the morning, until eleven or twelve at night, which many of them do, to the great injury of their health; with a family, which many of them have, the greatest number will be six, seven, perhaps eight per week! When we take into view, rent, occasional want of employment, sickness, and the support of children, we shall have some slight idea of the distresses of the numerous widows, who are devoted to this most miserable of employments. May I not ask, who, duly weighing these things, will have the hardness of heart to involve in one general, sweeping denunciation, the distressed poor, as if their sufferings were the penalties of idleness and dissipation?

Although I know how extremely difficult it is to eradicate inveterate prejudices, such as many of our citizens entertain on this subject, yet I fondly hope those prejudices will lose much of their weight and influence, when the following facts are calmly and dispassionately considered. Thousands of our labouring people travel hundreds of miles in quest of employment on canals, at 62½, 75, and 87½ cents per day, paying a dollar and a half or two dollars per week for their board, leaving families behind, depending on them for support. They labour frequently in marshy grounds, where they inhale pestiferous miasmata, which destroy their health, often irrecoverably. They return to their poor families, broken hearted, and with ruined constitutions, with a sorry pittance, most laboriously earned, and take to their beds, sick, and unable to work. Hundreds are swept off annually, many of them leaving numerous and helpless families. Notwithstanding their wretched fate, their places are quickly supplied by others, although death stares them in the face. Hundreds are most laboriously employed on turnpikes, working from morning till night, at from half a dollar to three quarters per day, exposed to the broiling sun in summer, and all the inclemency of our severe winters. There is always a redundance of wood pilers in our cities, whose wages are so low, that their utmost efforts do not enable them to earn more than from thirty-five to fifty cents per day. The painful situation of a watchman is an object of desire. There never is a want of scavengers; and, finally, there is no employment whatever, how disagreeable, or loathsome, or dangerous, or deleterious soever it may be, or however reduced the wages, that does not find persons willing to follow it, rather than beg or steal. With respect to females, what I have already stated is abundantly sufficient for their justification. Surely these facts are overwhelming, and ought to rescue the character of the labouring classes from the mass of obloquy by which they are too often unjustly aspersed.

Essays on the Public Charities of Philadelphia (Philadelphia, 1830), 171–173.

STUDY QUESTIONS

1. According to Carey, most poor people actually had jobs. By his reckoning, why then were so many impoverished?
2. What sorts of jobs did poor people in antebellum cities tend to have?

Moral Reform and Prostitution

One aspect of urban poverty that particularly troubled Mathew Carey was its disproportionate effect on young women, who were left especially vulnerable by limited employment opportunities and who not infrequently turned to prostitution as a means of survival. Similarly concerned were members of organizations like the New York Female Moral Reform Society, which had hundreds of auxiliaries less than a decade after its founding in the 1830s. Deeply religious, alarmed by sexual vice, and convinced that much of the urban misery confronted by poor women grew from that sort of vice, those involved in female moral reform societies undertook missionary and charity work among prostitutes and other poor women in slums like New York's Five Points. They tried to protect women and get them to abandon lives of prostitution by offering moral counseling and safe places to live. Moreover, they assaulted male "licentiousness" by lobbying for laws that would make soliciting a prostitute a crime, pledging not to associate with men who countenanced such behavior, and publishing stories in newspapers like the New York society's Advocate of Moral Reform *about male sexual immorality and its female victims. These efforts, however, were not uncontroversial. By frankly dealing with sexual matters and tackling a double standard by which Americans winked at male sexual dalliances while morally condemning the women they dallied with, the middle-class women involved in female moral reform societies were hardly the delicate creatures most men expected them to be.*

Working among Society's "Outcasts" (1836)

We give to our readers this week, a short extract from the journal of our Missionary, who is diligently and faithfully laboring among the outcasts in the abodes of sin and misery. We shall continue these reports from time to time, as our limits will permit, and in our next, hope to give our friends a full exposition of our views and feelings on the subject of missionary labor, and a Magdalen Asylum. In the meantime we will only state, that the meetings on the Sabbath and during the week at the Five Points, have become full to overflowing, and our Missionary is very anxious, that a chapel should be built and opened in that neighborhood immediately, under the direction of our society. The family in whose house the meetings are now held, have been converted to God since their residence there, and they are unwilling to leave the degraded spot, because they feel that God has called them and placed them there, to labor for him. Their attachment to the cause has been evinced by the hiring of an additional room to accommodate those who come there, to learn the way of life and salvation. We feel that the plan of a chapel, which would draw in, not only abandoned females, but many *sailors*, who resort in great numbers to the Points, is a very *important one*, and deserves the consideration of the Christian public.

New-York, April 29, 1836.
From the above date to May the 9th, I have not kept a regular account of my labors. I have visited the highest and lowest order of brothels. I have exhorted publicly and privately and delivered many tracts. I have been reviled and threatened by the wicked; and I have been encouraged too by the same class with tears confessing their sins. Br.———, a student from a theological seminary spent a week laboring with me. Our prayer meetings at the Points are crowded. Many young men from the country were present at our last meeting and seemed loth to quit the place.—They appeared deeply sensible of the worth of their souls. Some of the abandoned females generally attend. One cried aloud and brought a great concourse to the door of the place of our meeting. She proposed leaving the place, but wanted some wine first.—Several have proposed leaving. I have told them where they could call, when they were ready to seek a better world.

May 10th. From this date up to the 15th I have spent part of my time in visiting at the Points—attending on anniversary meetings—prayer meetings—preachings, &c. I preached 3 times this day in Sixth Avenue, near the Society House. E—R—, on her way to this place of religious worship, was assailed by a base wretch who seized her arm making use of the most obscene language, and beckoning to several others, his associates in sin to come and aid him in preventing her escape.—She succeeded however in getting from his grasp, and by running escaped further molestation. By her request after meeting, I went with her to her residence. On her way back, one of the party who was in company with the person who insulted her was discovered, but seeing me with her, he decamped speedily. I have no doubt there was a plot laid to entrap her on her return to her residence. Thus it seems that a female is in danger in the streets of this city, not only at night, but during the hours of the day.

May 16th. Visited some families. Among others a man apparently near death, but rejoicing in the hope of soon being in possession of the land of promise. I had however to learn that two of his connections were abandoned females and a younger sister of these girls then present, was thought to be about following their steps. She was affectionately admonished, but with what effect I know not.

May 17th. I was called in by a mother to use my influence for her abandoned daughter. I accordingly went to 95 Division-street, where I found the ruined child. I asked her if she was disposed to forsake her present course, and was answered in the affirmative. After prayer, and some instructions relative to her future course, I told her she could come to the Society house. Lord grant this may prove to be a brand plucked from the burning.

May 18th. In company with brother C. I went to my field of labor. Went into a larger elegantly furnished house in Leonard-street. We were very civilly treated in this house; where we read the word of God, and exhorted these wretched women to repentance. They were serious, and even requested us to come again. We went on visiting, and found some who profess to be Christians. We prayed, and rejoiced that God had not left himself without witnesses, even at the Five points. Heard of several girls who were disposed to forsake their sins: our meetings are owned of the Lord in stirring up these girls to feel the need of repentance and pardon.

Founding an Auxiliary in Otsego County, New York (1837)

Dear Sisters—It gives me pleasure to inform you of the organization of a Female Moral Reform Society in Springfield, Otsego co., N.Y., auxiliary to the N.Y. Female Moral Reform Society. Our society was formed in September and now numbers about 100. Hurtful prejudices have existed and still do exist against any effort of the kind, but as a general thing ignorant and suspicious characters are the most violent in their opposition. It is a source of grief, that some even professing godliness are found in the ranks of the infidel and libertine on this subject. They object against the introduction of such papers in their families as the "Advocate of Moral Reform," on account of the indelicacy of the subject of which it treats, and for fear of poisoning the virtuous sensibilities of their children. It would be well, however, here to remark, that with some of the objectors I am personally and particularly acquainted, and am confident that they are the most indelicate, obscene, and even vulgar individuals in their own families of any in town. Let me present you with the "Pledge" of our society:

"Believing that licentiousness is a prominent sin of our land and of the world; peculiarly offensive to God; destructive of the happiness of families, and ruining the souls and bodies of our fellow-creatures; and believing we are bound to lend our influence to encourage those who are making efforts to stay this mighty flood of iniquity, we, as friends of virtue, unitedly pledge ourselves to endeavor to promote chastity in ourselves and others, according to the scripture definition of the word. And for the accomplishment of this object we will abstain from every thing, in thought, manner, dress, or conversation, calculated to produce or promote this evil. And believing that the licentious man is equally, and even more guilty than the licentious female, we do pledge ourselves to abstain from all social intercourse with those of either sex known to be licentious."

Agreeable to an article of the constitution, the ladies at their quarterly meeting made provision to be publicly addressed by a minister friendly to the cause. The Rev. Wm. Lochead, of Cherry Valley, being invited, was present, and gave a faithful picture of the vice with the remedies, for which he received the unanimous thanks of a highly respectable number of the first ladies of town present on the occasion.

Calling for Action—A Sample Petition to a State Legislature (1838)

Petition

TO THE HONOURABLE THE LEGISLATURE OF THE STATE OF———.

Whereas certain vices exist in this community, viz. Seduction and Adultery, which are most degrading to moral and accountable beings, and as destructive to the best interests of individuals, families, and society at large, as theft, burglary, and arson; and whereas no efficient measures have yet been taken by your honourable body for their suppression, in consequence of which their continued prevalence is filling our almshouses and penitentiaries, and prisons with the victims of want and crime, rending the hearts of fathers and mothers, and causing unutterable anguish to be felt through all the relations of life; and whereas the enforcement of salutary laws would tend greatly to diminish this amount of human wo, and suppress extensively those sins which are a "reproach to any people;"— And whereas the Legislature of this State has the constitutional power to enact such laws as the nature of the case imperiously demands,—

We, therefore, the undersigned, Women of this State, and of the county of———, respectfully and earnestly pray your honourable body at this session of the legislature, to pass an act, whereby the perpetrators of the aforesaid crimes of seduction and adultery shall be punished with imprisonment, for such term of time as shall be sufficient to make the penalty "a terror to evil doers."

Advocate of Moral Reform (July 15, 1836) 101–102; (February 1, 1837) 207; October 1, 1838, p. 152.

STUDY QUESTIONS

1. What kinds of things did female reform society members do and see on their visits to poor urban women?
2. Why do you think "hurtful prejudices" existed against female reform societies and their activities?

The "Romanist" Threat and How to Meet It

Although many reform movements advanced goals that would be deemed liberal or progressive by modern standards, hardly all movements could be classified as such. Members of the nativist movement, for example, articulated a distinctly conservative and even reactionary vision for America's future as they sought to rouse people against growing numbers of immigrants in American cities, and especially against Irish Catholic immigrants who arrived in the United States by the hundreds of thousands between the 1830s and the 1850s. Thomas R. Whitney, a lawyer from New York City, was especially active in nativist circles. He was involved in creating several anti-immigrant political parties that called for reforming naturalization laws and for laws barring the foreign-born from political office. He also helped found the Order of United Americans, a semisecret fraternal organization designed to cultivate anti-immigrant political activism and nativist cultural and political education among young men. Although neither the parties nor the fraternal society ever became especially large, as the number of Irish immigrants increased in the late 1840s and early 1850s, so did sympathy for nativist goals, and in the mid-1850s nativists launched a new political entity known as the American Party. Labeled by its opponents the "Know-Nothing Party," it was remarkably successful, briefly taking over the Massachusetts state legislature and garnering more than 850,000 votes in the 1856 presidential election. In A Defence of the American Policy, *Whitney, who successfully ran for Congress in 1855, describes what he saw as the dangers of Catholicism and immigrants, and explains the aims of the Order of United Americans.*

Thomas R. Whitney, *A Defence of the American Policy, as Opposed to the Encroachments of Foreign Influence* (1856)

Papal Aspirations in the United States

The Course of Jesuitism is so subtle and insidious; it performs its work by such slow, and almost imperceptible degrees, that the people most directly interested, the Americans, are the last to take the alarm. Each change that is made in our old Protestant system and customs, towards the papal intention is so slight as to attract no particular notice, the more especially as the changes are made ostensibly under the sanction of one or the other of the political parties; and as each party has vied with its opponent in efforts to secure the Roman Catholic vote, neither has ventured to expose the encroachment when it has been made by the other; hence we have not realized the amount of progress actually made. But if we look back, and contemplate the aggregate of those changes, and draw a comparison of the past with the present, the extent of Roman Catholic encroachments become palpable and startling.

When the Republic was established, Romanism could scarcely be said to have had an existence in the land. Certainly, it had no influence—it made no pretensions—it was modest, humble, solicitous. As a religion, it took its place side by side with Protestant creeds, scarce visible in the preponderating numbers of surrounding churches. A Romish priest could not be recognized by his attire and demeanor, from his Protestant neighbor. The external forms and ceremonies of the Church were humbly kept from view, and the whole demeanor of priest and layman was that of unostentatious Christianity.

But what a change has taken place in the demeanor, and the numerical power of that Church, since the foundation of the Republic! Its humility has been changed to defiant audacity; a bold, commanding ostentation has taken the place of its retiring simplicity. It builds its nunneries, its Jesuit colleges, its churches, in every nook and corner of the land, and it consecrates them in all the pomp and formulae of its ancient pride, surrounded by the drawn swords and bayonets of its martial legions, who are organized, commissioned, and armed *as a part of the militia of the State*. It *baptizes* its *bells* amid superstitious trappings and ceremonies adapted to the palmiest days of its benumbing power. It holds it councils of bishops who issue their edicts in conformity with the despotic character of its government. It sends its nuncio to decide a controversy between a bishop and his congregation, and the nuncio decides *against* the people, and in violation of the law of the land, and the principles of Republicanism. It tampers with our public men and our public policy, and has already, in most of the States, erased from their constitutions, that conservative feature which prevented clerical interference in political affairs. It has perverted legitimate and authentic history whenever that history portrayed its own enormities. It has driven the Word of God from many of our public and district schools. It has obtained the control of our post-office department, and secured the chief-justice of the United States. It has increased numerically, from comparatively nothing, to about four millions, and now, self-confident, it claims to possess a controlling political influence in the affairs of the country.

The Order of United Americans

The organization of this order took place on the 21st of December, 1844, in the city of New York. At that time several gentlemen, entertaining a solemn conviction of the dangers which overhang our institutions, from the nefarious designs of Jesuitism, from the rapidly-increasing influences exerted upon them from abroad, and from the ignorant masses of Europeans who were permitted to share in the elective franchise, as also from the glaring habits of corruption to which our politicians had descended; having witnessed also the futility of previous attempts to awaken the popular mind to a true sense of those evils, or to overcome the united and secret combination of organized demagogues by means of an open party, and anticipating that a like result would follow the effort then being made—resolved to adopt some plan by which those deleterious influences might be met on their own terms, and with their own weapons. The most potent weapon employed by the unscrupulous politicians, as well as by the natural foes of American Republicanism—the followers of Loyola—was the *secrecy* with which their machinations were planned and carried out, and it was determined that the same weapon (secrecy) should be employed to check their operations, and thwart their designs.

It was observable, also, that the political education of the young men of the country was confided entirely to the partisan schools, and very few graduated and stood forth upon the platform of manhood with any ideas of political duty beyond the mere essentials of a democratic or a whig success. They understood very distinctly, because they were so trained to believe, that to the party into whose lap they had chanced to fall when they emerged from boyhood, the whole country, if not the whole world, was indebted for every vestige of liberty remaining, and for all that might be garnered up for future use—hence, when their party was triumphant, they were given to understand that "the country was safe," and they could return to their workshops and counters, and continue their avocations with the most perfect assurance that there would be no more danger until the next election. In their estimation the highest qualification of a politician was to be found in his tact for getting the "right" votes into the ballot-box, and keeping out the "wrong" ones, and the most accomplished statesman was he who could make his measures tell best for "the party." The idea of legislating for the people was not *obsolete* with them, because they had never entertained it—it had not been among the rudiments of their education; it was a thing Utopian—heard of but unknown. Thus the *spirituel* of our political element was rapidly degenerating into a mere factional system, while the pernicious elements of radicalism, superstition, and ignorance, were held aloof as make-weights to be thrown into either scale which would afford the largest remuneration.

A system that would afford a school of patriotism to the young, purify the *morale* of the political atmosphere, and by awakening a *home pride*, a spirit of American nationality among the people, neutralize and stifle those imported theories which were being rapidly engrafted upon our time-honored republican customs and sentiments, was a something desirable, at least, if not imperatively necessary as a measure of self-protection. The formation of a politico-benevolent institution, beyond the reach of the corrupting influences of partisan demagogues, was therefore determined upon. An institution which, as one of its features, should receive into its membership young men who were soon to enter upon the discharge of their political duties, and thus, by bring them into a social contact with men of maturer years and experience, afford to them opportunities for a more rational and patriotic political instruction than could be obtained under the corrupting influences of mere partisans and factionists—an institution that should be strictly national in its character, and entirely American in its policy and its membership; one that would, in its political character and action, eschew all partisan attachments and prejudices, moving unitedly in whatever direction the ultimate good of the country should demand, whether in the choice of men, of the adoption of measures—an institution that would encourage study, oratory, and research, and impart information to the young by addresses and discussions in political science, and general history, and especially on topics relating to American history, and thus by intuition bring about a more conservative, healthy, and patriotic train of political thought in the great American mind.

Such was the general outline of a plan for the formation of a society for the purposes which I have already stated. As an additional bond of unity, a beneficiary feature, something of the nature of Odd Fellowship, was added to the plan, and upon this basis the Order of United Americans was ushered into existence.

A Defence of the American Policy, as Opposed to the Encroachments of Foreign Influence (1856), 80–82, 258–261.

STUDY QUESTIONS

1. What threats did Whitney see to the United States coming from Catholics and Catholic influence? How did he see the major political parties as being complicit in that threat?

2. Why did Whitney believe young native-born Americans needed a new kind of political education? How would the Order of United Americans carry out this education?

A Working-Class Radical Critiques the Industrial Order

Urban reforms frequently addressed issues of particular relevance to the poor and working classes, but no reform grounded in the urban experience gained the involvement of more actual working-class people than did the labor movement. The expansion of wage work was one of the most profound changes wrought by the antebellum industrial order; and particularly for artisans and craftspeople accustomed to controlling their own labor, the factory system and employer pressures to work longer hours under restricted conditions raised troubling questions about their independence, the value of their work, and ultimately, the respect they received in society. Afraid that their status and material circumstances would be reduced to those of common laborers, skilled members of the working class began demanding reforms to the economic system. Among the more radical reformers was Thomas Skidmore. A machinist living in New York City, in 1829 Skidmore published The Rights of Man to Property! *a scathing appraisal of how private property unjustly enabled its owners to accumulate wealth and power by living off the labor of others without working themselves. Skidmore instead advocated the equitable redistribution of property, the abolition of inheritance, and a system in which all people could work on terms of relative equality free from exploitative wage labor relations. Skidmore argued that these changes should take place democratically, but in being an assault on the wealthy and a call to arms for the poor, his work nonetheless envisioned a very different socioeconomic organization than that developing in pre–Civil War America.*

Thomas Skidmore, *The Rights of Man to Property!* (1829)

One thing must be obvious to the plainest understanding; that as long as property is unequal; or rather, as long as it is so enormously unequal, as we see it at present, that those who possess it, *will* live on the labor of others, and themselves perform none, or if any, a very disproportionate share, of that toil which attends them as a condition of their existence, and without the performance of which, they have no *just* right to preserve or retain that existence, even for a single hour.

It is not possible to maintain a doctrine to the contrary of this position, without, at the same time, maintaining an absurdity no longer tolerated in enlightened countries; that a part, and that a very great part, of the human race, are doomed, of right, to the slavery of toil, while others are born, only to enjoy.

I, for one, disavow every such doctrine. Even if it be admitted that the present possessors of property, in any country, are the true and rightful owners of it, beyond any question, still I maintain that they have no just right to use it in such a manner, as to extract from others, the result of their labors, for the purpose of exempting themselves from the necessity of laboring as much as others must labor, for a like amount of enjoyment. The moment that any possessor of property, makes such use of it, I care not how, nor under the sanction of what law, or system of laws, as to live in idleness, partial or total, thus supporting himself, more or less, on the labors of others; that moment he contravenes and invades the rights of others; and has placed himself in the condition which would justify the party injured, in dispossessing the aggressor, of the instrument of his aggression.

But the work which I thus present to the consideration of my fellow citizens and others, does not rest here the defence of its principles. It does not rest contented with merely showing, in this way, that men have no right to their property, (as they call it) when they use it, for the purpose of converting their fellow beings into slaves to labor for their use. It goes farther. It attempts to shew, that the whole system of the laws of property, in all countries, is such: that no man has any just and true title to his possessions at all: that they are in fact, possessions growing out of injustice, perpetrated by all governments, from time immemorial and continued down to the present hour. It depends then upon the *success* of this attempt, whether I have added strength to the position I have assumed, that *all men should live on their own labor, and not on the labor of others*. If, in the course of the following pages, I have shewn that the present possessors of enormous property, (I mean more *particularly* these,) have no just title to their possessions; and if it is apparent, as I trust it is, than when property is enormously unequal, that the men of toil, of all countries, can never have the full enjoyment of their labor; it will be conceded, no doubt, that I have shewn enough to justify my fellow citizens in pulling down the present edifice of society, and to induce them to build a new one in its stead, provided I have also shewn how to organize this new government in such a manner as to compel all men, without exception, to labor as much as others must labor, for the same amount of enjoyment; or, in default thereof, to be deprived of such enjoyment altogether. Of this, however, it is for the reader, and for every reader, to judge.

The Rights of Man to Property! (New York, 1829), 3–6.

STUDY QUESTIONS

1. Why, according to Skidmore, was private property ownership often unjust?
2. Do you agree with Skidmore that no one is entitled to live off the labor of others?

Taking Political Action: Working Men's Parties

Seeing independent political organization as one mechanism for making practical changes in workers' lives, northeastern labor reformers founded several Working Men's parties in the early 1830s and put forward their own candidates for a variety of municipal and state-level offices. Ultimately, however, this strategy had limited success. Activists fought among themselves, with some pushing for far-reaching goals along the lines proposed by Skidmore and others insisting upon more moderate reforms like expanding public education and making the legal and political systems fairer and more responsive to workers' needs. Moreover, the major political parties alternately accused Working Men's parties of being radicals and pried away potential voters by claiming (usually falsely) to support workers' issues themselves. The address below, delivered at the 1830 general meeting of the New York City Working Men's Party, suggests the challenges labor reformers faced in trying to make forceful demands while simultaneously insisting they were not the wild-eyed outliers critics accused them of being.

Address to the Working Men's Party of New York City (1830)

When the Working Men say they want men who will honestly support their principles, it becomes necessary distinctly to state what their principles are.

They hold that the only legitimate object of legislation are the defence of the lives, liberties, and *equal individual* rights of the governed; and that *all* legislation beyond this is mischievious; therefore.

They disapprove all monopolies. They conceive them to be a benefit only to the few, and injury to the many. They seek their total abolition, not violently or suddenly, but constitutionally and quietly. They are opposed to bank chartering, as a monopoly; to exclusive auctioneering, as a monopoly; to privileged corporations, as monopolies; in a word, to each and every law and regulation, by which wealth is favored at the expense of poverty, and intrigueing speculations at the expense of the people.

They disapprove a system of civil law according to which the rich or the influential only, stand a chance fair of obtaining legal redress. Such they consider our present clumsy, complicated, perplexining, tedious, and partial system of law to be. They especially disapprove our present laws for the collection of debts, as without force for the rogue, and often equally injurious to the honest creditor and debtor. They conceive that so long as justice is sold as at present, it will be purchased by the rich, and withheld from him who cannot pay for it. They protest against the present system of law, therefore, as virtually and unjustly depriving a citizen of his unalienable rights, if he have not a heavy purse to purchase and secure them.

They are opposed to a strong government, and to [s]umptuary laws. They think that the United States require neither; and they have observed, that such governments and laws rather lead to oppression in the few, than subordination in the many. They especially object to the paying of debts being secured at the expense of the liberty of the citizen, and to any crime being punished with death.

They are opposed to all ecclesiastical interference in secular affairs, and to all legislation on religion. They consider religion a private, not a public concern; and they believe that those who desire to amalgamate political and religious questions are actuated by ambition, not by piety. They consider the attempt to stop the mails on Sunday an ecclesiastical encroachment, dangerous and unconstitutional.

They are opposed to every law that savors of a standing army in time of peace; and to our present compulsory militia system, as productive of no one good effect, while it encourages intemperance and vanity, and oppresses the poor, by requiring of him a vexatious, useless service, to the injury of his business.

They view the present district system as injurious—They desire to see it changed, so that there shall be as many districts as representatives; because, thus only they believe, can the political machines of the present ruling faction be broken up, and its ill-gotten and abused influence destroyed.

But there is one measure which still remains to be spoken of, and which they consider of more importance than all the rest, inasmuch as it secures and perpetuates every political right they possess, or may hereafter obtain. It is a system of PUBLIC EDUCATION, such as shall place within the reach of all equal facilities for the intellectual cultivation and rational training of their offspring; a system which "shall unite under the same roof the son of the rich and of the poor, the widow's charge and the orphan;" and which shall combine a knowledge of the practical arts with that of the useful sciences. To this great measure their thoughts and feelings tend, as to that which will break down, and can alone safely break down, the great wall of partition which has hitherto separated theory and practice—knowledge and industry—science and labor. Thus do they hope to see all men and women cultivated, and all useful. They hope to see the same class producers and consumers. Instead of the mind being exclusively cultivated at the expense of the body, or the body slavishly over-wrought to the injury of the mind, they hope to see a nation of equal fellow citizens, all trained to produce and all permitted to enjoy. By equal, intellectual cultivation only, are equal rights secured; and without knowledge to employ them, all rights are comparatively useless.

Unless this safeguard of liberty is secured, and by the enlightening of the mass, the axe of knowledge is laid at the root of aristocracy, there is effected, as it were, nothing. The best labors are lost, and the success of the present is ever hazarded in the future. As the FIRST AND CHIEF of their objects, therefore, the Mechanics and Working Men put forward a system of Equal, Republican, Scientific, Practical EDUCATION.

Having thus stated plainly and briefly what *are* their principles and chief objects, it remains to state what *are not*.

They have been spoken of as recommending an Equal Division of Property. They have never recommended, and they utterly disapprove any such proposal. They disapprove it, both as impracticable and inefficient; impracticable, because the feeling and judgment of the people are opposed to it; and inefficient, because an equal division to-day, will not secure equality to-morrow. They disapprove of it as a bone of useless, wordy contention.

They have been spoken of as *Infidels*. They, like the mass of their fellow citizens throughout these states, have every shade of religious opinion. As individuals, they are orthodox, heterodox, religious, sceptical. As a political body, they have no religious nor irreligious character whatever. They abstain, with especial care, from all mixing up of theological with political questions, and they seek only to secure to themselves and their posterity, INVIOLABLE RELIGIOUS FREEDOM.

They have been spoken of as levellers and disorganizers. They are emphatically the reverse. They seek to raise all by the mild and efficient aid of Public Education; and to secure a tranquil government by the only means which can secure it—the diffusion of intelligence, and the implanting of virtuous habits universally among those who shall compose the next generation.

They condemn all violence; all sumptuary laws; all hurried reforms; all sudden, unprepared changes. They think these are usually changes of men, not of measures. But they approve, and will advocate, a gradual, searching, thorough reformation of the body politic; a reformation that shall purge it of its aristocracy, its corruption, and its expensive, unrepublican excrescences.

These are the principles the Mechanics and Working Men of this city advocate. They will support for office those men, and those men only, whom they believe sincerely to hold such principles as these; and whom they see able and ready to advocate the same in the councils of the nation. Should they, in their first choice, be deceived, they will change their public servants again and again, until they find those who will legislate honestly for the true interests of the people.

Workingman's Advocate, September 18, 1830.

STUDY QUESTIONS
1. What demands did the New York Working Men's Party have? Why was public education more important to them than their other demands?
2. Why do you think opponents attacked Working Men's parties as being radicals and socialists? Do they seem particularly radical to you?

Unions, Strikes, and the Ten-Hour Day

By the mid-1830s, Working Men's parties had effectively ceased to exist. But the conditions that so troubled many in the laboring classes continued to worsen. That reality led to the embrace of new strategies for advancing labor's goals. Especially popular was the creation of labor unions that tried to coordinate worker activities both within and across trade lines. Many small labor associations existed prior to the 1830s, but during that decade workers began organizing citywide groups and, in a few instances, unions that were even national in scope. Among the most persistent complaints of these early unions was that employers kept imposing longer hours than the ten-hour day laborers believed allowed for both reasonable productivity and a reasonable standard of living. When employers dismissed their complaints, workers began to strike. Although unionizing and striking for a ten-hour day hardly seem revolutionary by modern standards, it was not clear that such activities were even legal prior to the 1840s, and a number of labor leaders were tried and convicted of conspiracy for their actions. Unionizing and striking may not have been the radicalism of Thomas Skidmore, and the momentum labor gained in the 1830s was gutted by economic depression late in the decade. Nonetheless, as the articles below from the Workingman's Advocate *newspaper suggest, insisting that ownership did not automatically entail total control of a workplace was to question an absolute vision of private property ascendant in antebellum America and to argue that profit ought not to be the only important thing in economic life.*

The Ten Hour System (1832)

None but the rankest aristocrats or the most thoughtless politicians have opposed by argument, the adoption of the ten hour system, for it must certainly be the *essence* of aristocracy or *idiotic* thought-lessness that would argue that men may not dispose of their own labor in such quantities as may suit themselves.

The *sellers of labor* now very generally see that the less there is of that as well as of every other saleable article in the market, *the better price the article will bring*; and *seeing this*, it will be difficult to induce them to cause a *glut*.

But the keeping up the price of labor, will not be the only nor the chief advantage of the ten hour system. The chief advantage of it will be, that it will enable the *sellers of labor* to devote two or three hours each day to the acquisition of *knowledge*, particularly *political* knowledge.—It will enable them to inquire and ascertain why they are enabled to obtain *only* a bare subsistence by laboring ten hours out of every twenty-four, while many who never performed any kind of useful labor, either mental or bodily, enjoy in plenty the fruits of the earth, and accumulate wealth. *This*, and more, will the ten hours system do, and therefore it is a very good system; but it will not be a *panacea* for all the evils of government. *That* must be sought after when the ten hour system is adopted.

Turn Outs: Strikes in Massachusetts and New Jersey (1835)

This is a proud day for the friends of EQUAL RIGHTS, and a sorrowful one for those who live upon prey and plunder. The Journeymen House Wrights of [Boston] struck this morning at six o'clock, for the "TEN HOUR SYSTEM," almost to a man. They met in front of the State House at an early hour, where they were addressed by several of their body, in an eloquent and forcible manner; after which the great Anthem of Liberty, the Marseilles Hymn, was sung by the assembled multitude. "Ye sons of freedom awake to glory," rung upon the morning breeze like the voice of doom. They then formed a procession, with a band of music, and marched through all the principal streets in the most perfect good order and decorum; their ranks continually swelling, until they numbered SEVERAL HUNDRED. At "high noon," "the witching hour when *sloths* do walk," they paraded in State street, and halted under the very noses of the rag-money Nabobs, and indolent drones, "*disorganizing*" their sweet tempers most effectually.

The blow is struck—and it will stay struck; no cowardly timeserving, no slavish truckling, no "*fear and trembling*," will accompany this great work of salvation. Every other means have been tried in vain, and the independent journeymen, after submitting for years * * * to a yoke that bowed them to the earth with the non-combativeness of Job, and the quiet of the dove, have at last determined to "live free or die." They have for years been patient as the fox in the brambles, while a vulture brood of blood-suckers have been gorging themselves almost to bursting; but that time has gone by. "They know their rights, and knowing dare maintain them."

It will be seen, also, by the following article from the Paterson Courier, that a very necessary turn out has taken place in that town. We are somewhat surprised, however, at the moderation of their demands. It is not melancholy to think that such means are necessary to prevent *children*, every one of whom ought to be at school, from being worked over *eleven hours a day!*

TURN OUT.—Meetings have been held almost every evening for the last six or eight days by the parents of those children who have been engaged in the Mills of this town and are standing out for a reduction of the hours of labor, for the purpose of inducing the Mill owners to reduce the working hours from 13 1/2 to 11. This has not yet been accomplished. If the employers cannot pay the same price for 11 hours they did for 13 1/2 and make a reasonable profit, then we say compromise the matter. Eleven hours is abundant for either man or beast to labor. We understand a committee appointed at one of the meetings (at the request of two or three of the employers) politely invited every Mill owner to attend a conference meeting, which they [the nobility] considered as an insult. We knew that a Cotton Mill and Carriage were the insignias of distinction, yet we were astonished at this injudicious course,— the interest and prosperity of the town demanded concessions from both parties, and when an opportunity offered to compromise, they should have embraced it. The "strike," has assumed the appearance of determined resistance on both sides. The operatives have formed an association similar to a Trade's Union auxiliary, and have appointed a committee to receive whatever donations may be offered for those who may stand in need of assistance,—we understand from one of the committee that little short of $150 has already been received for that purpose, and that signatures have been obtained for a small sum weekly while the stand out continues.

The aristocracy are opposed to any and every plan for the protection of the working classes—the Trade's Union has been pronounced a political machine, calculated to overthrow the liberties of our country.—'Tis true the working men, the wealth of our land, are making rapid strides towards the extinction of mock nobility—they are determined no longer to yield to the influence of the usurping employer, but will have their rights; yet, we have very little to fear from their political influence. When they get the ascendency the employer will condescend to confer with those in his employ.

Workingman's Advocate, June 2, 1832, and July 25, 1835.

STUDY QUESTIONS

1. What benefits did labor reformers feel workers would gain from a ten-hour day?
2. What words would you use to characterize the rhetoric of labor reformers? Were they angry? Defiant? Righteous? Sarcastic? Something else?

Institutions

A European Assessment of the Penitentiary System

Although antebellum reformers involved in issues like poverty and prostitution rarely absolved those they hoped to help of culpability for their circumstances, they were more inclined than previous generations of Americans to recognize that systemic change to social problems would not come simply from convincing individuals to make different moral choices. Reformers saw self-discipline and religious virtue as foundations of character and social order, but many also realized those mores were likelier to be instilled in environments where they seemed worth embracing. The sense that environment shaped character played an even more powerful role in plans of reformers who focused on people most Americans deemed deviant or defective. Rather than abandoning such individuals as social outcasts or considering their situations hopeless, these reformers believed they could be made socially useful by spending time in new kinds of specialized institutions. There, they could be isolated from dangerous or unhealthy influences and subjected to routines designed to inculcate respectability and self-control, reemerging as orderly and productive citizens. Instead of ascribing crime to innate human depravity and subjecting criminals to corporal punishment, for example, reformers insisted that upbringing and environment led to crime and that it would be more effective and humane to rehabilitate criminals than to brutalize them. Reformers began successfully lobbying state governments to create facilities known as penitentiaries where inmates could be quarantined and their energies focused on remaking themselves through a regimen that combined forced labor, strict discipline, silence, and solitude. Below, Frenchmen Alexis de Tocqueville and Gustave Beaumont record some of their thoughts after having spent several

105

months in 1831 touring American penitentiaries at the behest of the French government. While Beaumont and Tocqueville came away impressed with some innovations of the penitentiary system, they were also skeptical of the extent to which it would thoroughly transform the lives of convicts, as vaunted by its boosters.

Gustave de Beaumont and Alexis de Tocqueville, *On the Penitentiary System in the United States and Its Application in France* (1833)

Whoever has studied the interior of prisons and the moral state of their inmates, has become convinced that communication between these persons renders their moral reformation impossible, and becomes even for them the inevitable cause of an alarming corruption. This observation, justified by the experience of every day, has become in the United States an almost popular truth; and the publicists who disagree most respecting the way of putting the penitentiary system into practice, fully agree on this point, that no salutary system can possibly exist without the separation of criminals.

* * *

This separation, which prevents the wicked from injuring others, is also favorable to himself.

Thrown into solitude he reflects. Placed alone, in view of his crime, he learns to hate it; and if his soul be not yet surfeited with crime, and thus have lost all taste for anything better, it is in solitude, where remorse will come to assail him.

* * *

Yet, whatever may be the crime of the guilty prisoner, no one has the right to take life from him, if society decree merely to deprive him of his liberty. Such, however, would be the result of absolute solitude, if no alleviation of its rigors were offered.

This is the reason why labor is introduced into the prison. Far from being an aggravation of the punishment, it is a real benefit to the prisoner.

But even if the criminal did not find in it a relief from his sufferings, it nevertheless would be necessary to force him to it. It is idleness which has led him to crime; with employment he will learn how to live honestly.

* * *

Thoroughly convinced of these truths, the founders of the new penitentiary at Philadelphia, thought it necessary that each prisoner should be secluded in a separate cell during day as well as night.

They have thought that absolute separation of the criminals can alone protect them from mutual pollution, and they have adopted the principle of separation in all its rigor. According to this system, the convict, once thrown into his cell, remains there without interruption, until the expiration of his punishment. He is separated from the whole world; and the penitentiaries, full of malefactors like himself, but every one of them entirely isolated, do not present to him even a society in the prison. * * *

As solitude is in no other prison more complete than in Philadelphia, nowhere, also, is the necessity of labor more urgent. At the same time, it would be inaccurate to say, that in the Philadelphia penitentiary labor is imposed; we may say with more justice that the favor of labor is granted. When we visited this penitentiary, we successfully conversed with all its inmates. There was not a single one among them who did not speak of labor with a kind of gratitude, and who did not express the idea that without the relief of constant occupation, life would be insufferable.

What would become, during the long hours of solitude, without this relief, of the prisoner, given up to himself, a prey to the remorses of his soul and the terrors of his imagination? Labor gives to the solitary cell an interest; it fatigues the body and relieves the soul.

It is highly remarkable, that these men, the greater part of whom have been led to crime by indolence and idleness, should be constrained by the torments of solitude, to find in labor their only comfort. By detesting idleness, they accustom themselves to hate the primary cause of their misfortune; and labor, by comforting them, makes them love the only means, which when again free, will enable them to gain honestly their livelihood.

The founders of the Auburn prison acknowledged also the necessity of separating the prisoners, to prevent all intercourse among themselves, and to subject them to the obligation of labor; but they follow a different course in order to arrive at the same end.

In this prison * * * the prisoners are locked up in their solitary cells at night only. During day they work together in common workshops, and as they are subjected to the law of rigorous silence, though united, they are yet in fact isolated. Labor in common and in silence forms then the characteristic trait which distinguishes the Auburn system from that of Philadelphia.

Owing to the silence to which the prisoners are condemned, this union of the prisoners, it is asserted, offers no inconvenience, and presents many advantages.

They are united, but no moral connection exists among them. They see without knowing each other. They are in society without any intercourse; there exists among them neither aversion nor sympathy. The criminal, who contemplates a project of escape, or an attempt against the life of his keepers, does not know in which of his companions he may expect to find assistance. Their union is strictly material, or, to speak more exactly, their bodies are together, but their souls are separated; and it is not the solitude of the body which is important, but that of the mind. * * *

Their union in the workshops has, therefore, nothing dangerous: it has, on the contrary, it is said, an advantage peculiar to it, that of accustoming the prisoners to obedience.

What is the principal object of punishment in relation to him who suffers it? It is to give him the habits of society, and first to teach him to obey.

* * *

There are in America as well as in Europe, estimable men whose minds feed upon philosophical reveries, and whose extreme sensibility feels the want of some illusion. These men, for whom philanthropy has become a matter of necessity, find in the penitentiary system a nourishment for this generous passion. Starting from abstractions which deviate more or less from reality, they consider man, however far advanced in crime, as still susceptible of being brought back to virtue. They think that the most infamous being may yet recover the sentiment of honor; and pursuing consistently this opinion, they hope for an epoch when all criminals may be radically reformed, the prisons be entirely empty, and justice find no crimes to punish.

Others, perhaps without so profound a conviction, pursue nevertheless the same course; they occupy themselves continually with prisons; it is the subject to which all the labors of their life bear reference. Philanthropy has become for them a kind of profession, and they have caught the *monomanie* of the penitentiary system, which to them seems the remedy for all the evils of society.

We believe that both overrate the good to be expected from this institution, of which the real benefit can be acknowledged without attributing to it imaginary effects.

* * *

[I]f it be true that the radical reformation of a depraved person is only an accidental instead of being a natural consequence of the penitentiary system, it is nevertheless true that there is another kind of reformation, less thorough than the former, but yet useful for society, and which the system we treat of seems to produce in a natural way.

We have no doubt, but that the habits of order to which the prisoner is subjected for several years, influence very considerably his moral conduct after his return to society.

* * *

Perhaps, leaving the prison he is not an honest man, but he has contracted honest habits. He was an idler; now he knows how to work. His ignorance prevented him from pursuing a useful occupation; now he knows how to read and to write; and the trade which he has learnt in the prison, furnishes him the means of existence which formerly he had not. Without loving virtue, he may detest the crime of which he has suffered the cruel consequences, and if he is not more virtuous he has become at least more judicious; his morality is not honor, but interest. His religious faith is perhaps neither lively nor deep; but even supposing that religion has not touched his heart, his mind has contracted habits of order, and he possesses rules for his conduct in life; without having a powerful religious conviction, he has acquired a taste for moral principles which religion affords; finally, if he has not become in truth better, he is at least more obedient to the laws, and that is all which society has the right to demand.

If we consider the reformation of convicts under this point of view, it seems to us to be obtained, in many cases, through the system which we are considering; and those Americans who have the least confidence in the radical regeneration of criminals, believe, nevertheless, in the existence of a reformation reduced to these more simple terms.

On the Penitentiary System in the United States and Its Application in France (Carbondale, 1964), 55, 56–58, 80, 89–90.

STUDY QUESTIONS
1. How did the Auburn system and the Philadelphia system differ? What elements did they have in common, and how were those elements designed to bring about reformation of criminals?
2. What did Tocqueville and Beaumont think were reasonable goals to which the penitentiary might aspire, and what did they think was beyond its capacity to perform?

Retrieving Wayward Youth

Historians have long debated the extent to which middle-class reformers sought to control the behavior of the poor and working class and inculcate them with values that would facilitate the stable development of industrial capitalism. Whatever the relative merits of different sides of this debate, it is hard to avoid the conclusion that a desire for social control played an important role in the creation of private charitable institutions known as Houses of Refuge. Part schools and part prisons, Houses of Refuge (and their public counterparts, known as Reform Schools) admitted delinquent, abandoned, and impoverished children, the numbers of which seemed to be increasing in the antebellum era. During the several years children spent on average as inmates, they were subjected to an educational, labor, and disciplinary regimen that was supposed to dissuade them from engaging in crime, impart them with Christianity, and teach them skills that would help them lead upright lives and gain employment upon release. Benevolent concern for their charges undoubtedly motivated reformers involved with Houses of Refuge, and in most facilities officials tried—at least rhetorically—to replicate some elements of family governance they believed inmates lacked. Ultimately, however, fears of disorder and a sense that young people outside the middle classes sometimes needed to be forced into conformity played obvious roles in the institutions' design and administration.

Conceiving the House of Refuge: Report of the Board of Managers for the Society for the Prevention of Pauperism, New York, 1823

Connected with Juvenile Delinquency there is a subject which the Board beg leave to lay before the public and our civil authorities, which, if acted upon, they are confident would greatly reform and prevent the increase of young offenders. It is the project of a House of Refuge for Young Delinquents when discharged from prison. Let us for a moment dwell upon the condition and feelings of a youth when he is let loose from prison upon the termination of his punishment. How hopeless and helpless is his case; without money, without friends, without the means of gaining his bread, even with the sweat of his brow, and, above all, without character. No hand is extended to guide him on his way; no tongue speaks to him the voice of comfort; no smile of welcome lights up the face of friendship. All who know him shun him; he bears the mark of Cain upon him; all hands bid him depart; all doors are closed against him. He feels as if the world were a desert, and he alone in it; as if the prison he left contained all his friends and all his ties, and as if its gate, when it closed upon him, shut him out from a home. Thus viewing the world, and thus viewed by the world, can he repent and reform? No opportunity is given him to do so. He is driven to seek the haunts of lawless men, for such alone will receive him; he is compelled to theft and robbery, because he cannot starve. He is sought after and tempted by old offenders, who are always on the watch for young proselytes to join them in their depredations upon society, and he is again convicted and punished, and again let loose upon the world, riper in years and iniquity. This is no picture of the fancy, no story of exaggeration; it is the history of hundreds of our youth who are annually discharged from our prisons and again and again recommitted to them. Ask our officers of justice and judges, and they will tell you that the statement is true. They will tell you that the faces of young offenders grow familiar to them, from the frequency of their conviction; and that they do not know what to do with them, as imprisonment works no repentance.

An establishment, that would afford to them temporary refuge after they are discharged from prison, would rescue many from destruction, and would be an application of charity and philanthropy of the noblest kind. A House of Refuge, the Society believe, is equally desired by those who have the administration of our criminal law, who have expressed the greatest confidence in its success. We have official information that between one and two hundred young persons, from the age of seven to fourteen years, are annually brought before the police, on charges involving various degrees of crime; and it is the opinion of our magistrates that all between those ages can, by proper means, be reformed, and made useful members of society. The superintendents of the House of Refuge should possess a knowledge of character, and understand the avenues to the heart. They should first endeavor to effect a change in the mind, to restore independence and pride of principle, to give strength to virtuous dispositions, and stability to good intentions. Unless the heart is corrupt indeed, and sunk deep in guilt, the youth would undergo a change of feeling and character, and he would look upon crime with greater abhorrence, because he himself has been a criminal. Human nature is not so uniformly depraved as to be criminal from the love of crime, but oftener from necessity or accident, a bad education or evil example. No doubt the guilty often pause and tremble in their career, and would return to virtue if they could.

To support a House of Refuge, would require funds, to procure by hiring, or otherwise, a suitable building where they would receive moral and religious instruction, and be taught some of the most simple mechanic arts.

The greater part of the young convicts are the children of poor and abandoned parents, and commence their career by street begging and petty pilfering. Those who preferred it (and there would doubtless be many), when their minds were properly wrought upon, their character changed, and the seeds of virtuous principles had taken root, might be bound out in the country to farmers, or sent to sea as apprentices to masters of vessels. The offender now feels that he has regained his character; he hopes the world has forgiven, and, perhaps forgotten, his offense; and he feels himself once more to be a part of society. If but one out of ten could, by such an establishment, be saved from ruin, it would repay all the effort of founding and maintaining it. It should be supported by subscribers and contributors, and placed under the direction of benevolent and competent men, many of whom our city can boast, who would gladly undertake it. The Legislature, convinced of its utility and economy to the public treasury, in saving them the support of many convicts, would doubtless patronize it by ample contributions.

Statistics and Daily Workings of Select Houses of Refuge and Schools of Reform, 1857

Title	Location	No. of Inmates	Division of Time	Avg. Period of Detention	Deaths, Last 12 mos.	Escapees, Last 12 mos.	Avg. Age of Inmates	Employment of Inmates
House of Refuge	Randall's Isl'd N. York	426 male, 51 female	7 hrs. labor, 4.5 hrs. school, 1.5 hrs. meals, 9.5 hrs. sleep, 1.5 hrs. recreation	16 months	3	4	13.5	Shoemaking, chair seat & wire cloth making, farming, &c.
House of Reformation	Boston, Mass.	158, all male	5 hrs. labor, 5 hrs. school, 1.5 hrs. meals, 9.5 hrs. sleep, 3 hrs. recreation	18 months	0	0	12	Shoe making and knitting
House of Refuge	Cincinnati, Ohio	191 male, 37 female	7 hrs. labor, 4.5 hrs. school, 1.5 hrs. meals, 9.5 hrs. sleep, 1.5 hrs. recreation	14 months	0	19	13	Broom and brush making, shoe making, knitting

State Reform School	Cape Elizabeth, Maine	208, all male	6 hrs. labor, 4.5 hrs. school, 1.5 hrs. meals, 9 hrs. sleep, 3.5 hrs. recreation	14.5 months	1	0	13.5	Shoe, chair, brick making, farming, tailoring
State Reform School	West Meriden, Conn.	170, all male	6 hrs. labor, 4.5 hrs. school, 1 hrs. meals, 9.5 hrs. sleep, 3 hrs. recreation	18 months	0	1	12	Farming, burnishing, basket making, tailoring
House of Refuge	Baltimore, Md.	125 male, 23 female	6.5 hrs. labor, 4 hrs. school, 1.5 hrs. meals, 9 hrs. sleep, 3 hrs. recreation	12 months	0	3	12.5	Making shoes, tailoring, farming, gardening, knitting

Methods of Discipline

"HOUSE OF REFUGE," NEW YORK.—Discipline based on the principle of rewards and punishments. Lost character and standing may be redeemed by repentance and good conduct, specially noted in every department. Punishments are prescribed by the By-laws of the Managers, and are: 1st. Privation of play and exercise; 2d. Sent supperless to bed; 3d. Bread and water for meals; 4th Solitary confinement in cells; 5th. Corporal punishment.

* * *

"STATE REFORM SCHOOL," CAPE ELIZABETH.—Simple reprimand; demerit marks; dismission from certain confidential employments; dismission from trusts of honor; passage from a higher to a lower grade; loss of a single meal; detention during play hours; diet of bread and water for a short time; confinement in a light room, and corporal punishment. No corporal punishment or confinement is resorted to except in the fourth grade. Teachers and overseers may reprimand, deprive of a single meal, and give marks of demerit; but all cases of much importance must be reported to the Superintendent daily, in writing. At 7 o'clock in the evening of each day, all cases reported are examined by the Superintendent.

* * *

"HOUSE OF REFUGE," BALTIMORE.—By instruction in moral and religious principles; by the observance of system in all things; by constant employment; by rigid subordination to the rules of the House. These are our aims, regulated, in administration, by the law of kindness. For misdemeanors, the punishments are: privation of meals, or parts of meals; confinement in dormitories for short periods, and, when necessary, confinement in dark rooms. Corporal punishment only allowed by special order of the Executive Committee—in the gravest cases, by sentence delivered in form by the Committee; in no case to the girls. In the schools, the punishments are specially defined by the School Committee, sanctioned by the Board.

Educational Plans

"HOUSE OF REFUGE," NEW YORK.—Mental, moral and religious. Mental or intellectual education extends to a practical knowledge of the common English branches. Moral instruction includes a knowledge of the principles of right and wrong, with the duties all owe to each other and their obligations to society. Religious instruction relates to the great truths contained in the Bible, including the schemes of redemption and salvation of man through Christ, and the obligations of man to his Maker.

* * *

"HOUSE OF REFUGE," CINCINNATI.—Physical, intellectual, moral, and religious. Physical, as far as to become acquainted with simple mechanical arts, and a thorough training in industrious habits. Intellectual extends to a knowledge of the elementary branches taught in public schools. Moral inculcates a knowledge of the great principles of right and wrong, teaches their duty to their fellowman, and instructs them in their various relations to society. Religious, teaches them their dependence on God and the principles of the gospel contained in the New Testament. Devotional exercises are had morning and evening, and religious instruction given, on the Sabbath, in Sabbath-school and chapel.

* * *

"STATE REFORM SCHOOL," C[APE] ELIZABETH.— Instruction in reading, writing, grammar, geography, arithmetic, and singing during four hours of each day.

* * *

"HOUSE OF REFUGE," BALTIMORE.—A plain English education, consisting of spelling, reading, writing, arithmetic, grammar, history, geography, with the use of maps, music; Sabbath-schools and Bible classes. Religious services are regularly and voluntarily conducted on the Sabbath by ministers of various denominations, and daily morning and evening devotions are strictly observed.

System of Governance

The only true mode to reform delinquent youth is, by the adoption of family government. In this all agree. The only distinction remaining is, whether they are conducted on the congregated family system, or on a family system, segregated into several groups. All profess, and in truth aim to govern upon the principle of the family, with one object, one interest, one heart, one head, and one altar. Thus, in at least one of our congregated institutions, the superintendent, his officers, and the inmates sit at table in the same dining-hall, while over the head of the table is the printed motto: "We are one family."

Proceedings of the First Convention of Managers and Superintendents of Houses of Refuge and Schools of Reform in the United States of America (New York, 1857), 81–82, 85, 86, 88, 90, 91, 93, 94, 95.

STUDY QUESTIONS

1. Why did those who created the first Houses of Refuge believe young criminals were in need of special attention even after serving time in jail?
2. Describe the daily routine and disciplinary regimen administered at Houses of Refuge. How effective do you think these institutions likely were in carrying out their goals?

Treating the Insane

Few reformers who believed in the power of institutions to change lives faced greater skepticism than those who worked to improve care for the mentally ill, because into the early nineteenth century, most Americans viewed the mentally ill as being practically beyond help. Unless maintained at home by family members, the insane were often confined to poorhouses or jails in abominable conditions. But as the number of people suffering from mental illnesses seemed to rise, and as medical professionals increasingly attributed that rise to the stresses and strains of modern "civilization," reformers began arguing that insanity was susceptible to treatment. What patients needed, they concluded, was a humane environment that helped them regain control over their faculties. In 1843, Dorothea Dix sent to the Massachusetts legislature a report exposing physical abuse and material deprivation routinely endured by the insane throughout the state. Her efforts created a scandal that led to an expansion of the state's mental hospital, and she convinced several other states to build new hospitals over the ensuing decade. Among them was the New Jersey State Lunatic Asylum in Trenton. Founded in 1848, it was the first in the United States to be built on the institutional plans of Thomas Story Kirkbride. Then the lead physician at the Pennsylvania Hospital for the Insane, Kirkbride favored an architectural model and care regimen known as "moral treatment" in which the mentally ill were treated kindly while living in surroundings designed to facilitate the recovery of sanity. Though only partially fulfilling their promise, more than two dozen American mental hospitals were built on the Kirkbride plan by the end of the nineteenth century.

Dorothea Dix Appeals to the Massachusetts Legislature (1843)

I come to present the strong claims of suffering humanity. I come to place before the Legislature of Massachusetts the condition of the miserable, the desolate, the outcast. I come as the advocate of helpless, forgotten, insane, and idiotic men and women; of beings, sunk to a condition from which the most unconcerned would start with real horror; of beings wretched in our Prisons, and more wretched in our Alms-Houses. And I cannot suppose it needful to employ earnest persuasion, or stubborn argument, in order to arrest and fix attention upon a subject, only the more strongly pressing in its claims, because it is revolting and disgusting in its details.

* * *

I proceed, gentlemen, briefly to call your attention to the present state of Insane Persons confined within this Commonwealth, in *cages, closets, cellars, stalls, pens! Chained, naked, beaten with rods,* and *lashed* into obedience!

* * *

Danvers. November; visited the almshouse; a large building, much out of repair; understand a new one is in contemplation. Here are from fifty-six to sixty inmates; one idiotic; three insane; one of the latter in close confinement at all times.

Long before reaching the house, wild shouts, snatches of rude songs, imprecations, and obscene language, fell upon the ear, proceeding from the occupant of a low building, rather remote from the principal building to which my course was directed. Found the mistress, and was conducted to the place, which was called "*the home*" of the *forlorn* maniac, a young woman, exhibiting a condition of neglect and misery blotting out the faintest idea of comfort, and outraging every sentiment of decency. She had been, I learnt, "a respectable person; industrious and worthy; disappointments and trials shook her mind, and finally laid prostrate reason and self-control; she became a maniac for life! She had been at Worcester Hospital for a considerable time, and had been returned as incurable." The mistress told me she understood that, while there, she was "comfortable and decent." Alas! what a change was here exhibited! She had passed from one degree of violence and degradation to another, in swift progress; there she stood, clinging to, or beating upon, the bars of her caged apartment, the contracted size of which afforded space only for increasing accumulations of filth, a *foul* spectacle; there she stood with naked arms and dishevelled hair; the unwashed frame invested with fragments of unclean garments, the air so extremely offensive, though ventilation was afforded on all sides save one, that it was not possible to remain beyond a few moments without retreating for recovery to the outward air. Irritation of body, produced by utter filth and exposure, incited her to the horrid process of tearing off her skin by inches; her face, neck, and person were thus disfigured to hideousness; she held up a fragment just rent off; to my exclamation of horror, the mistress replied: "oh, we can't help it; half the skin is off sometimes; we can do nothing with her; and it makes no difference what she eats, for she consumes her own filth as readily as the food which is brought her."

* * *

Groton. A few rods removed from the poorhouse is a wooden building upon the road-side, constructed of heavy board and plank; it contains one room, unfurnished, except so far as a bundle of straw constitutes furnishing. There is no window, save an opening half the size of a sash, and closed by a board shutter; in one corner is some brick-work surrounding an iron stove, which in cold weather serves for warming the room. The occupant of this dreary abode is a young man, who has been declared incurably insane. He can move a measured distance in his prison; that is, so far as a strong, heavy chain, depending from an *iron collar which invests his neck*, permits. In fine weather, and it was pleasant when I was there in June last, the door is thrown open, at once giving admission to light and air, and affording some little variety to the solitary in watching the passers-by. But that portion of the year which allows of open doors is not the chiefest part; and it may be conceived, without drafting much on the imagination, what is the condition of one who, for days and weeks, and months, sits in darkness and alone, without employment, without object. It may be supposed that paroxysms of frenzy are often exhibited, and that the tranquil state is rare in comparison with that which incites to violence. This I was told is the fact.

I may here remark that severe measures, in enforcing rule, have in many places been openly revealed. I have not seen chastisement administered by stripes, and in but few instances have I seen the *rods* and *whips*, but I have seen blows inflicted, both passionately and repeatedly.

I have been asked if I have investigated the causes of insanity? I have not; but I have been told that this most calamitous overthrow of reason, often is the result of a life of sin; it is sometimes, but rarely, added, they must take the consequences; they deserve no better care! Shall man be more just than God; he who causes his sun, and refreshing rains, and life-giving influence, to fall alike on the good and the evil? Is not the total wreck of reason, a state of distraction, and the loss of all that makes life cherished, a retribution sufficiently heavy, without adding to consequences so appalling, every indignity that can bring still lower the wretched sufferer? Have pity upon those who, while they were supposed to lie hid in secret sins, "have been scattered under a *dark veil of forgetfulness*; over whom is spread a heavy night, and who unto themselves are more grievous than the darkness."

Memorial to the Legislature of Massachusetts (Boston, 1843), 4, 7, 17–18.

Thomas S. Kirkbride on the Means of Restoring Sanity (1854)

Having referred to the unfavorable results of an habitual use of restraint and seclusion in a Hospital for the Insane, it is proper to indicate in more detail some of the means by which these unfortunate effects may be obviated.

A properly constructed building, admitting of a liberal classification of the patients, and the employment of an adequate number of intelligent and kind assistants, has already been referred to as being indispensable for such an object. The design, in establishing every such institution, being the restoration and comfort of the afflicted, the relief of their families, and the protection of the community, there can be no question but that it is sound economy to provide everything that will effect these objects promptly and in the most thorough manner.

Without adequate provision for out-door exercise and occupation for the patients, and a liberal supply of means of amusement, the excitement of the wards, and the violent and mischievous propensities of their inmates, will be apt to be such as to require modes of management that might otherwise be easily dispensed with. The first cost of some of these arrangements will necessarily be considerable, but the ultimate results can hardly fail to be so gratifying as to satisfy the most rigid stickler for economy, that the only wise course is to provide liberally of everything likely to be beneficial to the patients.

The farm and garden offer admirable means of useful occupation to the insane at certain periods of the disease, for, useful as they are to a large number, no greater indiscretion could be committed than attempting to set all insane men at work in every stage of their malady. To those accustomed to such pursuits, as well as to many who have been differently occupied, regular moderate labor in the open fields or in the garden contributes most essentially to their comfort, and tends to promote their recovery. Labor, then, is one of our best remedies; it is as useful in improving the health of the insane, as in maintaining that of the sane. It is one of the best anodynes for the nervous, it composes the restless and excited, promotes a good appetite and a comfortable digestion, and gives sound and refreshing sleep to many who would without it pass wakeful nights.

The provision of adequate and comfortable workshops, in a convenient position, and under the care of competent superintendents, may be made a source of profit to an institution, and furnish another means of labor of an interesting kind to a large number of the insane.

The usual means of amusement, which demand active muscular exercise, should not be neglected. A Gymnasium, suitable in its fitting up, for insane men, and a Calisthenum for insane women, will be found useful. The various games of ball, the exercise of using a car on a circular railroad, the care of domestic animals, as well as regular walks on the grounds or in the neighborhood, are also among the kinds of exercise that will be enjoyed by many patients; while means of carriage riding seem almost indispensable for many, who from physical and other causes cannot resort to the more active forms which have already been referred to.

Within doors, the means of keeping a comfortable house are, in addition to the medical treatment, the constant presence among the patients of intelligent attendants, active supervisors and judicious teachers or companions, always ready to check the commencement of excitement, to separate quarrelsome individuals, and to change the train of thought of those who seem disposed to be troublesome. The means to effect the objects in view are very numerous, and the tact of an individual is shown in selecting those that are most applicable to a case.

The introduction of regular courses of lectures, interesting exhibitions of various kinds, and musical entertainments in the lecture-rooms of our Hospitals for the Insane, has done much to break up the monotony of hospital life, which is so common a source of complaint among the insane.

Regular courses of instruction in well furnished school-rooms, reading aloud by the teachers to the patients of the more excited wards, the use of well selected libraries, the inspection of collections of curiosities, the use of musical instruments, and various games, are all among the many means which an ingenious Superintendent will suggest for the benefit and amusement of his patients, and which ought to be provided for in every institution for the insane.

On the Construction, Organization and General Arrangements of Hospitals for the Insane (Philadelphia, 1854), 61–63.

STUDY QUESTIONS

1. What tactics did Dorothea Dix use in her appeal to Massachusetts legislators? Why do you think she was able to convince them to reform mental health care?

2. What were some of the basic provisions of the Kirkbride plan for treating insanity? How did they reflect the notion that a proper environment was the key to rehabilitation and the recovery of mental health?

Creating Common Schools

Institutions rarely succeeded as their supporters imagined. Underfunded and understaffed penitentiaries and insane asylums frequently regressed into the very soul-deadening, repressive, and physically brutalizing places they were designed to be improvements upon, their inmates effectively warehoused rather than rehabilitated. But institutional reform was not wholly as bleak as those realities suggest. When it came to education, for example, the idea that public institutions could have broader social utility bore significant fruit. Dozens of residential schools for the deaf and the blind opened before the Civil War, and most northern states created publicly funded elementary education systems that gave children outside the wealthy classes access to regular schooling for the first time in American history. As educational reformers like Horace Mann of Massachusetts imagined them, these "common schools" would improve prospects for poor and working-class children by imparting to them the knowledge and skills they needed to succeed economically, and the schools would provide cultural instruction that would further the civic participation of children from varying ethnic and religious backgrounds. For all of Mann's optimism, however, it is clear that reformers engineered common schools to mold disorderly children into a particular kind of American citizen. The structure of the school day, with its strictly regimented schedule, its insistence on punctuality and obedience to authority, and its dependence on teaching through memorization and repetition, helped inculcate desirable behaviors for workers in a capitalist society. The curriculum, meanwhile, emphasized moralistic, biblical, and patriotic lessons in the hope that future generations would embrace middle-class Protestant values. Members of the working class often supported the creation of common schools, but given the ideological agenda at work, they were not uncontroversial institutions.

Horace Mann on the Promise of Universal Education (1848)

Under the providence of God, our means of education are the grand machinery by which the "raw material" of human nature can be worked up into inventors and discoverers, into skilled artisans and scientific farmers, into scholars and jurists, into the founders of benevolent institutions, and the great expounders of ethical and theological science. By means of early education, those embryos of talent may be quickened which will solve the difficult problems of political and economical law; and by them, too, the genius may be kindled which will blaze forth in the poets of humanity. Our schools, far more than they have done, may supply the presidents and professors of colleges, and superintendents of public instruction, all over the land; and send, not only into our sister States, but across the Atlantic, the men of practical science to superintend the construction of the great works of art. Here, too, may those judicial powers be developed and invigorated which will make legal principles so clear and convincing as to prevent appeals to force; and, should the clouds of war ever lower over our country, some hero may be found the nursling of our schools, and ready to become the leader of our armies, that best of all heroes who will secure the glories of a peace, unstained by the magnificent murders of the battle-field.

* * *

I proceed, then, in endeavoring to show how the true business of the schoolroom connects itself, and becomes identical, with the great interests of society. The former is the infant, immature state of those interests; the latter their developed, adult state. As "the child is father to the man," so may the training of the schoolroom expand into the institutions and fortunes of the State.

* * *

Now, two or three things will doubtless be admitted to be true, beyond all controversy, in regard to Massachusetts. By its industrial condition, and its business operations, it is exposed, far beyond any other State in the Union, to the fatal extremes of overgrown wealth and desperate poverty. Its population is far more dense than that of any other State. It is four or five times more dense than the average of all the other States taken to-gether; and density of population has always been one of the proximate causes of social inequality. According to population and territorial extent, there is far more capital in Massachusetts— capital which is movable, and instantaneously available—than in any other State in the Union; and probably both these qualifica-tions respecting population and territory could be omitted with-out endangering the truth of the assertion. * * * If this be so, are we not in danger of naturalizing and domesticating among our-selves those hideous evils which are always engendered between capital and labor, when all the capital is in the hands of one class, and all the labor is thrown upon another?

Now, surely nothing but universal education can counterwork this tendency to the domination of capital and the servility of labor. If one class possesses all the wealth and the education, while the residue of society is ignorant and poor, it matters not by what name the relation between them may be called: the latter, in fact and in truth, will be the servile dependents and subjects of the former. But, if education be equably diffused, it will draw property after it by the strongest of all attractions; for such a thing never did happen, and never can happen, as that an intelligent and practical body of men should be permanently poor. Property and labor in different classes are essentially antagonistic; but property and labor in the same class are essentially fraternal. The people of Massachusetts have, in some degree, appreciated the truth, that the unexampled prosperity of the State—its comfort, its competence, its general intelligence and virtue—is attributable to the education, more or less perfect, which all its people have received: but are they sensible of a fact equally important; namely, that it is to this same education that two-thirds of the people are indebted for not being to-day the vassals of as severe a tyranny, in the form of capital, as the lower classes of Europe are bound to in the form of brute force?

Education then, beyond all other devices of human origin, is a great equalizer of the conditions of men,—the balance-wheel of the social machinery. I do not here mean that it so elevates the moral nature as to make men disdain and abhor the oppression of their fellow-men. This idea pertains to another of its attributes. But I mean that it gives each man the independence and the means by which he can resist the selfishness of other men. It does better than to disarm the poor of their hostility toward the rich: it prevents being poor. Agrarianism is the revenge of poverty against wealth. The wanton destruction of the property of others—the burning of hay-ricks and corn-ricks, the demolition of machinery because it supersedes hand-labor, the sprinkling of vitriol on rich dresses—is only agrarianism run mad. Education prevents both the revenge and the madness. On the other hand, a fellow-feeling for one's class or caste is the common instinct of hearts not wholly sunk in selfish regards for person or for family. The spread of education, by enlarging the cultivated class or caste, will open a wider area over which the social feelings will expand; and, if this education should be universal and complete, it would do more than all things else to obliterate factitious distinctions in society.

The main idea set forth in the creeds of some political reformers, or revolutionizers, is, that some people are poor *because* others are rich. This idea supposes a fixed amount of property in the community, which by fraud or force, or arbitrary law, is unequally divided among men; and the problem presented for solution is, how to transfer a portion of this property from those who are supposed to have too much to those who feel and know that they have too little. At this point, both their theory and their expectation of reform stop. But the beneficent power of education would not be exhausted, even though it should peaceably abolish all the miseries that spring from the co-existence, side by side, of enormous wealth and squalid want. It has a higher function. Beyond the power of diffusing old wealth, it has the prerogative of creating new. It is a thousand times more lucrative than fraud, and adds a thousand-fold more to a nation's resources than the most successful conquests. Knaves and robbers can obtain only what was before possessed by others. But education creates or develops new treasures,—treasures not before possessed or dreamed of by any one.

Annual Reports of the Secretary of the Board of Education of Massachusetts for the Years 1845–1848 (Boston, 1891), 228, 233, 250–252.

STUDY QUESTIONS

1. What did Horace Mann mean when he wrote that "the true business of the schoolroom connects itself, and becomes identical, with the great interests of society"?

2. How did Mann see public education as decreasing class divisions in the United States? Do you think public education serves these purposes today?

Temperance

A Founding Father's Medical Advice

The temperance movement, whose supporters sought to limit or end alcohol consumption in the United States, had wider support than any other antebellum reform. Perfectly fusing together the religious and family mores of middle-class evangelicals, broader secular materialist notions of personal well-being and national improvement, and a desire for social order, temperance both exemplified many elements of the reform impulse and garnered the participation of millions of Americans. Moreover, temperance attested to reformers' optimism, because drinking was so ubiquitous in public and private life in the early-nineteenth century that Americans consumed on average more than three times what they drink today. Concerns about alcohol were evident, however, as early as the late eighteenth century. One of the first to sound a warning about its dangers was Benjamin Rush, a prominent Philadelphia physician, signer of the Declaration of Independence, and author of a popular 1784 pamphlet in which he argued that distilled alcoholic beverages were addictive and led to physical diseases and social ills. By the time the American temperance movement really took root in the 1820s, many of its activists would find Rush's beliefs in the moderate health benefits of beer, cider, and wine unacceptably accommodating of a substance they believed viciously destructive. Nonetheless, antebellum temperance supporters would repeatedly cite Rush's work. In particular, the "moral and physical thermometer" that Rush used to represent visually the increasingly pernicious effects of increasingly strong liquor would be reprinted and adapted by other authors over and over again throughout the nineteenth century.

Benjamin Rush, *A Moral and Physical Thermometer* (illustration, 1790)

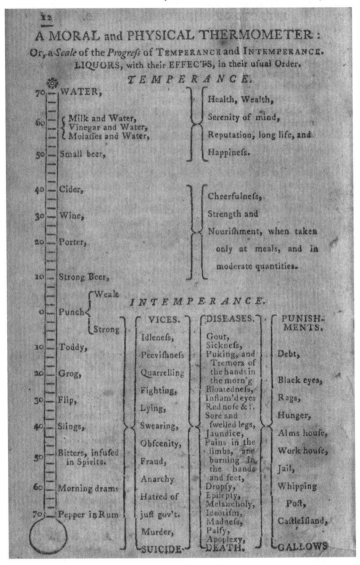

An Inquiry into the Effects of Spirituous Liquors on the Human Body (Boston, 1790), 12. (*The Library Company of Philadelphia*)

STUDY QUESTIONS

1. What sorts of consequences did Rush believe followed from excessive consumption of alcohol?
2. Why do you think Rush distinguished between the health consequences of drinking fermented beverages like beer and wine, and distilled beverages like rum?

A Call to Action

Temperance advocates like Benjamin Rush made little headway in the early republic. Indeed, per capita consumption of alcohol actually increased over the initial decades of the nineteenth century. At the same time, however, heavy drinking, particularly in the eyes of middle-class evangelicals, seemed antithetical to the work ethic, the family model, and the religious faith becoming central to antebellum American life. Presbyterian minister Lyman Beecher, for example, was among America's most prominent clergymen when he published a series of sermons in 1825 railing against alcohol consumption. Arguing that intemperance was unacceptable in all circumstances, Beecher concluded that alcohol ravaged individuals and families; that it undermined national prosperity, strength, and morality; and that voluntary associations ought to undertake a public campaign to convince Americans of the dangers they faced. Beecher's sermons were reprinted often in the antebellum era, and they helped inspire the creation of the American Temperance Society. Founded in 1826, the ATS successfully transformed scattered temperance calls into a mass movement. Within a decade, its leaders claimed thousands of local and state affiliates and two million individual pledges to abstain from alcohol forever, and thousands of small distilleries closed as per capita liquor consumption dropped by more than half in the 1830s alone. Suddenly, temperance had become a critical component of American respectability, while hard liquor had acquired cultural associations with sin, sickness, and poverty that it had rarely had before and that it has yet to escape completely. Here, Beecher recognizes that trying to eliminate drinking was daunting. But he insists that American Christians could accomplish anything they set their minds to, and that failure's costs were too high to ignore.

Lyman Beecher, *Six Sermons on the Nature, Occasions, Signs, Evils, and Remedy of Intemperance* (1825)

But it will be said,—"What can be done?"—and ten thousand voices will reply, "Nothing—oh nothing—men always have drunk to excess, and they always will; there is so much capital embarked in the business of importation and distillation—and so much supposed gain in vending ardent spirits—and such an insatiable demand for them—and such ability to pay for them by high-minded, wilful, independent freemen—that nothing can be done."

Then farewell, a long farewell, to all our greatness! The present abuse of ardent spirits has grown out of what was the prudent use of it, less than one hundred years ago; then there was very little intemperance in the land—most men, who drank at all, drank temperately. But if the prudent use of ardent spirits one hundred years ago, has produced such results as now exist, what will the present intemperate use accomplish in a century to come? Let no man turn off his eye from this subject, or refuse to reason, and infer—there is a moral certainty of a wide extended ruin, without reformation. The seasons are not more sure to roll, the sun to shine, or the rivers to flow—than the present enormous consumption of ardent spirits is sure to produce the most deadly consequences to the nation. They will be consumed in a compound ratio—and there is a physical certainty of the dreadful consequences. Have you taken the dimensions of the evil, its manifold and magnifying miseries, its sure-paced and tremendous ruin? And shall it come unresisted by prayer, and without a finger lifted to stay the desolation?

What if all men had cried out, as some did, at the commencement of the revolutionary struggle—"Alas! we must submit—we must be taxed—nothing can be done—Oh the fleets and armies of England—we cannot stand before them!!" Had such counsels prevailed, we should have abandoned a righteous cause, and forfeited that aid of Heaven, for which men are always authorized to trust in God, who are disposed to do his will.

Nothing can be done! Why can nothing be done? Because the intemperate will not stop drinking, shall the temperate keep on and become drunkards? Because the intemperate cannot be reasoned with, shall the temperate become madmen? And because force will not avail with men of independence and property, does it follow that reason, and conscience, and the fear of the Lord, will have no influence?

And because the public mind is now unenlightened, and un-awakened, and unconcentrated, does it follow that it cannot be enlightened, and aroused, and concentrated in one simultaneous and successful effort? Reformations as much resisted by popular feeling, and impeded by ignorance, interest, and depraved obsti-nacy, have been accomplished, through the medium of a rectified public opinion, and no nation ever possessed the opportunities and the means that we possess, of correctly forming the public opinion—nor was a nation ever called upon to attempt it by mo-tives of such imperious necessity. Our all is at stake—we shall per-ish if we do not effect it. There is nothing that ought to be done, which a free people cannot do.

The science of self-government is the science of perfect govern-ment, which we have yet to learn and teach, or this nation, and the world, must be governed by force. But we have all the means, and none of the impediments, which hinder the experiment amid the dynasties and feudal despotisms of Europe. And what has been done justifies the expectation that all which yet remains to be done will be accomplished. The abolition of the slave trade, an event now almost accomplished, was once regarded as a chimera of be-nevolent dreaming. But the band of Christian heroes, who conse-crated their lives to the work, may some of them survive to behold it achieved. This greatest of evils upon earth, this stigma of human nature, wide-spread, deep-rooted, and intrenched by interest and state policy, is passing away before the unbending requisitions of enlightened public opinion.

No great melioration of the human condition was ever achieved without the concurrent effort of numbers, and no extended, well-directed application of moral influence, was ever made in vain. Let the temperate part of the nation awake, and reform, and concen-trate their influence in a course of systematic action, and success is not merely probable, but absolutely certain. And cannot this be accomplished?—cannot the public attention be aroused, and set in array against the traffick in ardent spirits, and against their use?

With just as much certainty can the public sentiment be formed and put in motion, as the waves can be moved by the breath of heaven—or the massy rock, balanced on the precipice, can be pushed from its centre of motion;—and when the public sentiment once begins to move, its march will be as resistless as the same rock thundering down the precipice. Let no man then look upon our condition as hopeless, or feel, or think, or say, that nothing can be done. The language of Heaven to our happy nation is, "be it unto thee even as thou wilt," and there is no despondency more fatal, or more wicked, than that which refuses to hope, and to act, from the apprehension that nothing can be done.

Six Sermons on the Nature, Occasions, Signs, Evils, and Remedy of Intemperance (Boston, 1828), 83–87.

STUDY QUESTIONS

1. How did Beecher respond to those who argued that drinking was so ingrained in American culture that nothing could be done to eradicate it?
2. Who did Beecher believe bore responsibility for leading the temperance charge?

The Washingtonian Movement

For all the successes of temperance reformers in the 1820s and 1830s, they failed to reach thousands who arguably were most in need of reform. The leaders and the rank-and-file members of groups like the American Temperance Society were overwhelmingly evangelicals. Many were essentially sober people even before taking a temperance pledge, and they spent more time drawing attention to the damage caused by alcohol than on trying to help alcoholics break their habits. By contrast, the Washingtonian movement, founded in Baltimore in 1840, shied away from clerical leadership and religious moralizing, aiming instead to have men who had overcome serious drinking problems tell their stories and offer support to those still struggling with sobriety. In 1842, Abraham Lincoln, then a lawyer and a member of the Illinois House of Representatives, spoke to the

Springfield Washingtonians. Though never a drunk himself, he explained why he felt the Washingtonian approach to temperance was bearing fruit and how their ultimate triumph would benefit the nation.

Abraham Lincoln, An Address Delivered before the Springfield Temperance Society, on the 22d February, 1842

Although the Temperance cause has been in progress for near twenty years, it is apparent to all, that it is, *just now*, being crowned with a degree of success, hitherto unparalleled.

* * *

For this new and splendid success, we heartily rejoice. That that success is so much greater *now* than *heretofore*, is doubtless owing to rational causes; and if we would have it to continue, we shall do well to enquire what those causes are. The warfare heretofore waged against the demon of Intemperance, has, some how or other, been erroneous. Either the champions engaged, or the tactics they adopted, have not been the most proper. These champions for the most part, have been Preachers, Lawyers, and hired agents. Between these and the mass of mankind, there is a want of *approachability*, if the term be admissible, partially at least, fatal to their success. They are supposed to have no sympathy of feeling or interest, with those very persons whom it is their object to convince and persuade.

And again, it is so easy and so common to ascribe motives to men of these classes, other than those they profess to act upon. The *preacher*, it is said, advocates temperance because he is a fanatic, and desires a union of Church and State; the *lawyer*, from his pride and vanity of hearing himself speak; and the *hired agent*, for his salary. But when one, who has long been known as a victim of intemperance, bursts the fetters that have bound him, and appears before his neighbors "clothed, and in his right mind," a redeemed specimen of long lost humanity, and stands up with tears of joy trembling in eyes, to tell of the miseries *once* endured, *now* to be endured no more forever; of his once naked and starving children, now clad and fed comfortably; of a wife long weighed down with woe, weeping, and a broken heart, now restored to health, happiness, and renewed affection; and how easily it all is done, once it is resolved to be done; however simple his language, there is a logic, and an eloquence in it, that few, with human feelings, can resist. They cannot say that *he* desires a union of church and state, for he is not a church member; they cannot say *he* is vain of hearing himself speak, for his whole demeanor shows, he would gladly avoid speaking at all; they cannot say *he* speaks for pay for he receives none, and asks for none. Nor can his sincerity in any way be doubted; or his sympathy for those he would persuade to imitate his example, be denied.

In my judgment, it is to the battles of this new class of champions that our late success is greatly, perhaps chiefly, owing. But, had the old school champions themselves, been of the most wise selecting, was their *system* of tactics, the most judicious? It seems to me, it was not. Too much denunciation against dram sellers and dram-drinkers was indulged in. This, I think, was both impolitic and unjust. It was *impolitic*, because, it is not much in the nature of man to be driven to any thing; still less to be driven about that which is exclusively his own business; and least of all, where such driving is to be submitted to, at the expense of pecuniary interest, or burning appetite. When the dram-seller and drinker, were incessantly told, not in the accents of entreaty and persuasion, diffidently addressed by erring man to an erring brother; but in the thundering tones of anathema and denunciation * * * that *they* were the authors of all the vice and misery and crime in the land; that *they* were the manufacturers and material of all the thieves and robbers and murderers that infested the earth; that *their* houses were the workshops of the devil; and that *their persons* should be shunned by all the good and virtuous, as moral pestilences—I say, when they were told all this, and in this way, it is not wonderful that they were slow, *very slow*, to acknowledge the truth of such denunciations, and to join the ranks of their denouncers, in a hue and cry against themselves.

* * *

But I have said that denunciations against dram-sellers and dram-drinkers, are *unjust* as well as impolitic. Let us see.

I have not enquired at what period of time the use of intoxicating drinks commenced; nor is it important to know. It is sufficient that to all of us who now inhabit the world, the practice of drinking them, is just as old as the world itself,—that is, we have seen the one, just as long as we have seen the other. * * *

So too, it was every where a respectable article of manufacture and of merchandize. The making of it was regarded as an honorable livelihood; and he who could make most, was the most enterprising and respectable. * * * Universal public opinion not only tolerated, but recognized and adopted its use.

It is true, that even *then*, it was known and acknowledged, that many were greatly injured by it; but none seemed to think the injury arose from the *use* of a *bad thing*, but from the *abuse* of a *very good thing*. The victims to it were pitied, and compassionated, just as now are, the heirs of consumptions, and other hereditary diseases. Their failing was treated as a *misfortune*, and not as a *crime*, or even as a *disgrace*.

If, then, what I have been saying be true, is it wonderful, that *some* should think and act *now*, as *all* thought and acted *twenty years ago*? And is it *just* to assail, *contemn*, or despise them, for doing so? The universal *sense* of mankind, on any subject, is an argument, or at least an *influence* not easily overcome. * * *

Another error, as it seems to me, into which the old reformers fell, was, the position that all habitual drunkards were utterly incorrigible, and therefore, must be turned adrift, and damned without remedy, in order that the grace of temperance might abound to the temperate *then*, and to all mankind some hundred years *thereafter*. There is in this something so repugnant to humanity, so uncharitable, so cold-blooded and feelingless, that it never did, nor ever can enlist the enthusiasm of a popular cause. We could not love the man who taught it—we could not hear him with patience. The heart could not throw open its portals to it. The generous man could not adopt it. It could not mix with his blood. It looked so fiendishly selfish, so like throwing fathers and brothers overboard, to lighten the boat for our security—that the noble minded shrank from the manifest meanness of the thing.

* * *

By the Washingtonians, this system of consigning the habitual drunkard to hopeless ruin, is repudiated. *They* adopt a more enlarged philanthropy. *They* go for present as well as future good. *They* labor for all *now* living, as well as all *hereafter* to live. *They* teach *hope* to all—*despair* to none. As applying to *their* cause, *they* deny the doctrine of unpardonable sin.

* * *

To these *new champions*, and this *new* system of tactics, our late success is mainly owing; and to *them* we must chiefly look for the final consummation. The ball is now rolling gloriously on, and none are so able as *they* to increase its speed, and its bulk—to add to its momentum, and its magnitude. Even though unlearned in letters, for this task, none others are so well educated. To fit them for this work, they have been taught in the true school. *They* have been in *that* gulf, from which they would teach others the means of escape. *They* have passed that prison wall, which others have long declared impassable; and who that has not, shall dare to weigh opinions with *them*, as to the mode of passing.

* * *

If the relative grandeur of revolutions shall be estimated by the great amount of human misery they alleviate, and the small amount they inflict, then, indeed, will this be the grandest the world shall ever have seen. Of our political revolution of '76, we all are justly proud. It has given us a degree of political freedom, far exceeding that of any other of the nations of the earth. In it the world has found a solution of that long mooted problem, as to the capability of man to govern himself. In it was the germ which has vegetated, and still is to grow and expand into the universal liberty of mankind.

But with all these glorious results, past, present, and to come, it had its evils too. It breathed forth famine, swam in blood and rode on fire; and long, long after, the orphan's cry, and the widow's wail, continued to break the sad silence that ensued. These were the price, the inevitable price, paid for the blessings it bought.

Turn now, to the temperance revolution. In *it*, we shall find a stronger bondage broken; a viler slavery, manumitted; a greater tyrant deposed. In *it*, more of want supplied, more disease healed, more sorrow assuaged. By *it* no orphans starving, no widows weeping. By *it*, none wounded in feeling, none injured in interest. Even the dram-maker, and dram seller, will have glided into other occupations *so* gradually, as never to have felt the shock of change; and will stand ready to join all others in the universal song of gladness.

And what a noble ally this, to the cause of political freedom. With such an aid, its march cannot fail to be on and on, till every son of earth shall drink in rich fruition, the sorrow quenching draughts of perfect liberty. Happy day, when, all appetites controled, all passions subdued, all matters subjected, *mind*, all conquering *mind*, shall live and move the monarch of the world. Glorious consummation! Hail fall of Fury! Reign of Reason, all hail!

"An Address Delivered before the Springfield Temperance Society, on the 22d February, 1842," *The Collected Works of Abraham Lincoln*, Roy P. Basler, ed. (New Brunswick, N.J., 1959), vol. 1, 271–273, 274–275, 276, 278–279.

STUDY QUESTIONS
1. Why did Lincoln think "preachers, lawyers, and hired agents" were relatively unsuccessful and unpersuasive temperance speakers?
2. What did Lincoln envision as the consequences of temperance reform for the United States?

Temperance Propaganda and the Road to Prohibition

Like supporters of many reform movements, temperance advocates spread their message in a variety of ways. They sent lecturers on public speaking tours. They circulated millions of pages of pamphlet literature, tracts, newspapers, and organizational reports. They penned songs, published lithograph and woodcut images, and wrote fiction. Temperance propaganda can seem absurd to modern eyes, with images and stories that were frequently lurid, melodramatic, sensational, moralistic, manipulative, or hopelessly sentimental. But it spoke to the serious concerns many Americans had about the dangers alcohol posed to their families, their health, their values, their prosperity, and the future of their country. And it was both very effective and extremely popular. Below are two examples of materials used in support of the temperance cause.

First are several lithographs published in the late 1840s by the printing firm of Currier and Ives. One, entitled "The Drunkards Progress," details how temperance reformers saw even casual drinking as leading inevitably to habitual use and total ruin. Next is a pair of images entitled "The Tree of Temperance" and "The Tree of Intemperance." Many variations of this juxtaposition appeared in nineteenth-century America, as it presented an easily understood message about the supposed consequences of a life of drinking as opposed to a life of abstinence.

Second is an excerpt from the most popular temperance novel of all time, Timothy Arthur's Ten Nights in a Bar-Room. *First published in 1854, Arthur's work describes the slow but steady disintegration of the fictional town of Cedarsville in the years after a man named Simon Slade opens the "Sickle and Sheaf" tavern. Selling hundreds of thousands of copies and rivaling Harriet Beecher Stowe's abolitionist novel* Uncle Tom's Cabin *in its appeal,* Ten Nights in a Bar-Room *ultimately concludes with a call for legally banning the manufacture and sale of alcohol. Although Lyman Beecher had suggested in his 1825 sermons that such laws might ultimately be beneficial, only by the 1850s did a large number of temperance reformers come to favor legislative prohibition as a superior strategy to moral persuasion for making America a dry nation. In 1851, Maine became the first state to ban the sale and manufacture of alcoholic beverages, and over the next several years more than a dozen states and hundreds of counties and towns followed. Ultimately, prohibition failed, and only a small number of places still had such laws by the outbreak of the Civil War. But that would not shake the conviction of some temperance reformers that morality had to be legislated for the public good.*

The Drunkard's Progress, from the First Glass to the Grave (illustration, 1840)

(The Granger Collection, New York)

The Tree of Temperance
(illustration, 1840)

The Tree of Intemperance
(illustration, 1840s)

(*Library of Congress*)

T. S. Arthur,
Ten Nights in a Bar-Room (1854)

Below, the narrator, a traveler, relates the conversation of two men from the town of Cedarsville as they react to the news that the son of a local judge had become a drunkard and lost nearly all his money to a professional gambler at the "Sickle and Sheaf" tavern.

The man, who had until now been sitting quietly in a chair, started up, exclaiming as he did so—

"Merciful heaven! I never dreamed of this! Whose sons are safe?"

"No man's," was the answer of the gentleman in whose office we were sitting—"No man's—while there are such open doors to ruin as you may find at the 'Sickle and Sheaf.' Did not you vote the anti-temperance ticket at the last election?"

"I did," was the answer; "and from principle."

"On what were your principles based?" was inquired.

"On the broad foundations of civil liberty."

"The liberty to do good or evil, just as the individual may choose?"

"I would not like to say that. There are certain evils against which there can be no legislation that would not do harm. No civil power in this country has the right to say what a citizen shall eat or drink."

"But may not the people, in any community, pass laws, through their delegated law-makers, restraining evil-minded persons from injuring the common good?"

"Oh, certainly—certainly."

"And are you prepared to affirm, that a drinking-shop, where young men are corrupted, ay, destroyed, body and soul—does not work an injury to the common good?"

"Ah! but there must be houses of public entertainment."

"No one denies this. But can that be a really Christian community which provides for the moral debasement of strangers, at the same time that it entertains them? Is it necessary that, in giving rest and entertainment to the traveler, we also lead him into temptation?"

"Yes—But—but—it is going too far to legislate on what we are to eat and drink. It is opening too wide a door for fanatical oppression. We must inculcate temperance as a right principle. We must teach our children the evils of intemperance, and send them out into the world as practical teachers of order, virtue, and sobriety. If we do this, the reform becomes radical, and in a few years there will be no bar-rooms, for none will crave the fiery poison."

"Of little value, my friend, will be, in far too many cases, your precepts, if temptation invites our sons at almost every step of their way through life. Thousands have fallen, and thousands are now tottering, soon to fall. Your sons are not safe; nor are mine. We cannot tell the day nor the hour when they may weakly yield to the solicitation of some companion, and enter the wide open door of ruin. And are we wise and good citizens to commission men to do the evil work of enticement? To encourage them to get gain in corrupting and destroying our children? To hesitate over some vague ideal of human liberty when the sword is among us, slaying our best and dearest? Sir! while you hold back from the work of staying the flood that is desolating our fairest homes, the black waters are approaching your own doors."

There was a startling emphasis in the tones with which this last sentence was uttered; and I did not wonder at the look of anxious alarm that it called to the face of him whose fears it was meant to excite.

"What do you mean, sir?" was inquired.

"Simply, that your sons are in equal danger with others."

"And is that all?"

"They have been seen, of late, in the bar-room of the 'Sickle and Sheaf.'"

"Who says so?"

"Twice within a week I have seen them going in there," was answered.

"Good heavens! No!"

"It is true, my friend. But who is safe? If we dig pits, and conceal them from view, what marvel if our own children fall therein?"

"My sons going to a tavern?" The man seemed utterly con-
founded. "How can I believe it? You must be in error, sir."

"No. What I tell you is the simple truth. And if they go
there—"

The man paused not to hear the conclusion of the sentence, but
went hastily from the office.

"We are beginning to reap as we have sown," remarked the
gentleman, turning to me as his agitated friend left the office. "As I
told them in the commencement it would be, so it is happening.
The want of a good tavern in Cedarville was over and over again
alleged as one of the chief causes of our want of thrift, and when
Slade opened the 'Sickle and Sheaf,' the man was almost glorified.
The gentleman who has just left us failed not in laudation of the
enterprising landlord; the more particularly, as the building of the
new tavern advanced the price of ground on the street, and made
him a few hundred dollars richer. Really, for a time, one might have
thought, from the way people went on, that Simon Slade was going
to make every man's fortune in Cedarville. But all that has been
gained by a small advance in property, is as a grain of sand to a
mountain, compared with the fearful demoralization that has
followed.'"

Ten Nights in a Bar-Room (London, 1855), 89–91.

STUDY QUESTIONS

1. Which do you think conveyed the temperance message more
   effectively and convincingly—images or fiction? Why?
2. Why do you think temperance reformers, having already successfully persuaded so many Americans to stop drinking, felt it
   necessary by the 1850s to advocate total legal prohibition of
   alcohol?

Abolitionism

An Appeal to Militant Antislavery

The movement against slavery had a tortuous history in the United States. While principled opposition to slavery was almost unheard of before the American Revolution, the rhetoric of liberty and equality gave antislavery enough momentum in the late eighteenth century such that northern states slowly phased the institution out of existence, and even some southern states passed laws making it easier for masters to emancipate slaves. Nonetheless, white racism remained ubiquitous, and the emergence of cotton as a cash crop around the turn of the nineteenth century made slaves more valuable and abolition less palatable. By the 1820s, support for abolition was restricted largely to northern free people of color, and those white Americans who did hope to end slavery mostly backed colonizationist schemes to remove people of African descent from the country altogether. Colonization retained significant white support long into the nineteenth century, but it was never especially practical, and by the end of the 1820s the small number of black Americans who had ever supported colonization had largely soured on it. The 1829 publication of David Walker's Appeal . . . to the Colored Citizens of the World *signaled that a more forceful antislavery movement was on the rise. Walker was born a free person of color in North Carolina, and he settled as an adult in Boston, where he ran a used clothing store and became active in black abolitionist organizations. Deeply rooted in his Christian faith and his indignation toward white hypocrisy and brutality, Walker's* Appeal *was a blistering assault on colonization, racism, and especially on slavery. Seeing no grounds for compromise or reason for delaying slavery's end, Walker ultimately called on slaves themselves to overthrow the institution by violence if necessary. Walker was found dead on his shop's door-step in 1830.*

David Walker, *Walker's Appeal . . . to the Colored Citizens of the World* (1829)

Now let us reason—I mean you of the United States, whom I believe God designs to save from destruction, if you will hear. For I declare to you, whether you believe it or not, that there are some on the continent of America, who will never be able to repent. God will surely destroy them, to show you his disapprobation of the murders they and you have inflicted on us. I say, let us reason; had you not better take our body, while you have it in your power, and while we are yet ignorant and wretched, not knowing but a little, give us education, and teach us the pure religion of our Lord and Master, which is calculated to make the lion lay down in peace with the lamb, and which millions of you have beaten us nearly to death for trying to obtain since we have been among you, and thus at once, gain our affection while we are ignorant? Remember Americans, that we must and shall be free and enlightened as you are, will you wait until we shall, under God, obtain our liberty by the crushing arm of power? Will it not be dreadful for you? I speak Americans for your good. We must and shall be free I say, in spite of you. You may do your best to keep us in wretchedness and misery, to enrich you and your children; but God will deliver us from under you. And wo, wo, will be to you if we have to obtain our freedom by fighting. Throw away your fears and prejudices then, and enlighten us and treat us like men, and we will like you more than we do now hate you, and tell us now no more about colonization, for America is as much our country, as it is yours.—Treat us like men, and there is no danger but we will all live in peace and happiness together. For we are not like you, hard hearted, unmerciful, and unforgiving. What a happy country this will be, if the whites will listen. What nation under heaven, will be able to do any thing with us, unless God gives us up into its hand?

* * *

If any are anxious to ascertain who I am, know the world, that I am one of the oppressed, degraded and wretched sons of Africa, rendered so by the avaricious and unmerciful, among the whites.—If any wish to plunge me into the wretched incapacity of a slave, or murder me for the truth, know ye, that I am in the hand of God, and at your disposal. I count my life not dear unto me, but I am ready to be offered at any moment. For what is the use of living, when in fact I am dead. But remember, Americans, that as miserable, wretched, degraded and abject as you have made us in preceding, and in this generation, to support you and your families, that some of you, (whites) on the continent of America, will yet curse the day that you ever were born. You want slaves, and want us for your slaves!!! My colour will yet, root some of you out of the very face of the earth!!!!!! You may doubt it if you please. I know that thousands will doubt— they think they have us so well secured in wretchedness, to them and their children, that it is impossible for such things to occur. So did the antideluvians doubt Noah, until the day in which the flood came and swept them away. So did the Sodomites doubt, until Lot had got out of the city, and God rained down fire and brimstone from Heaven upon them, and burnt them up. So did the king of Egypt doubt the very existence of a God; he said, "who is the Lord, that I should let Israel go?" Did he not find to his sorrow, who the Lord was, when he and all his mighty men of war, were smothered to death in the Red Sea? So did the Romans doubt, many of them were really so ignorant, that they thought the whole of mankind were made to be slaves to them; just as many of the Americans think now, of my colour. But they got dreadfully deceived.

* * *

See your Declaration Americans!!! Do you understand your own language? Hear your language, proclaimed to the world, July 4th, 1776—"We hold these truths to be self evident—that ALL MEN ARE CREATED EQUAL!! that they are *endowed by their Creator with certain unalienable rights*; that among these are life, *liberty*, and the pursuit of happiness!!" Compare your own language above, extracted from your Declaration of Independence, with your cruelties and murders inflicted by your cruel and unmerciful fathers and yourselves on our fathers and on us—men who have never given your fathers or you the least provocation!!!!!!

Hear your language further! "But when a long train of abuses and usurpation, pursuing invariably the same object, evinces a design to reduce them under absolute despotism, it is their *right*, it is their *duty*, to throw off such government, and to provide new guards for their future security."

Now, Americans! I ask you candidly, was your sufferings under Great Britain, one hundredth part as cruel and tyranical as you have rendered ours under you? Some of you, no doubt, believe that we will never throw off your murderous government and "provide new guards for our future security." If Satan has made you believe it, will he not deceive you? Do the whites say, I being a black man, ought to be humble, which I readily admit? I ask them, ought they not to be as humble as I? or do they think that they can measure arms with Jehovah? Will not the Lord yet humble them? or will not these very coloured people whom they now treat worse than brutes, yet under God, humble them low down enough? Some of the whites are ignorant enough to tell us, that we ought to be submissive to them, that they may keep their feet on our throats. And if we do not submit to be beaten to death by them, we are bad creatures and of course must be damned, &c. If any man wishes to hear this doctrine openly preached to us by the American preachers, let him go into the Southern and Western sections of this country—I do not speak from hear say—what I have written, is what I have seen and heard myself. No man may think that my book is made up of conjecture—I have travelled and observed nearly the whole of those things myself, and what little I did not get by my own observation, I received from those among the whites and blacks, in whom the greatest confidence may be placed.

The Americans may be as vigilant as they please, but they cannot be vigilant enough for the Lord, neither can they hide themselves, where he will not find and bring them out.

Walker's Appeal . . . to the Colored Citizens of the World (Boston, 1830), 78–79, 81–83, 85–86.

STUDY QUESTIONS

1. How does David Walker draw on both Christianity and the language of the American Revolution to make an argument

against slavery? Which do you think was more significant? Which is more effective?

2. What did Walker suggest the consequences would be for white Americans if they did not bring slavery to an end?

The Emergence of Garrison

Radical antislavery had its roots among the black population, but only when white support for such ideas spread did the seeds of abolitionism planted by African Americans grow into a substantial social movement. That whites were drawn to this form of abolitionism may seem surprising, but the abolitionist critique of slavery was a consummate expression of the reform spirit. Abolitionists argued that slavery mocked American ideals of freedom, that it was a sin preventing the nation from achieving redemption, that forced labor cheapened the value of hard work, and that slave families were routinely destroyed through sale and the sexual predations of white men on enslaved women. Abolitionists thus combined democratic individualism, Christian millennialism, middle-class family norms, and emerging economic ideals to make the case that slavery degraded everyone involved and disgraced American secular and religious values. The most important figure in making this argument to white Americans was William Lloyd Garrison. Born and raised in New England, Garrison had some initial interest in colonization, but by 1830 he had repudiated it as wholly inadequate to the cause of undoing slavery. Garrison instead began advocating immediate emancipation and the full social and political enfranchisement of black Americans as the only morally just course. In 1831, at the age of twenty-five, he began publishing The Liberator *to serve as the newspaper of this immediatist position. As his first editorial suggests, Garrison was strident, absolutely dedicated, and ferociously stubborn, and he made many enemies with his views, his writings, and his personality. He also exemplified the righteousness and perfectionism many reformers brought to their work.*

To the Public, *The Liberator*, January 1, 1831

During my recent tour for the purpose of exciting the minds of the people by a series of discourses on the subject of slavery, every place that I visited gave fresh evidence of the fact, that a greater revolution in public sentiment was to be effected in the free states— *and particularly in New-England*—than at the south. I found contempt more bitter, opposition more active, detraction more relentless, prejudice more stubborn, and apathy more frozen, than among slave owners themselves. Of course, there were individual exceptions to the contrary. This state of things afflicted, but did not dishearten me. I determined, at every hazard, to lift up the standard of emancipation in the eyes of the nation, *within sight of Bunker Hill and in the birth place of liberty.* That standard is now unfurled; and long may it float, unhurt by the spoliations of time or the missiles of a desperate foe—yea, till every chain be broken, and every bondman set free! Let southern oppressors tremble—let their secret abettors tremble—let their northern apologists tremble—let all the enemies of the persecuted blacks tremble.

* * *

Assenting to the "self-evident truth" maintained in the American Declaration of Independence, "that all men are created equal, and endowed by their Creator with certain inalienable rights—among which are life, liberty and the pursuit of happiness," I shall strenuously contend for the immediate enfranchisement of our slave population. * * *

I am aware, that many object to the severity of my language; but is there not cause for severity? I *will be* as harsh as truth, and as uncompromising as justice. On this subject, I do not wish to think, or speak, or write, with moderation. No! no! Tell a man whose house is on fire, to give a moderate alarm; tell him to moderately rescue his wife from the hand of the ravisher; tell the mother to gradually extricate her babe from the fire into which it has fallen;— but urge me not to use moderation in a cause like the present. I am in earnest—I will not equivocate—I will not excuse—I will not retreat a single inch—AND I WILL BE HEARD. The apathy of the people is enough to make every statue leap from its pedestal, and to hasten the resurrection of the dead.

It is pretended, that I am retarding the cause of emancipation by the coarseness of my invective, and the precipitancy of my measures. *The charge is not true.* On this question my influence,—humble as it is,—is felt at this moment to a considerable extent, and shall be felt in coming years—not perniciously, but beneficially   not as a curse, but as a blessing; and posterity will bear testimony that I was right. I desire to thank God, that he enables me to disregard "the fear of man which bringeth a snare," and to speak his truth in its simplicity and power.

The Liberator, January 1, 1831.

STUDY QUESTIONS
1. Did Garrison find more resistance to abolitionism in the North or the South?
2. Why did Garrison reject adopting more moderate rhetoric in assaulting slavery?

The Founding of the American Anti-Slavery Society

As an editor, Garrison believed language had the power to change minds, but he was also instrumental in formally organizing abolitionists to take concrete action and spread the message. Toward the end of 1833, he and roughly sixty others met in Philadelphia and founded the American Anti-Slavery Society to coordinate abolitionist activities in the United States. Popular especially in the northeast, by 1838 the Anti-Slavery Society claimed 1,300 local chapters and 250,000 members.

Declaration of the National Anti-Slavery Convention (1833)

The Convention, assembled in the City of Philadelphia to organize a National Anti-Slavery Society, promptly seize the opportunity to promulgate the following DECLARATION OF SENTIMENTS, as cherished by them in relation to the enslavement of one-sixth portion of the American people.

More than fifty-seven years have elapsed since a band of patriots convened in this place, to devise measures for the deliverance of this country from a foreign yoke. The corner-stone upon which they founded the TEMPLE OF FREEDOM was broadly this—"that all men are created equal; that they are endowed by their Creator with certain inalienable rights; that among these are life, LIBERTY, and the pursuit of happiness." At the sound of their trumpet-call, three millions of people rose up as from the sleep of death, and rushed to the strife of blood; deeming it more glorious to die instantly as freemen, than desirable to live one hour as slaves. —They were few in number—poor in resources; but the honest conviction that TRUTH, JUSTICE, and RIGHT were on their side, made them invincible.

We have met together for the achievement of an enterprise, without which, that of our fathers is incomplete, and which, for its magnitude, solemnity, and probable results upon the destiny of the world, as far transcends theirs, as moral truth does physical force.

* * *

[T]hose, for whose emancipation we are striving,—constituting at the present time at least one-sixth part of our countrymen,—are recognised by the laws, and treated by their fellow beings, as marketable commodities—as goods and chattels—as brute beasts;—are plundered daily of the fruits of their toil without redress;—really enjoy no constitutional nor legal protection from licentious and murderous outrages upon their persons;—are ruthlessly torn asunder—the tender babe from the arms of its frantic mother—the heart-broken wife from her weeping husband—at the caprice or pleasure of irresponsible tyrants;—and, for the crime of having a dark complexion, suffer the pangs of hunger, the infliction of stripes, and the ignominy of brutal servitude. They are kept in heathenish darkness by laws expressly enacted to make their instruction a criminal offence.

These are the prominent circumstances in the condition of more than TWO MILLIONS of our people, the proof of which may be found in thousands of indisputable facts, and in the laws of the slaveholding States.

Hence we maintain—

That in view of the civil and religious privileges of this nation, the guilt of its oppression is unequalled by any other on the face of the earth;—and, therefore,

That it is bound to repent instantly, to undo the heavy burden, to break every yoke, and to let the oppressed go free.

We further maintain—

That no man has a right to enslave or imbrute his brother—to hold or acknowledge him, for one moment, as a piece of merchandise—to keep back his hire by fraud—or to brutalize his mind by denying him the means of intellectual, social and moral improvement.

The right to enjoy liberty is inalienable. To invade it, is to usurp the prerogative of Jehovah. Every man has a right to his own body—to the products of his own labor—to the protection of law—and to the common advantages of society. It is piracy to buy or steal a native African, and subject him to servitude. Surely the sin is as great to enslave an AMERICAN as an AFRICAN.

Therefore we believe and affirm—

That there is no difference, *in principle*, between the African slave trade and American slavery;

That every American citizen, who retains a human being in involuntary bondage, is [according to Scripture] a MAN-STEALER;

That the slaves ought instantly to be set free, and brought under the protection of law;

That if they had lived from the time of Pharaoh down to the present period, and had been entailed through successive generations, their right to be free could never have been alienated, but their claims would have constantly risen in solemnity;

That all those laws which are now in force, admitting the right of slavery, are therefore before God utterly null and void; being an audacious usurpation of the Divine prerogative, a daring infringement on the law of nature, a base overthrow of the very foundations of the social compact, a complete extinction of all the relations, endearments and obligations of mankind, and a presumptuous transgression of all the holy commandments—and that therefore they ought to be instantly abrogated.

We further believe and affirm—

That all persons of color who possess the qualifications which are demanded of others, ought to be admitted forthwith to the enjoyment of the same privileges, and the exercise of the same prerogatives, as others; and that the paths of preferment, of wealth, and of intelligence, should be opened as widely to them as to persons of a white complexion.

We maintain that no compensation should be given to the planters emancipating their slaves—

Because it would be a surrender of the great fundamental principle that man cannot hold property in man;

Because SLAVERY IS A CRIME, AND THEREFORE IT IS NOT AN ARTICLE TO BE SOLD;

Because the holders of slaves are not the just proprietors of what they claim;—freeing the slaves is not depriving them of property, but restoring it to the right owner;—it is not wronging the master, but righting the slave—restoring him to himself;

Because immediate and general emancipation would only destroy nominal, not real property: it would not amputate a limb or break a bone of the slaves, but by infusing motives into their breasts, would make them doubly valuable to the masters as free laborers; and

Because if compensation is to be given at all, it should be given to the outraged and guiltless slaves, and not to those who have plundered and abused them.

We regard, as delusive, cruel and dangerous, any scheme of expatriation which pretends to aid, either directly or indirectly, in the emancipation of the slaves, or to be a substitute for the immediate and total abolition of slavery.

We fully and unanimously recognise the sovereignty of each State, to legislate exclusively on the subject of the slavery which is tolerated within its limits. We concede that Congress, *under the present national compact,* has no right to interfere with any of the slave States, in relation to this momentous subject.

But we maintain that Congress has a right, and is solemnly bound, to suppress the domestic slave trade between the several States, and to abolish slavery in those portions of our territory which the Constitution has placed under its exclusive jurisdiction.

We also maintain that there are, at the present time, the highest obligations resting upon the people of the free States, to remove slavery by moral and political action, as prescribed in the Constitution of the United States. They are now living under a pledge of their tremendous physical force to fasten the galling fetters of tyranny upon the limbs of millions in the southern States;— they are liable to be called at any moment to suppress a general insurrection of the slaves;—they authorise the slave owner to vote for three-fifths of his slaves as property, and thus enable him to perpetuate his oppression;—they support a standing army at the south for its protection;—and they seize the slave who has escaped into their territories, and send him back to be tortured by an enraged master or a brutal driver.

This relation to slavery is criminal and full of danger; IT MUST BE BROKEN UP.

These are our views and principles—these, our designs and measures. With entire confidence in the overruling justice of God, we plant ourselves upon the Declaration of our Independence, and upon the truths of Divine Revelation, as Upon the EVERLASTING ROCK.

We shall organize Anti-Slavery Societies, if possible, in every city, town and village of our land.

We shall send forth Agents to lift up the voice of remonstrance, of warning, of entreaty and rebuke.

We shall circulate, unsparingly and extensively, anti-slavery tracts and periodicals.

We shall enlist the PULPIT and the PRESS in the cause of the suffering and the dumb.

We shall aim at a purification of the churches from all participation in the guilt of slavery.

We shall encourage the labor of freemen over that of the slaves, by giving a preference to their productions;—and

We shall spare no exertions nor means to bring the whole nation to speedy repentance.

Our trust for victory is solely in GOD. We may be personally defeated, but our principles never. TRUTH, JUSTICE, REASON, HUMANITY, must and will gloriously triumph. Already a host is coming up to the help of the Lord against the mighty, and the prospect before us is full of encouragement.

Submitting this DECLARATION to the candid examination of the people of this country, and of the friends of liberty all over the world, we hereby affix our signatures to it;—pledging ourselves that, under the guidance and by the help of Almighty God, we will do all that in us lies, consistently with this Declaration of our principles, to overthrow the most execrable system of slavery that has ever been witnessed upon earth—to deliver our land from its deadliest curse—to wipe out the foulest stain which rests upon our national escutcheon—and to secure to the colored population of the United States all the rights and privileges which belong to them as men and as Americans—come what may to our persons, our interests, or our reputations—whether we live to witness the triumph of JUSTICE, LIBERTY and HUMANITY, or perish untimely as martyrs in this great, benevolent and holy cause.

The Liberator, December 14, 1833.

STUDY QUESTIONS

1. For what reasons did the American Anti-Slavery Society argue that slavery ought to be abolished? Why did they reject any plans for emancipation that would include colonization or that would compensate slaveholders for their property?
2. What tactics did the American Anti-Slavery Society announce they intended to use to bring their message to the American people?

Abolition as a Transatlantic Movement

As suggested by the English inspirations for Bible and tract societies, and by the interest of individuals like Tocqueville in penitentiaries, the cultural and intellectual currents that created America's age of reform were not restricted to the United States. Many movements had foreign parallels, perhaps none more significant than abolitionism, which had a prominent counterpart in Great Britain. Although England abolished slavery domestically in the 1770s, British merchants continued to play central roles in the Atlantic slave trade and hundreds of thousands of slaves toiled in British West Indian colonies. Toward the end of the eighteenth century, however, societies began proliferating in England that campaigned for abolition of the slave trade. Agitation by these groups resulted in Britain's abolishing the trade in 1807, a path followed by the United States the next year. English abolitionism was reinvigorated in the 1820s, this time with the goal of abolishing slavery itself throughout the British Empire. In 1833, Parliament passed the Slavery Abolition Act, which emancipated nearly 800,000 West Indian slaves by compensating slaveholders and establishing an apprenticeship system for former slaves as a transition to full freedom.

An Act for the Abolition of Slavery Throughout the British Colonies (1833)

An Act for the Abolition of Slavery throughout the *British* Colonies; for promoting the Industry of the Manumitted Slaves; and for compensating the Persons hitherto entitled to the Services of such Slaves.

Whereas divers Persons are holden in Slavery within divers of His Majesty's Colonies, and it is just and expedient that all such Persons should be Manumitted and set free, and that a reasonable Compensation should be made to the Persons hitherto entitled to the Services of such Slaves for the Loss which they will incur by being deprived of their Right to such Services: And whereas it is also expedient that Provision should be made for promoting the Industry and securing the good Conduct of the Persons so to be manumitted, for a limited Period after such their Manumission: And whereas it is necessary that the Laws now in force in the said several Colonies should forthwith be adapted to the new State and Relations of Society therein, which will follow upon such general Manumission as aforesaid of the said Slaves; and that, in order to afford the necessary time for such adaptation of the said Laws, a short Interval should elapse before such Manumission should take effect;

Be it therefore enacted by the King's most Excellent Majesty, by and with the Advice and Consent of the Lords Spiritual and

Temporal, and Commons, in this present Parliament assembled, and by the Authority of the same, THAT, from and after the first Day of *August* One thousand eight hundred and thirty-four all Persons who in conformity with the Laws now in force in the said Colonies respectively shall on or before the first Day of *August* One thousand eight hundred and thirty-four have been duly registered as Slaves in any such Colony * * * shall by force and virtue of this Act * * * become and be apprenticed Labourers * * *

II. And be it further enacted, That during the Continuance of the Apprenticeship of any such apprenticed Labourer such Person or Persons shall be entitled to the Services of such apprenticed Labourer as would for the Time being have been entitled to his or her Services as a Slave if this Act had not been made.

* * *

V. And be it further enacted, That no Person * * * shall continue in such Apprenticeship beyond the first Day of *August* One thousand eight hundred and forty; and that during such his or her Apprenticeship no such * * * apprenticed Labourer * * * shall be bound or liable, by virtue of such Apprenticeship, to perform any Labour in the Service of his or her Employer or Employers for more than forty-five Hours in the whole in any One Week.

* * *

XII. And be it further enacted, That, subject to the Obligations imposed by this Act, or to be imposed by any such Act of General Assembly, Ordinance, or Order in Council as herein-after mentioned, upon such apprenticed Labourers as aforesaid, all and every the Persons who on the said first Day of *August* One thousand eight hundred and thirty-four shall be holden in Slavery within any such *British* Colony as aforesaid shall upon and from and after the said first Day of *August* One thousand eight hundred and thirty-four become and be to all Intents and Purposes free and discharged of and from all Manner of Slavery, and shall be absolutely and for ever manumitted; and that the Children thereafter to be born to any such Persons, and the Offspring of such Children shall in like Manner be free from their Birth; and that from, and after the said first Day of *August* One thousand eight hundred and thirty-four Slavery shall be and is hereby utterly and for ever abolished and declared unlawful throughout the *British* Colonies, Plantations, and Possessions Abroad.

* * *

XXIV. And whereas, towards compensating the Persons at present entitled to the Services of the Slaves to be manumitted and set free by virtue of this Act for the Loss of such Services, His Majesty's most dutiful and loyal Subjects the Commons of *Great Britain* and *Ireland* in Parliament assembled have resolved to give and grant to His Majesty the Sum of Twenty Millions Pounds Sterling.

* * *

XXXIII. And for the Distribution of the said Compensation Fund and the Apportionment thereof amongst the several Persons who may prefer Claims thereon, be it enacted, That it shall and may be lawful for His Majesty from Time to Time, by a Commission under the Great Seal of the United Kingdom, to constitute and appoint such Persons, not being less than Five, as to His Majesty shall seem meet, to be Commissioners of Arbitration for inquiring into and deciding upon the Claims to Compensation, which may be pre-ferred to them under this Act.

---

www.pdavis.nl/Legis_07.htm.

STUDY QUESTIONS

1. How exactly would the apprenticeship plans of the British work? Do these plans seem fair and reasonable to you?
2. At what point would slavery be formally abolished in the British colonies?

The Culture of Abolitionism

As suggested by the popularity of temperance fiction like Ten Nights in a Bar-Room, *reform movements succeeded in drawing adherents and gaining attention in part by drawing on and contributing to popular culture. Few movements did this more extensively than abolitionism. Its supporters wrote novels, songs, plays, and memoirs. They produced broadsides and engravings. They held fairs to raise money, and they manufactured figurines, medallions, decorative plates, games, needlework, and dolls. In these ways and others, abolitionists made their cause more than a matter of political or social agitation—abolitionism became in some measure a lived experience that could be read, heard, enacted, and seen in a wide variety of public and private spaces. In the 1840s, for example, one could see the horrors of slavery depicted in periodicals like the* American Anti-Slavery Almanac, *attend a meeting where selections from* The Anti-Slavery Harp *songbook might be sung, or visit an antislavery fair and purchase* The Anti-Slavery Alphabet, *part of a large body of juvenile abolitionist literature designed to help parents acculturate their children to the cause.*

Illustrations of the American Anti-Slavery Almanac for 1840 (**illustration, 1840**)

The Anti-Slavery Harp, compiled by William W. Brown (1848)

I AM AN ABOLITIONIST
AIR — Auld Lang Syne

I am an Abolitionist!
   I glory in the name:
Though now by Slavery's minions hiss'd
   And covered o'er with shame,
It is a spell of light and power—
   The watchword of the free:—
Who spurns it in the trial-hour,
   A craven soul is he!

I am an Abolitionist!
   Then urge me not to pause;
For joyfully do I enlist
   In FREEDOM'S sacred cause:
A nobler strife the world ne'er saw,
   Th'enslaved to disenthral;
I am a soldier for the war,
   Whatever may befall!

I am an Abolitionist!
   Oppression's deadly foe;
In God's great strength will I resist,
   And lay the monster low;
In God's great name do I demand,
   To all be freedom given,
That peace and joy may fill the land,
   And songs go up to heaven!

I am an Abolitionist!
   No threats shall awe my soul,
No perils cause me to desist,
   No bribes my acts control;

A freeman will I live and die,
In sunshine and in shade,
And raise my voice for liberty,
Of nought on earth afraid.

GET OFF THE TRACK
AIR — Dan Tucker

Ho! the car Emancipation
Rides majestic thro' our nation,
Bearing on its train the story,
Liberty! a nation's glory.
Roll it along, thro' the nation,
Freedom's car, Emancipation!
* * *

Men of various predilections,
Frightened, run in all directions;
Merchants, editors, physicians,
Lawyers, priests, and politicians.
Get out of the way! every station!
Clear the track of 'mancipation!
* * *

Now again the bell is tolling,
Soon you'll see the car-wheels rolling;
Hinder not their destination,
Chartered for Emancipation.
Wood up the fire! keep it flashing,
While the train goes onward dashing.
* * *

See the people run to meet us;
At the depots thousands greet us;
All take seats with exultation,
In the Car Emancipation.
Huzza! Huzza!! Emancipation
Soon will bless our happy nation,
Huzza! Huzza!! HUZZA!!!

The Anti-Slavery Harp, compiled by William W. Brown (Boston, 1848), 17–18, 25–26.

The Anti-Slavery Alphabet (1847)

TO OUR LITTLE READERS.

Listen, little children, all,
Listen to our earnest call:
You are very young, 'tis true,
But there's much that you can do.
Even you can plead with men
That they buy not slaves again,
And that those they have maybe
Quickly set at liberty.
They may hearken what *you* say,
Though from *us* they turn away.
Sometimes, when from school you walk,
You can with your playmates talk,
Tell them of the slave child's fate,
Motherless and desolate.
And you can refuse to take
Candy, sweetmeat, pie or cake,
Saying "no"—unless 'tis free—
"The slave shall not work for me."
Thus, dear little children, each
May some useful lesson teach;
Thus each one may help to free
This fair land from slavery.

A is an Abolitionist—
A man who wants to free
The wretched slave—and give to all
An equal liberty.

B is a Brother with a skin
Of somewhat darker hue,
But in our Heavenly Father's sight,
He is as dear as you.

C is the Cotton-field, to which
This injured brother's driven,
When, as the white-man's *slave*, he toils
From early morn till even.

D is the Driver, cold and stern,
Who follows, whip in hand,
To punish those who dare to rest,
Or disobey command.

E is the Eagle, soaring high;
An emblem of the free;
But while we chain our brother man,
Our type he cannot be.

F is the heart-sick Fugitive,
The slave who runs away,
And travels through the dreary night,
But hides himself by day.

G is the Gong, whose rolling sound,
Before the morning light,
Calls up the little sleeping slave,
To labor until night.

H is the Hound his master trained,
And called to scent the track
Of the unhappy fugitive,
And bring him trembling back.

I is the Infant, from the arms
Of its fond mother torn,
And, at a public auction, sold
With horses, cows, and corn.

J is the Jail, upon whose floor
That wretched mother lay,
Until her cruel master came,
And carried her away.

K is the Kidnapper, who stole
That little child and mother—
Shrieking, it clung around her, but
He tore them from each other.

L is the Lash, that brutally
He swung around its head,
Threatening that "if it cried again,
He'd whip it till 'twas dead."

M is the Merchant of the north,
Who buys what slaves produce—
So they are stolen, whipped and worked,
For his, and for our use.

N is the Negro, rambling free
In his far distant home,
Delighting 'neath the palm trees' shade
And cocoa-nut to roam.

O is the Orange tree, that bloomed
Beside his cabin door,
When white men stole him from his home
To see it never more.

P is the Parent, sorrowing,
And weeping all alone—
The child he loved to lean upon,
His only son, is gone!

Q is the Quarter, where the slave
On coarsest food is fed,
And where, with toil and sorrow worn,
He seeks his wretched bed.

R is the "Rice-swamp, dank and lone,"
Where, weary, day by day,

He labors till the fever wastes
His strength and life away.

S is the Sugar, that the slave
Is toiling hard to make,
To put into your pie and tea,
Your candy, and your cake.

T is the rank Tobacco plant,
Raised by slave labor too:
A poisonous and nasty thing,
For gentlemen to chew.

U is for Upper Canada,
Where the poor slave has found
Rest after all his wanderings,
For it is British ground!

V is the Vessel, in whose dark,
Noisome, and stifling hold,
Hundreds of Africans are packed,
Brought o'er the seas, and sold.

W is the Whipping post,
To which the slave is bound,
While on his naked back, the lash
Makes many a bleeding wound.

X is for Xerxes, famed of yore;
A warrior stern was he
He fought with swords; let truth and love
Our only weapons be.

Y is for Youth—the time for all
Bravely to war with sin;
And think not it can ever be
Too early to begin.

Z is a Zealous man, sincere,
Faithful, and just, and true;
An earnest pleader for the slave—
Will you not be so too?

The Anti-Slavery Alphabet (Philadelphia, 1847).

STUDY QUESTIONS

1. What sorts of themes did abolitionists stress in their images, songs, and children's literature?
2. How do you imagine the culture of abolition helped strengthen the movement?

Abolitionsm Fractures

The American Anti-Slavery Society grew and the antislavery movement became more prominent over the course of the 1830s, but they were also extremely controversial. White southerners resented being morally condemned for slaveholding and claimed abolitionists encouraged life-threatening slave insurrections, while white northerners thought the abolitionist movement's biracialism scandalous and worried that antislavery agitation would destabilize and divide the nation. By the mid-1830s, abolitionists faced repression and violence nearly everywhere in the United States. The vehemence of the public reaction in turn helped fragment the movement internally by exacerbating tensions between people with varying ideas about strategy and tactics. Moderates felt the movement ought to engage politics and the law more directly, avoid taking unnecessarily inflammatory positions, and generally chart a course that might attract greater public support. By contrast, radicals, led by Garrison, concluded that the American political and legal systems had been impossibly tainted by slavery, that direct engagement with them undercut the moral purity necessary for a movement that understood slavery as a sin, and that, if anything, abolitionists ought to embrace their arguments about human equality and government corruption more wholeheartedly. Such stances led the radical faction toward support for feminism and pacifism, but even some abolitionists who agreed with Garrison in principle felt he was becoming so inflexible and outrageous to social conventions that he threatened to do more harm than good for the antislavery cause. These tensions came to a head at the American Anti-Slavery Society's annual meeting in 1840, when the appointment of a woman to the previously all-male business committee prompted hundreds of delegates to walk out in protest. As suggested by the following selection from the address of the American and Foreign Anti-Slavery Society formed by the dissenters, however, far more than the "woman question" alone provoked the schism.

Address of the American and Foreign Anti-Slavery Society (1840)

At the recent meeting of the Society, the acting President nominated a woman on the business committee, associated with eleven men * * * This was considered a test vote of the relative strength of the "woman's rights," and constitutional parties, assembled; and it was believed, that the act of placing a woman on the business committee, was merely an initiatory step to the introduction of other measures, FOREIGN to the original principles and designs of the anti-slavery enterprise, all tending to divert the minds of abolitionists from the cause of the poor slave, and the rights of the free people of color. * * * Several men, nominated to serve on the business committee, immediately declined serving, in consequence of the act of the majority, and others afterwards withdrew. They stated, that the innovation seemed to them repugnant to the constitution of the Society—that it was throwing a fire-brand into anti-slavery meetings—that it was contrary to the Scriptures and the usages of the civilized world—and that it tended to destroy the efficiency of female anti-slavery action.

But the question of "woman's rights" is not the only matter of difference between the adherents to the old society, and the friends of the new association; nor is it the chief cause of the difficulty, though it happened to come up first and prominently at the late meeting. At the formation of the American Anti-Slavery Society, the lawfulness of human government was recognized, and it was a fundamental principle, that political action was both expedient and proper. Recently, however, the same persons belonging to the anti-slavery ranks, who are contending for what they call "woman's rights" * * * deny the obligation of forming, supporting, or yielding obedience to civil government, and refuse to affirm the *duty* of political action. * * * Styling themselves "non-resistants," and professing to be opposed to all physical force * * * they seem determined to carry forward their favorite theories and practices, at all events, even if the great moral enterprise in which they and we originally embarked, should retrograde, and be justly offensive to those who might otherwise join the anti-slavery ranks, and help on the cause of impartial liberty to a glorious consummation. That there are such we do not entertain a doubt. We wish them to understand distinctly, that it will be no part of our design to break up existing organizations in church or state, but only to wake up and give impetus to the usual forms of social action; and the special object will be, by light and love, to secure appropriate church action in the several religious connexions. With regard to political action, while we recognize the rightfulness of government, and shall urge political action as a duty, we shall not go *as a society* with the machinery of party political arrangements, but leave that for the action of individual citizens. Neither shall we denounce those as recreants who may differ from us in regard to the *best mode* of such action. It will also be our endeavor to promote the "equal security, protection and improvement of the people of color," a duty that has been greatly neglected—to which we have not sufficiently attended—and which should be a leading object with every Anti-Slavery Association.

On the evening of May 13th, a preliminary meeting was held of some of those who were dissatisfied with the recent action of the American Anti-Slavery Society, to consider the subject of forming a new association. * * * And after prayerful consideration, it was unanimously resolved that it is best to separate from the old Society and to organize a new association on the same great fundamental principles, with enlarged objects. * * * On the next day a general meeting was notified, and numerously attended. About three hundred members of the American Anti-Slavery Society enrolled their names, and organized a Convention, which held its sessions during three days. A draft of a constitution was reported by a committee, its provisions fully discussed, and the same was finally adopted with great unanimity. * * * [T]he constitution contemplates enlarged action with reference to the slave trade, and especially co-ordinate action with the British and Foreign Anti-Slavery Society. This was a prominent motive in assuming the designation of the new Society. We wish to embrace within our operations the cause of the enslaved throughout the world, and to co-operate with our brethren in Great Britain, France, &c., in wise and judicious plans for the abolition of the slave trade, and *the system that produces it.*

* * *

Let it not be imagined that the Society has any desire to wage war upon any other association. Far from it. It has been a source of grief to the true friends of the slave—and of exultation to the enemies of human rights—to see a denunciatory spirit towards brethren professionally engaged in the sublime cause of emancipation, and to witness those who formerly endured unjustly so much reproach together—estranged or hostile. But our objects, being simply the peaceful deliverance of the slave, and the restoration of our fellow-citizens of color to *the same* rights and privileges with the rest of the community, do not require the adoption of any such policy. An enforced uniformity of action, a subjugation of the widespread anti-slavery hosts to the decrees of one central power, a necessity to follow the footsteps of any earthly leader, or to spend our breath in glorifying any man of like passions with ourselves, form no part of our plan of operations. So far as our own conduct can influence the future, the two divisions of the anti-slavery body will henceforth plead the cause of the slave, without criminating or recriminating each other; both will labor for the speedy and peaceful triumph of humanity and freedom; and God, and not man, will receive all the glory of the universal triumph of liberty. Should this, happily, be the case, all concerned may hereafter look back upon the circumstances that brought about a separation, with devout gratitude, as an occurrence that accelerated the progress of the cause. Let the eyes of all be directed to those great systems of iniquity for the extinction of which we have associated together, beseeching the God of all grace to smile upon our efforts, and crown them with His blessing.

The Liberator, June 19, 1840.

STUDY QUESTIONS

1. The opponents of Garrison noted that the selection of a woman to the American Anti-Slavery Society's business committee touched off a walkout at the Society's convention, but they insisted that it was not "the chief cause of the difficulty" between the Society's factions. What instead was the root of the rift?

2. In what ways did the founders of the American and Foreign Anti-Slavery Society say their organization would act differently from the American Anti-Slavery Society?

The Garrisonian Embrace of Pacifism and Nonresistance

As the founders of the American and Foreign Anti-Slavery Society noted, radical abolitionists increasingly distanced themselves from any kind of engagement with what they viewed as a corrupt government, a position that led many of them toward associations with the antebellum peace movement. Given the widespread dedication of reformers to human progress and the creation of a holy society, it is unsurprising that a movement emerged to eliminate the destructiveness and perceived sinfulness of war. The first national pacifist organization was the American Peace Society (APS). Founded in 1828, the APS brought together individuals with a range of perspectives on whether violence could ever be justified, and its leaders advocated creating institutions like an international court and a Congress of Nations to resolve disputes between countries before hostilities erupted. Ultimately, however, like the abolitionists, the antebellum peace movement fragmented. Many with particularly radical understandings of coercion as a sin, including William Lloyd Garrison, were drawn to the anarchistic philosophy of nonresistance. Rejecting the legitimacy of all human governments and all forms of violence, even in self-defense, nonresistants insisted instead that total withdrawal from civil society was the only path to a truly Christian life. In September 1838, Garrison led a convention in Boston that established the New England Non-Resistance Society as an alternative to moderate groups like the APS.

Declaration of Sentiments, Adopted by the Peace Convention (1838)

ASSEMBLED in Convention, from various sections of the American Union, for the promotion of peace on earth and good will among men, we, the undersigned, regard it as due to ourselves, to the cause which we love, to the country in which we live, and to the world, to publish a DECLARATION, expressive of the principles we cherish, the purposes we aim to accomplish, and the measures we shall adopt to carry forward the work of peaceful, universal reformation.

We cannot acknowledge allegiance to any human government; neither can we oppose any such government by a resort to physical force. We recognize but one KING and LAWGIVER, one JUDGE and RULER of mankind. We are bound by the laws of a kingdom which is not of this world; the subjects of which are forbidden to fight; in which MERCY and TRUTH are met together, and RIGHTEOUSNESS and PEACE have kissed each other; which has no state lines, no national partitions, no geographical boundaries; in which there is no distinction of rank, or division of caste, or inequality of sex; the officers of which are PEACE, its exactors RIGHTEOUSNESS, its walls SALVATION, and its gates PRAISE; and which is destined to break in pieces and consume all other kingdoms.

Our country is the world, our countrymen are all mankind. We love the land of our nativity only as we love all other lands. The interests, rights, liberties of American citizens are no more dear to us than are those of the whole human race. Hence, we can allow no appeal to patriotism, to revenge any national insult or injury. The PRINCE OF PEACE, under whose stainless banner we rally, came not to destroy, but to save, even the worst of enemies. He has left us an example, that we should follow his steps.

* * *

We register our testimony, not only against all wars, whether offensive or defensive, but all preparations for war; against every naval ship, every arsenal, every fortification; against the militia system and a standing army; against all military chieftains and soldiers; against all monuments commemorative of victory over a foreign foe, all trophies won in battle, all celebrations in honor of military or naval exploits; against all appropriations for the defense of a nation by force and arms, on the part of any legislative body; against every edict of government requiring of its subjects military service. Hence, we deem it unlawful to bear arms, or to hold a military office.

As every human government is upheld by physical strength, and its laws are enforced virtually at the point of the bayonet, we cannot hold any office which imposes upon its incumbent the obligation to compel men to do right, on pain of imprisonment or death. We therefore voluntarily exclude ourselves from every legislative and judicial body, and repudiate all human politics, worldly honors, and stations of authority. If *we* cannot occupy a seat in the legislature or on the bench, neither can we elect *others* to act as our substitutes in any such capacity.

It follows, that we cannot sue any man at law, to compel him by force to restore any thing which he may have wrongfully taken from us or others; but, if he has seized our coat, we shall surrender up our cloak, rather than subject him to punishment.

We believe that the penal code of the old covenant, AN EYE FOR AN EYE, AND A TOOTH FOR A TOOTH, has been abrogated by JESUS CHRIST; and that, under the new covenant, the forgiveness, instead of the punishment of enemies, has been enjoined upon all his disciples, in all cases whatsoever. To extort money from enemies, or set them upon a pillory, or cast them into prison, or hang them upon a gallows, is obviously not to forgive, but to take retribution. * * *

The history of mankind is crowded with evidences, proving that physical coercion is not adapted to moral regeneration; that the sinful dispositions of men can be subdued only by love; that evil can be exterminated from the earth only by goodness; that it is not safe to rely upon an arm of flesh, upon man whose breath is in his nostrils, to preserve us from harm; that there is great security in being gentle, harmless, long-suffering, and abundant in mercy; that it is only the meek who shall inherit the earth, for the violent who resort to the sword are destined to perish with the sword. Hence, as a measure of sound policy,—of safety to property, life, and liberty,—of public quietude and private enjoyment,—as well as on the ground of allegiance to HIM who is KING OF KINGS, and LORD OF

LORDS,—we cordially adopt the non-resistance principle; being confident that it provides for all possible consequences, will ensure all things needful to us, is armed with omnipotent power, and must ultimately triumph over every assailing force.

* * *

Having thus briefly, but frankly, stated our principles and purposes, we proceed to specify the measures we propose to adopt, in carrying our object into effect.

We expect to prevail, through THE FOOLISHNESS OF PREACHING—striving to commend ourselves unto every man's conscience, in the sight of GOD. From the press, we shall promulgate our sentiments as widely as practicable. We shall endeavor to secure the co-operation of all persons, of whatever name or sect. The triumphant progress of the cause of TEMPERANCE and of ABOLITION in our land, through the instrumentality of benevolent and voluntary associations, encourages us to combine our own means and efforts for the promotion of a still greater cause. Hence, we shall employ lecturers, circulate tracts and publications, form societies, and petition our state and national governments, in relation to the subject of UNIVERSAL PEACE. It will be our leading object to devise ways and means for effecting a radical change in the views, feelings and practices of society, respecting the sinfulness of war, and the treatment of enemies.

In entering upon the great work before us, we are not unmindful that, in its prosecution we may be called to test our sincerity, even as in a fiery ordeal. It may subject us to insult, outrage, suffering, yea, even death itself. We anticipate no small amount of misconception, misrepresentation, calumny. Tumults may arise against us. The ungodly and violent, the proud and pharisaical, the ambitious and tyrannical, principalities and powers, and spiritual wickedness in high places, may combine to crush us. So they treated the MESSIAH, whose example we are humbly striving to imitate. If we suffer with him, we know that we shall reign with him. We shall not be afraid of their terror, neither be troubled. Our confidence is in the LORD ALMIGHTY, not in man. Having withdrawn from human protection, what can sustain us but that faith which overcomes the world? We shall not think it strange concerning the fiery trial which is to try us, as though some strange thing had happened unto us; but rejoice, inasmuch as we are partakers of CHRIST'S sufferings. Wherefore, we commit the keeping of our souls to GOD, in well-doing, as unto a faithful Creator. FOR EVERY ONE THAT FORSAKES HOUSES, OR BRETHREN, OR SISTERS, OR FATHER, OR MOTHER, OR WIFE, OR CHILDREN, OR LANDS, FOR CHRIST'S SAKE, SHALL RECEIVE A HUNDRED FOLD, AND SHALL INHERIT EVERLASTING LIFE.

The Liberator, September 28, 1838.

STUDY QUESTIONS

1. Why did nonresistants believe that all forms of coercion were sinful? How did that belief translate into their feelings about human governments?
2. Why did nonresistants reject the legitimacy of nation-states themselves?

The Emergence of Political Abolitionism

While disillusionment with the United States and insistence upon absolute moral purity led many radical abolitionists to distance themselves from American institutions, moderate members of the antislavery movement increased their participation in public life in the 1840s and tried to force change through more conventional democratic mechanisms. When it came to electoral politics, for example, moderates recognized that working directly with the major political parties brought limited gains, but they believed that running candidates under the banner of a separate antislavery party could yield significant influence and exposure for the cause. Although the Liberty Party, formed in 1840, never gained a large number of votes nationally, enough people in several states voted for the party in 1844 that Whig candidate Henry Clay lost the presidential election. More significantly, the Liberty Party broke ground for partisan political antislavery upon which the Free Soil and Republican parties would build in the future.

Liberty Party Platform (1844)

1. *Resolved*, That human brotherhood is a cardinal principle of true democracy, as well as pure Christianity, which spurns all inconsistent limitations; and neither the political party which repudiates it, nor the political system which is not based on it, can be truly democratic or permanent.

2. *Resolved*, That the Liberty party, placing itself upon this broad principle, will demand the absolute and unqualified divorce of the General Government from slavery, and also the restoration of equality of rights among men, in every State where the party exists, or may exist.

3. *Resolved*, That the Liberty party has not been organized for any temporary purpose by interested politicians, but has arisen from among the people in consequence of a conviction, hourly gaining ground, that no other party in the country represents the true spirit of the Constitution of the United States.

4. *Resolved*, That the Liberty party has not been organized merely for the overthrow of slavery; its first decided effort must, indeed, be directed against slave-holding as the grossest and most revolting manifestation of despotism, but it will also carry out the principle of equal rights into all its practical consequences and applications, and support every just measure conducive to individual and social freedom.

5. *Resolved*, That the Liberty party is not a sectional party, but a national party; was not originated in a desire to accomplish a single object, but in a comprehensive regard to the great interests of the whole country; is not a new party, nor a third party, but is the party of 1776, reviving the principles of that memorable era, and striving to carry them into practical application.

6. *Resolved*, That it was understood in the times of the Declaration and the Constitution, that the existence of slavery in some of the States was in derogation of the principles of American liberty, and

a deep stain upon the character of the country, and the implied faith of the States and the Nation was pledged that slavery should never be extended beyond its then existing limits, but should be gradually, and yet, at no distant day, wholly abolished by State authority.

* * *

8. *Resolved,* That the faith of the States and the Nation thus pledged, has been shamefully violated by the omission, on the part of many of the States, to take any measures whatever for the abolition of slavery within their respective limits; by the continuance of slavery in the District of Columbia, and in the Territories of Louisiana and Florida; by the legislation of Congress; by the protection afforded by national legislation and negotiation to slaveholding in American vessels, on the high seas, employed in the coastwise slave traffic; and by the extension of slavery far beyond its original limits, by acts of Congress admitting new slave States into the Union.

* * *

12. *Resolved,* That the provision of the Constitution of the United States which confers extraordinary political powers on the owners of slaves, and thereby constituting the two hundred and fifty thousand slaveholders in the slave States a privileged aristocracy; and the provisions for the reclamation of fugitive slaves from service, are anti-republican in their character, dangerous to the liberties of the people and ought to be abrogated.

* * *

14. *Resolved,* That the peculiar patronage and support hitherto extended to slavery and slaveholding by the General Government ought to be immediately withdrawn, and the example and influence of national authority ought to be arrayed on the side of liberty and free labor.

* * *

17. *Resolved,* That we regard voting in an eminent degree as a moral and religious duty, which, when exercised, should be by voting for those who will do all in their power for immediate emancipation.

18. *Resolved,* That this convention recommend to the friends of liberty in all those free States where any inequality of rights and

privileges exists on account of color, to employ their utmost energies to remove all such remnants and effects of the slave system.

National Party Platforms of the United States, compiled by J. M. H. Frederick (Akron, Ohio, 1896), 14–15.

STUDY QUESTIONS

1. What special and unjust considerations did supporters of the Liberty Party believe the national government gave to slavehold-ers that ought to be withdrawn?
2. Do you think the radical abolitionists were right that politics inherently corrupted the antislavery cause, or do you think that direct involvement with politics was an effective way to make real change when it came to slavery?

Women's Rights/Feminism

A Demand for Intellectual Equality

American women in the early nineteenth century had little formal economic, political, or legal power. Married women were especially restricted, as their legal identities were subsumed within those of their husbands and they were generally unable to own property or procure a divorce even from abusive men. But widespread discussions in the early republic about equality, the value of reason, and individual rights lent themselves to some broader questioning of sexual inequalities and hierarchies. Moreover, even though the emerging gender conventions of the era posited that women were domestic beings, they also presumed that women were especially moral beings. That assumption, in turn, led women to take on greater public roles in a variety of reform activities and to see their potential for acting in bolder ways than American women ever had. Frances "Fanny" Wright, however, was bolder than most. Indeed, she may have been the most notorious woman in antebellum America. Born in Scotland, in the 1820s Wright moved to the United States, became a citizen, and relentlessly called upon her adopted country to fulfill its egalitarian creed. Attacking all forms of discrimination and hierarchy, and railing against organized religion as a superstition impeding intellectual freedom, Wright supported abolitionism and utopian socialism and called for universal free secular education. More scandalously, she advocated the use of birth control, an end to traditional marriage, free love, and liberalized divorce laws. Wright was the first female newspaper editor in the United States and the first American woman to deliver a lecture series to a mixed-gender audience, and she saw her positions as being in keeping with women's equality. But she understood how shocking those positions were to most

Americans, for whom distinct (and by modern standards, profoundly unequal)
roles for men and women provided social order in keeping with God's will. Here,
in a selection from her 1828 lectures, Wright declaims against the forced igno-
rance of American women, arguing that failing to educate women denied them
not only equality but also their basic humanity.

Frances Wright,
Course of Popular Lectures (1836)

It is with delight that I have distinguished, at each successive meeting, the increasing ranks of my own sex. Were the vital principle of
human equality universally acknowledged, it would be to my fellow
beings without regard to nation, class, sect, or sex, that I should
delight to address myself. But until equality prevail in condition,
opportunity, and instruction, it is every where to the least favored in
these advantages, that I most especially and anxiously incline.

Nor is the ignorance of our sex a matter of surprise, when efforts, as violent as unrelaxed, are every where made for its
continuance.

It is not as of yore. Eve puts not forth her hand to gather the fair
fruit of knowledge. The wily serpent now hath better learned his
lesson; and, to secure his reign in the garden, beguileth her *not* to
eat. Promises, entreaties, threats, tales of wonder, and, alas! tales of
horror, are all poured in her tender ears. Above, her agitated fancy
hears the voice of a god in thunders; below, she sees the yawning
pit; and, before, behind, around, a thousand phantoms, conjured
from the prolific brain of insatiate priestcraft, confound, alarm, and
overwhelm her reason!

Oh! were that worst evil withdrawn which now weighs upon our
race, how rapid were its progress in knowledge! Oh! were men—
and, yet more, women, absolved from fear, how easily and speedily
and gloriously would they hold on their course in improvement!
The difficulty is not to convince, it is to *win attention*. Could truth
only be heard, the conversion of the ignorant were easy. And well
do the hired supporters of error understand this fact. Well do they
know, that if the daughters of the present, and mothers of the fu-

ture generation, were to drink of the living waters of knowledge, their reign would be ended—"their occupation gone." So well do they know it, that, far from obeying to the letter the command of their spiritual leader, "Be ye fishers of men," we find them every where *fishers of women*. Their own sex, old and young, they see with indifference swim by their nets; but closely and warily are their meshes laid, to entangle the female of every age.

Fathers and husbands! do ye not also understand this fact? Do ye not see how, in the mental bondage of your wives and fair companions, ye yourselves are bound? Will ye fondly sport yourselves in your imagined liberty, and say, "it matters not if our women be mental slaves?" Will ye pleasure yourselves in the varied paths of knowledge, and imagine that women, hoodwinked and unawakened, will make the better servants and the easier playthings?

* * *

However novel it may appear, I shall venture the assertion, that, until women assume the place in society which good sense and good feeling alike assign to them, human improvement must advance but feebly. It is in vain that we would circumscribe the power of one half of our race, and that half by far the most important and influential. If they exert it not for good, they will for evil; if they advance not knowledge, they will perpetuate ignorance. Let women stand where they may in the scale of improvement, their position decides that of the race. Are they cultivated?—so is society polished and enlightened. Are they ignorant?—so is it gross and insipid. Are they wise?—so is the human condition prosperous. Are they foolish?—so is it unstable and unpromising. Are they free?—so is the human character elevated. Are they enslaved?—so is the whole race degraded. Oh! that we could learn the advantage of just practice and consistent principles! that we could understand, that every departure from principle, how speciously soever it may appear to administer to our selfish interests, invariably saps their very foundation! that we could learn that what is ruinous to some is injurious to all; and that whenever we establish our own pretensions upon the sacrificed rights of others, we do in fact impeach our own liberties, and lower ourselves in the scale of being!

* * *

We see men who will aid the instruction of their sons, and condemn only their daughters to ignorance. "Our sons," they say, "will have to exercise political rights, may aspire to public offices, may fill some learned profession, may struggle for wealth and acquire it. It is well that we give them a helping hand; that we assist them to such knowledge as is going, and make them as sharp witted as their neighbors. "But for our daughters," they say—if indeed respecting them they say any thing—"for our daughters, little trouble or expense is necessary. They can never *be any thing*; in fact, they *are nothing*. We had best give them up to their mothers, who may take them to Sunday's preaching; and, with the aid of a little music, a little dancing, and a few fine gowns, fit them out for the market of marriage."

Am I severe? It is not my intention. I know that I am honest, and I fear that I am correct. Should I offend, however I may regret, I shall not repent it; satisfied to incur displeasure, so that I render service.

But to such parents I would observe, that with regard to their sons, as to their daughters, they are about equally mistaken. If it be their duty, as we have seen, to respect in their children the same natural liberties which they cherish for themselves—if it be their duty to aid as guides, not to dictate as teachers—to lend assistance to the reason, not to command its prostration,—then have they nothing to do with the blanks or the prizes in store for them, in the wheel of worldly fortune. Let possibilities be what they may in favor of their sons, they have no calculations to make on them. It is not for them to ordain their sons magistrates nor statesmen: nor yet even lawyers, physicians, or merchants. They have only to improve the one character which they receive at the birth. They have only to consider them as *human beings*, and to ensure them the fair and thorough developement of all the faculties, physical, mental, and moral, which distinguish their nature. In like manner, as respects their daughters, they have nothing to do with the injustice of laws, nor the absurdities of society. Their duty is plain, evidence, decided. In a daughter they have in charge a human being; in a son, the same. Let them train up these *human beings*, under the expanded wings of liberty. Let them seek *for* them and *with* them just knowledge; encouraging, from the cradle upwards, that useful curiosity which will lead them unbidden in the paths of free enquiry; and place them, safe and superior to the storms of life, in the security of well regulated, self-possessed minds, well grounded, well reasoned, conscientious opinions, and self-approved, consistent practice.

Course of Popular Lectures (New York, 1836), 38–39, 44–45, 52–53.

STUDY QUESTIONS

1. Why, according to Wright, did men systematically deny women access to knowledge, and what were the consequences of that denial for American society?
2. What did Wright see as the duty of parents toward their children?

A Comparative Context for Women's Equality

Women did not need to take public positions nearly as extreme as those of Fanny Wright to express their sense that antebellum gender inequalities were unjust. In 1835, for example, novelist Lydia Maria Child published a two-volume work entitled The History of the Condition of Women, in Various Ages and Nations. *Child neither called overtly for female equality nor made much of an explicit argument at all. Merely by describing women's positions in various societies over the course of thousands of years, however, she demonstrated the astonishing capacities of women to perform hard labor, exercise power, and undertake nearly any task performed by men even as they were denied many rights and privileges men assumed exclusively as their own. In so doing, Child implicitly questioned widely held notions in the United States about the "natural" domesticity, frailty, and passivity of women. As her discussion of Native American societies suggests, Child's ethnographic observations came loaded with her own racial, cultural, and other biases, but* The History of the Condition of Women *was nonetheless a pioneering achievement that challenged the accepted circumstances of American women by revealing how unusual and artificially imposed those circumstances were.*

Lydia Maria Child, *The History of the Condition of Women, in Various Ages and Nations* (1835)

Before America was settled by Europeans, it was inhabited by Indian tribes, which greatly resembled each other in the treatment of their women. Every thing except war and hunting was considered beneath the dignity of man. During long and wearisome marches, women were obliged to carry children, provisions, and hammocks on their shoulders; they had the sole care of the horses and dogs, cut wood, pitched the tents, raised the corn, and made the clothing. When the husband killed game, he left it by a tree in the forest, returned home, and sent his wife several miles in search of it. In most of the tribes, women were not allowed to eat and drink with men, but stood and served them, and then ate what they left.

When the Spaniards arrived in South America, the Indian women, delighted with attentions to which they had been entirely unaccustomed, often betrayed the conspiracies formed against them, supplied them with food, and acted as guides.

Father Joseph reproved a female savage on the banks of the Orinoco, because she destroyed her infant daughter. She replied, "I wish my mother had thus prevented the manifold sufferings I have endured. Consider, Father, our deplorable situation. Our husbands go out to hunt; we are dragged along with one infant at our breast, and another in a basket. Though tired with long walking, we are not allowed to sleep when we return, but must labor the whole night in grinding maize to make chica for them. They get drunk, and beat us, draw us by the hair of the head, and tread us under foot. And after a slavery of perhaps twenty years, what have we to comfort us? A young wife is then brought home, and permitted to abuse us and our children. What kindness can we show our daughters equal to putting them to death? Would to God my mother had put me under ground the moment I was born."

* * *

The Indian bridegroom generally pays his father-in-law for his bride; and even in their primitive form of society, he who can offer a large price is most likely to be acceptable to parents. Handsome

Indian girls are not unfrequently disposed of contrary to their inclinations. They are not permitted to marry relations within so near a degree of consanguinity as cousins. Suicide is common among the women of these savage tribes. When thwarted in love, or driven to desperation by ill usage, they frequently hang themselves to the branch of a tree, rush into the sea, or throw themselves from a precipice. The men very rarely destroy their own lives. They seldom have more than one wife at a time; but they change just when they please, interchange with each other, and lend to visiters, without scandal. When a wife becomes old, a younger one is often purchased; and the first one may either kill herself, or tamely submit to be the drudge of the family.

* * *

When it was proposed (either facetiously or otherwise) that women should be members of parliament, an Englishman objected to it, on the ground that a lady, who sat with committees of gentlemen, might sometimes meet with a species of impoliteness that would be embarrassing. If *this* be a reason why women should not transact public business, it is a fact exceedingly disgraceful to civilized men. Female captives taken by Indians, though treated with the most diabolical cruelty, according to their savage mode of warfare, have travelled with powerful warriors days and weeks, through the loneliest paths of the forest, and never been subjected to the slightest personal insult.

* * *

Both boys and girls are early taught to endure without a murmur the utmost rigors of climate, excess of labor, and the extremity of pain. It is common to try their fortitude by ordering them to hold their hands in the fire, till permission is given to withdraw them; and if even their countenances give indication of agony, it is deemed dishonorable. When taken captive in war they have need of their utmost powers of endurance; for their enemies exercise all their ingenuity in torture. Yet such is the force of education, that women, as well as men, will smile and utter jeering words, while their nails are pulled out by the roots, their feet crushed between stones, and their flesh torn with red-hot pincers.

It is an almost universal rule that women are more tender-hearted than men; but the North American Indians seem to furnish an exception. When a prisoner is tied to the stake, women are even more furious and active than men, in the work of cruelty.

* * *

The Indian women sometimes accompany the men on hunting excursions, for the purpose of bringing home the game; and in time of battle they often encourage and assist the warriors. In addition to the toilsome occupations already alluded to, they made garments of skins, sewed with sinews and thorns, wove neat mats and baskets, and embroidered very prettily with shells, feathers, and grass of various colors.

* * *

Indian women are usually well skilled in simple remedies, and are the physicians of their tribes. In some places, medicine is considered peculiarly efficacious if it is prepared and administered by the hand of a maiden. The healing art is intimately connected in their minds with magic, and medicines are seldom given without prayers and incantations, to avert the influence of evil spirits.

* * *

The women of the Hurons and Iroquois seem to have had more influence than was common among other tribes. Huron women might appoint a member of the council, and one of their own sex if they chose. They could prevail upon the warriors to go to battle, or to desist from it, according to their wishes. Among the Natchez, authority descended in an hereditary line both to male and female. It is a general rule with the American tribes that a man should be succeeded by his sister's children, not by his own.

The History of the Condition of Women, in Various Ages and Nations (London, 1835), vol. 2, 225–226, 230–232, 235, 237, 239, 241.

STUDY QUESTIONS

1. According to Child, what sorts of indignities and mistreatment did women face in Native American societies? What sorts of power and influence did they have?
2. How do you imagine that reading about women and their roles in other societies would lead Americans to reflect on the positions of women in their own?

The Abolitionist "Woman Question" Spurs Rebuke of Female Subordination

It was fitting that Lydia Maria Child frequently compared women's circumstances to those of slaves in her History of the Condition of Women. *Like many antebellum advocates of female equality, Child was an active abolitionist before taking a strong public position on women's rights and saw numerous parallels between the subjugation of blacks and women. Indeed, it made sense that calls for women's rights in the United States only became an organized movement in the context of abolitionism. The radical nature of the antislavery movement tended to attract activists more questioning of the broader social order than most reform movements did, and although abolitionist women understood they were not literally slaves, extending calls for black freedom and equality to women required only a short and obvious leap. A significant moment for the emergence of feminism from abolitionism came in 1837 when Congregationalist ministers in Massachusetts circulated a letter deploring public speaking by women as "unnatural." Written specifically in reaction to a northeastern lecture tour by abolitionists Angelina and Sarah Grimké, the letter both aggravated tensions among antislavery activists over the role of women in the movement and provoked written responses by the Grimké sisters that became classics of American feminist literature. In* Letters on the Equality of the Sexes, and the Condition of Woman, *first published in 1838, Sarah Grimké presented secular and religious arguments for women's equality, rejecting the ministers' positions against female public speaking as well as many of the cultural assumptions and legal and socioeconomic realities sustaining what she saw as the generally degraded status of American women.*

Sarah Grimké, *Letters on the Equality of the Sexes, and the Condition of Woman* (1838)

During the early part of my life, my lot was cast among the butterflies of the *fashionable* world; and of this class of women, I am constrained to say, both from experience and observation, that their education is miserably deficient; that they are taught to regard marriage as the one thing needful, the only avenue to distinction; hence to attract the notice and win the attentions of men, by their external charms, is the chief business of fashionable girls. They seldom think that men will be allured by intellectual acquirements, because they find, that where any mental superiority exists, a woman is generally shunned and regarded as stepping out of her "appropriate sphere," which, in their view, is to dress, to dance, to set out to the best possible advantage her person, to read the novels which inundate the press, and which do more to destroy her character as a rational creature, than any thing else. Fashionable women regard themselves, and are regarded by men, as pretty toys or as mere instruments of pleasure; and the vacuity of mind, the heartlessness, the frivolity which is the necessary result of this false and debasing estimate of women, can only be fully understood by those who have mingled in the folly and wickedness of fashionable life; and who have been called from such pursuits by the voice of the Lord Jesus, inviting their weary and heavy laden souls to come unto Him and learn of Him, that they may find something worthy of their immortal spirit, and their intellectual powers; that they may learn the high and holy purposes of their creation, and consecrate themselves unto the service of God; and not, as is now the case, to the pleasure of man.

There is another and much more numerous class in this country, who are withdrawn by education or circumstances from the circle of fashionable amusements, but who are brought up with the dangerous and absurd idea, that *marriage* is a kind of preferment; and that to be able to keep their husband's house, and render his situation comfortable, is the end of her being. Much that she does and says and thinks is done in reference to this situation; and to be married is too often held up to the view of girls as the sine qua non of human happiness and human existence. For this purpose more than for any other, I verily believe the majority of girls are trained. This is demonstrated by the imperfect education which is bestowed upon them, and the little pains taken to cultivate their minds, after they leave school, by the little time allowed them for reading, and by the idea being constantly inculcated, that although all household concerns should be attended to with scrupulous punctuality at particular seasons, the improvement of their intellectual capacities is only a secondary consideration, and may serve as an occupation to fill up the odds and ends of time. In most families, it is considered a matter of far more consequence to call a girl off from making a pie, or a pudding, than to interrupt her whilst engaged in her studies. This mode of training necessarily exalts, in their view, the animal above the intellectual and spiritual nature, and teaches women to regard themselves as a kind of machinery, necessary to keep the domestic engine in order, but of little value as the *intelligent* companions of men.

Let no one think, from these remarks, that I regard a knowledge of housewifery as beneath the acquisition of women. Far from it: I believe that a complete knowledge of household affairs is an indispensable requisite in a woman's education. * * * All I complain of is, that our education consists so almost exclusively in culinary and other manual operations. I do long to see the time, when it will no longer be necessary for women to expend so many precious hours in furnishing "a well spread table," but that their husbands will forego some of their accustomed indulgences in this way, and encourage their wives to devote some portion of their time to mental cultivation, even at the expense of having to dine sometimes on baked potatoes, or bread and butter.

* * *

There is another way in which the general opinion, that women are inferior to men, is manifested, that bears with tremendous effect on the laboring class, and indeed on almost all who are obliged to earn a subsistence, whether it be by mental or physical exertion—I allude to the disproportionate value set on the time and labor of men and of women. A man who is engaged in teaching, can always, I believe, command a higher price for tuition than a woman—even when he teaches the same branches, and is not in any respect superior to the woman. This I know is the case in boarding and other schools with which I have been acquainted, and it is so in every occupation in which the sexes engage indiscriminately. * * * In those employments which are peculiar to women, their time is estimated at only half the value of that of men. A woman who goes out to wash, works as hard in proportion as a wood sawyer, or a coal heaver, but she is not generally able to make more than half as much by a day's work. The low remuneration which women receive for their work, has claimed the attention of a few philanthropists, and I hope it will continue to do so until some remedy is applied for this enormous evil.

* * *

There is another class of women in this country, to whom I cannot refer, without feelings of the deepest shame and sorrow. I allude to our female slaves. Our southern cities are whelmed beneath a tide of pollution; the virtue of female slaves is wholly at the mercy of irresponsible tyrants, and women are bought and sold in our slave markets, to gratify the brutal lust of those who bear the name of Christians.

* * *

Nor does the colored woman suffer alone: the moral purity of the white woman is deeply contaminated. In the daily habit of seeing the virtue of her enslaved sister sacrificed without hesitancy or remorse, she looks upon the crimes of seduction and illicit intercourse without horror, and although not personally involved in the guilt, she loses that value for innocence in her own, as well as the other sex, which is one of the strongest safeguards to virtue. She lives in habitual intercourse with men, who she knows to be polluted by licentiousness, and often is she compelled to witness in her own domestic circle, those disgusting and heart-sickening jealousies and strifes which disgraced and distracted the family of Abraham. In addition to all this, the female slaves suffer every species of degradation and cruelty, which the most wanton barbarity can inflict; they are indecently divested of their clothing, sometimes tied up and severely whipped, sometimes prostrated on the earth, while their naked bodies are torn by the scorpion lash. * * * Can any American women look at these scenes of shocking licentiousness and cruelty, and fold her hands in apathy, and say, "I have nothing to do with slavery"? *She cannot and be guiltless.*

I cannot close this letter, without saying a few words on the benefits to be derived by men, as well as women, from the opinions I advocate, relative to the equality of the sexes. Many women are now supported, in idleness and extravagance, by the industry of their husbands, fathers, or brothers, who are compelled to toil out their existence, at the counting house, or in the printing office, or some other laborious occupation, while the wife and daughters and sisters take no part in the support of the family, and appear to think that their sole business is to spend the hard bought earnings of their male friends. I deeply regret such a state of things, because I believe that if women felt their responsibility, for the support of themselves, or their families it would add strength and dignity to their characters, and teach them more true sympathy for their husbands, than is now generally manifested,—a sympathy which would be exhibited by actions as well as words. Our brethren may reject my doctrine, because it runs counter to common opinions, and because it wounds their pride; but I believe they would be "partakers of the benefit" resulting from the Equality of the Sexes, and would find that woman, as their equal, was unspeakably more valuable than woman as their inferior, both as a moral and an intellectual being.

Letters on the Equality of the Sexes and the Condition of Woman (Boston, 1838), 46–49, 50–52, 53–55.

STUDY QUESTIONS

1. According to Grimké, how were most American women raised to view and understand marriage, and why did she feel such an upbringing did women a disservice?
2. How did Grimké make the case that slavery was bad for black and white women alike?

Planting the Seeds of a Movement

The burgeoning feminism of the preceding decades finally began coalescing into a movement in 1840, as fallout from the split within American abolitionism spilled across the Atlantic Ocean onto the floor of the World's Anti-Slavery Convention in London. Although organizers of that convention had called upon antislavery societies from around the world to send delegates, a controversy erupted about whether female delegates sent by some American groups ought to be recognized and seated. After some acrimonious debate, an overwhelming ma-

jority of conventioneers voted to exclude women from the proceedings. That evening, Lucretia Mott, one of the excluded delegates, and Elizabeth Cady Stanton, who was married to one of the male delegates, walked London's streets discussing what had transpired. They concluded that the time had come for women to agitate for their own emancipation independent of the antislavery struggle and that they would convene a women's rights convention on their return to the United States. Below are selections from speeches delivered on the convention floor by several male delegates on behalf of seating women, and a portion of Elizabeth Cady Stanton's recollection of meeting Lucretia Mott, from an address she delivered at Mott's funeral in 1881.

Voices at the World's Anti-Slavery Convention (1840)

Wendell Phillips, Massachusetts: Massachusetts has for several years acted on the principle of admitting women to an equal seat with men in the deliberative bodies of anti-slavery societies. When the Massachusetts Anti-Slavery Society received that paper [calling for the sending of delegates to London], it interpreted it, as it was its duty, in the broadest and most liberal sense. If there be any other paper emanating from the Committee limiting to one sex the qualification of membership, there is no proof, and as an individual I have no knowledge, that such a paper ever reached Massachusetts. We stand here in consequence of your invitation, and knowing our custom, as it must be presumed you did, we had a right to interpret "friends of the slave," to include women as well as men. In such circumstances we do not think it just or equitable to that State, nor to America in general, that after the trouble, the sacrifice, the self-devotion of a part of those who leave their families, and kindred, and occupations in their own land, to come 4000 miles to attend this World's Convention, they should be refused a place in its deliberations.

William Adam, Massachusetts: I will only add, if the ladies who have come from America are not deemed entitled, in consequence of the credentials they bear, to a place in this assembly, I feel for one that

I am not entitled to occupy such a position. My credentials proceed from the same persons, and from the same societies, and bear the same names as theirs. I have no other authority to appear amongst you, to take a place in your proceedings, and give a voice in your deliberations, than that right which is equally possessed by the ladies to whom a place among you has been denied. In the Society from which I have come, female exertion is the very life of us, and of all that we have done, and all we hope to do. To exclude females, would be to affix a stigma upon them.

George Bradburn, Massachusetts: [W]e are now told, that it would be outraging the tastes, habits, customs, and prejudices of the English people, to allow women to sit in this Convention. I have a great respect for the customs of Old England. But I ask, gentlemen, if it be right to set up the customs and habits, not to say prejudices, of Englishmen, as a standard, for the government, on this occasion, of Americans and of persons belonging to several other independent nations? It seems to me that it were, to say the least, very unadvisable to do so. I can see neither reason nor policy in so doing. Besides, I deprecate the principle of this objection. In America it would exclude from our Conventions all persons of colour; for there, customs, habits, tastes, prejudices, would be outraged by *their* admission. And I do not wish to be deprived of the aid of those who have done so much for our cause, for the purpose of gratifying any mere custom or prejudice. I know that women have furnished most essential aid in accomplishing what has been accomplished in the state of Massachusetts. If, in the legislature of that state, I have been able to do any thing in furtherance of this cause, by keeping on my legs eight or ten hours, day after day, it was mainly owing to the valuable assistance I derived from the *women* of Massachusetts. * * * In America, women have taken, and they continue to take, part in meetings of this sort. On the American Anti-Slavery platform, they stand as equals of the men, in respect, at least, of rights and privileges. The American Anti-Slavery Society has decided, that, as members of that body, they ought so to stand. It has been so decided in most of the local societies in Massachusetts, where the standard of abolitionism was first planted. And, with all deference to the abolitionists present, I say, that the best, the bravest, and those who have sacrificed most for this cause, are, with very few exceptions, decidedly on this side of the question. * * * Some one has said, that if women are admitted, they will take sides on this question. Well, what then? Have they not just as good right to take sides as we have?

George Thompson, England: It appears that we are prepared to sanction ladies in the employment of all means, so long as they are confessedly unequal with ourselves. It seems that the grand objection to their appearance amongst us is this, that it would be placing them on a footing of equality, and that, that, would be contrary to principle and custom. * * * Again, I ask, why are they excluded? Is it on the score of intellect? No gentleman, I am sure, will call their intellectual qualification in question. Is it on the score of principle? No gentleman will call that in question. Is it on the score of discretion? Putting this their present act in dispute out of the question, (in my opinion the noblest of their lives), they stand acknowledged by their countrymen and countrywomen to be irreproachable in the midst of a crooked and a perverse generation. Are they ineligible on the ground of their inferior zeal? Oh, that we all opposed slavery half as earnestly; then instead of being the opposers of their entrance into this Convention, we should feel ourselves honoured in admitting them.

William H. Ashurst, England: Are not these women as competent as yourselves to judge of the principles of Christianity, and to bring forth the best affections of our nature? If these are their qualifications, should you upon principle exclude them. It seems impossible for you or for any Christian men to draw that conclusion. * * * You are convened to influence society upon a subject connected with the kindliest feelings of our nature; and being the first assembly met to shake hands with other nations, and employ your combined efforts to annihilate slavery throughout the world, are you to commence by saying, "we will take away the rights of one-half of creation?" That is the principle which you are putting forward.

Proceedings of the General Anti-Slavery Convention (London, 1841), 24, 29–30, 33–34, 37.

Elizabeth Cady Stanton Recalls Meeting Lucretia Mott (1881)

In June, 1840, I met Mrs. Mott for the first time, in London. Crossing the Atlantic in company with James G. Birney, then the Liberty Party candidate for President, soon after the bitter schism in the anti-slavery ranks, he described to me as we walked the deck day after day, the women who had fanned the flames of dissension, and had completely demoralized the anti-slavery ranks. As my first view of Mrs. Mott was through his prejudices, no prepossessions in her favor biased my judgment. When first introduced to her at our hotel in Great Queen Street, with the other ladies from Boston and Philadelphia who were delegates to the World's Convention, I felt somewhat embarrassed, as I was the only lady present who represented the "Birney faction," though I really knew nothing of the merits of the division, having been outside the world of reforms. Still, as my husband and my cousin, Gerrit Smith, were on that side, I supposed they would all have a feeling of hostility toward me. However, Mrs. Mott, in her sweet, gentle way, received me with great cordiality and courtesy, and I was seated by her side at dinner.

No sooner were the viands fairly dispensed, than several Baptist ministers began to rally the ladies on having set the Abolitionists all by the ears in America, and now proposing to do the same thing in England. I soon found that the pending battle was on woman's rights, and that unwittingly I was by marriage on the wrong side. As I had thought much on this question in regard to the laws, Church action, and social usages, I found myself in full accord with the other ladies, combating most of the gentlemen at the table; our only champion, George Bradburn, was too deaf to hear a word that was said. In spite of constant gentle nudgings by my husband under the table, and frowns from Mr. Birney opposite, the tantalizing tone of the conversation was too much for me to maintain silence. Calmly and skillfully Mrs. Mott parried all their attacks, now by her quiet humor turning the laugh on them, and then by her earnestness and dignity silencing their ridicule and sneers. I shall never forget the look of recognition she gave me when she saw by my remarks that I fully comprehended the problem of woman's rights and wrongs. How beautiful she looked to me that day.

***

I found in this new friend a woman emancipated from all faith in man-made creeds, from all fear of his denunciations. Nothing was too sacred for her to question, as to its rightfulness in principle and practice. "Truth for authority, not authority for truth," was not only the motto of her life, but it was the fixed mental habit in which she most rigidly held herself. It seemed to me like meeting a being from some larger planet, to find a woman who dared to question to opinions of Popes, Kings, Synods, Parliaments, with the same freedom that she would criticize an editorial in the *London Times*, recognizing no higher authority than the judgment of a pure-minded, educated woman. When I first heard from the lips of Lucretia Mott that I had the same right to think for myself that Luther, Calvin, and John Knox had, and the same right to be guided by my own convictions, and would no doubt live a higher, happier life than if guided by theirs, I felt at once a new-born sense of dignity and freedom; it was like suddenly coming into the rays of the noon-day sun, after wandering with a rushlight in the caves of the earth.

Elizabeth Cady Stanton, Susan B. Anthony, and Matilda Joslyn Gage, eds., *History of Woman Suffrage* (New York, 1881), vol. 1, 419–420, 422.

STUDY QUESTIONS
1. What arguments did supporters of seating female delegates to the World's Anti-Slavery Convention muster on their behalf?
2. What about Lucretia Mott impressed Elizabeth Cady Stanton? Why was spending time with her in England such an important period in Stanton's life?

The Birth of the Women's Rights Movement

It would be eight years before the plan Elizabeth Cady Stanton and Lucretia Mott discussed in London for a women's rights convention came to fruition in the United States. The Seneca Falls Convention, named for the upstate New

York town where Stanton lived and the meeting took place, was organized quickly and somewhat by happenstance. But it became a historical touchstone for women's rights, shifting the argument for female equality firmly onto secular grounds and inspiring dozens of similar conventions across the Northeast and Midwest in the 1850s. Nearly three hundred people, including several dozen men, attended the Seneca Falls Convention. They unanimously adopted a Declaration of Sentiments (modeled directly on the Declaration of Independence) and nearly all the dozen proposed resolutions, which together laid out demands for redressing a wide variety of social, cultural, legal, and economic injustices and inequities. The only resolution that failed to pass unanimously was the demand that women be given the right to vote. Although suffrage would become in many ways the central issue for women's rights advocates until it was gained at the national level in 1920, in the antebellum era calling for women's direct participation in electoral politics was seen as so radical that even some supporters feared the wider public would never take the movement seriously if the convention formally advocated it.

Seneca Falls Declaration of Sentiments (1848)

DECLARATION OF SENTIMENTS

When, in the course of human events, it becomes necessary for one portion of the family of man to assume among the people of the earth a position different from that which they have hitherto occupied, but one to which the laws of nature and of nature's God entitle them, a decent respect to the opinions of mankind requires that they should declare the causes that impel them to such a course.

We hold these truths to be self-evident: that all men and women are created equal; that they are endowed by their Creator with certain inalienable rights; that among these are life, liberty, and the pursuit of happiness; that to secure these rights governments are instituted, deriving their just powers from the consent of the governed. Whenever any form of government becomes destructive of these ends, it is the right of those who suffer from it to refuse allegiance to it, and to insist upon the institution of a new government, laying its foundation on such principles, and organizing its powers in such form, as to them shall seem most likely to effect their safety and happiness. Prudence indeed, will dictate that governments long established should not be changed for light and transient causes; and accordingly all experience hath shown that mankind are more disposed to suffer, while evils are sufferable, than to right themselves by abolishing the forms to which they were accustomed. But when a long train of abuses and usurpations, pursuing invariably the same object evinces a design to reduce them under absolute despotism, it is their duty to throw off such government, and to provide new guards for their future security. Such has been the patient sufferance of the women under this government, and such is now the necessity which constrains them to demand the equal station to which they are entitled.

The history of mankind is a history of repeated injuries and usurpations on the part of man toward woman, having in direct object the establishment of an absolute tyranny over her. To prove this, let facts be submitted to a candid world.

He has never permitted her to exercise her inalienable right to the elective franchise.

He has compelled her to submit to laws, in the formation of which she had no voice.

He has withheld from her rights which are given to the most ignorant and degraded men—both natives and foreigners.

Having deprived her of this first right of a citizen, the elective franchise, thereby leaving her without representation in the halls of legislation, he has oppressed her on all sides.

He has made her, if married, in the eye of the law, civilly dead.

He has taken from her all right in property, even to the wages she earns.

He has made her, morally, an irresponsible being, as she can commit many crimes with impunity, provided they can be done in the presence of her husband. In the covenant of marriage, she is compelled to promise obedience to her husband, he becoming, to all intents and purposes, her master—the law giving him power to deprive her of her liberty, and to administer chastisement.

He has so framed the laws of divorce, as to what shall be the proper causes, and in case of separation, to whom the guardianship of the children shall be given, as to be wholly regardless of the happiness of women—the law, in all cases, going upon a false supposition of the supremacy of man, giving all power into his hands.

After depriving her of all rights as a married woman, if single, and the owner of property, he has taxed her to support a government which recognizes her only when her property can be made profitable to it.

He has monopolized nearly all the profitable employments, and from those she is permitted to follow, she receives but a scanty remuneration. He closes against her all the avenues to wealth and distinction which he considers most honorable to himself. As a teacher of theology, medicine, or law, she is not known.

He has denied her the facilities for obtaining a thorough education, all colleges being closed against her.

He allows her in Church, as well as State, but a subordinate position, claiming Apostolic authority for her exclusion from the ministry, and, with some exceptions, from any public participation in the affairs of the Church.

He has created a false public sentiment by giving to the world a different code of morals for men and women, by which moral delinquencies which exclude women from society, are not only tolerated, but deemed of little account in man.

He has usurped the prerogative of Jehovah himself, claiming it as his right to assign for her a sphere of action, when that belongs to her conscience and to her God.

He has endeavored, in every way that he could, to destroy her confidence in her own powers, to lessen her self-respect, and to make her willing to lead a dependent and abject life.

Now, in view of this entire disfranchisement of one-half the people of this country, their social and religious degradation—in view of the unjust laws above mentioned, and because women do feel themselves aggrieved, oppressed, and fraudulently deprived of their most sacred rights, we insist that they have immediate admission to all the rights and privileges which belong to them as citizens of the United States.

In entering upon the great work before us, we anticipate no small amount of misconception, misrepresentation, and ridicule; but we shall use every instrumentality within our power to effect our object. We shall employ agents, circulate tracts, petition the State and National legislatures, and endeavor to enlist the pulpit and the press in our behalf. We hope this Convention will be followed by a series of Conventions embracing every part of the county.

* * *

WHEREAS, The great precept of nature is conceded to be, that "man shall pursue his own true and substantial happiness." Blackstone in his Commentaries remarks, that this law of Nature being coeval with mankind, and dictated by God himself, is of course superior in obligation to any other. It is binding over all the globe, in all countries and at all times; no human laws are of any validity if contrary to this, and such of them as are valid, derive all their force, and all their validity, and all their authority, mediately and immediately, from this original; therefore,

Resolved, That such laws as conflict, in any way, with the true and substantial happiness of woman, are contrary to the great precept of nature and of no validity, for this is "superior in obligation to any other."

Resolved, That all laws which prevent woman from occupying such a station in society as her conscience shall dictate, or which place her in a position inferior to that of man, are contrary to the great precept of nature, and therefore of no force or authority.

Resolved, That woman is man's equal—was intended to be so by the Creator, and the highest good of the race demands that she should be recognized as such.

Resolved, That the women of this country ought to be enlightened in regard to the laws under which they live, that they may no longer publish their degradation by declaring themselves satisfied with their present position, nor their ignorance, by asserting that they have all the rights they want.

Resolved, That inasmuch as man, while claiming for himself intellectual superiority, does accord to woman moral superiority, it is pre-eminently his duty to encourage her to speak and teach, as she has an opportunity, in all religious assemblies.

Resolved, That the same amount of virtue, delicacy, and refinement of behavior that is required of woman in the social state, should also be required of man, and the same transgressions should be visited with equal severity on both man and woman.

Resolved, That the objection of indelicacy and impropriety, which is so often brought against woman when she addresses a public audience, comes with a very ill-grace from those who encourage, by their attendance, her appearance on the stage, in the concert, or in feats of the circus.

Resolved, That woman has too long rested satisfied in the circumscribed limits which corrupt customs and a perverted application of the Scriptures have marked out for her, and that it is time she should move in the enlarged sphere which her great Creator has assigned her.

Resolved, That it is the duty of the women of this country to secure to themselves their sacred right to the elective franchise.

Resolved, That the equality of human rights results necessarily from the fact of the identity of the race in capabilities and responsibilities.

Resolved, therefore, That, being invested by the Creator with the same capabilities, and the same consciousness of responsibility for their exercise, it is demonstrably the right and duty of woman, equally with man, to promote every righteous cause by every righteous means; and especially in regard to the great subjects of morals and religion, it is self-evidently her right to participate with her brother in teaching them, both in private and in public, by writing and by speaking, by any instrumentalities proper to be used, and in any assemblies proper to be held; and this being a self-evident truth growing out of the divinely implanted principles of human nature, any custom or authority adverse to it, whether modern or wearing the hoary sanction of antiquity, is to be regarded as a self-evident falsehood, and at war with mankind.

* * *

Resolved, That the speedy success of our cause depends upon the zealous and untiring efforts of both men and women, for the overthrow of the monopoly of the pulpit, and for the securing to woman an equal participation with men in the various trades, professions, and commerce.

Elizabeth Cady Stanton, Susan B. Anthony, and Matilda Joslyn Gage, eds., *History of Woman Suffrage* (New York, 1881), vol. 1, 70–73.

STUDY QUESTIONS

1. Why do you think the authors of the Seneca Falls Declaration of Sentiments chose to model it on the Declaration of Independence? Was this a smart tactic?
2. What "injuries and usurpations" did the Seneca Falls Declaration assert had been perpetrated on American women? What changes did they demand regarding the rights and social positions of women?

A Sign of Progress: Property Rights for Married Women

Although women's suffrage would not be achieved until long after the Civil War, the antebellum women's rights movement achieved some tangible progress by 1860, particularly in the legal realm. Numerous states liberalized their divorce laws, making it easier for women to escape troubled marriages. Several also passed laws allowing married women to maintain control over their own property. While some of these laws had little to do with women's rights and were geared instead toward protecting some of a family's assets from being seized for debt, laws like the one passed in New York State in 1860 were clear responses to agitation by female activists. New York had passed its first married woman's property act in 1848. But the 1860 legislation was more sweeping, giving married women control over their own property, enabling them to keep their own wages, permitting them to file lawsuits and enter contracts, providing for joint custody of children, and generally liberating married women in some significant measure from the near-total legal and economic dependence on their husbands that prevailed for much of the antebellum era. This step was a relatively small one toward true equality and independence for women, and it spoke only in limited measure to many concerns expressed by early feminists or to those of women outside the middle class. Nonetheless, the ability of women to take hold of their own economic destinies, which increased over the course of the nineteenth century, was a vital accomplishment.

New York Married Woman's Property Act (1860)

An Act Concerning the Rights and Liabilities of Husband and Wife. Passed March 20, 1860.

The People of the State of New York, represented in Senate and Assembly, do enact as follows:

SECTION 1. The property, both real and personal, which any married woman now owns, as her sole and separate property; that which comes to her by descent, devise, bequest, gift, or grant; that which she acquires by her trade, business, labor, or services, carried on or performed on her sole or separate account; that which a woman married in this State owns at the time of her marriage, and the rents, issues, and proceeds of all such property, shall notwithstanding her marriage, be and remain her sole and separate property, and may be used, collected, and invested by her in her own name, and shall not be subject to the interference or control of her husband, or liable for his debts, except such debts as may have been contracted for the support of herself or her children, by her as his agent.

§2. A married woman may bargain, sell, assign, and transfer her separate personal property, and carry on any trade or business, and perform any labor or services on her sole and separate account, and the earnings of any married woman from her trade, business, labor, or services shall be her sole and separate property, and may be used or invested by her in her own name.

§3. Any married woman possessed of real estate as her separate property may bargain, sell, and convey such property, and enter into any contract in reference to the same; but no such conveyance or contract shall be valid without the assent, in writing, of her husband, except as hereinafter provided.

§4. In case any married woman possessed of separate real property, as aforesaid, may desire to sell or convey the same, or to make any contract in relation thereto, and shall be unable to procure the assent of her husband as in the preceding section provided, in consequence of his refusal, absence, insanity, or other disability, such married woman may apply to the County Court in the county where she shall at the time reside, for leave to make such sale, conveyance, or contract, without the assent of her husband.

§5. Such application may be made by petition, verified by her, and setting forth the grounds of such application. If the husband be a resident of the county and not under disability from insanity or other cause, a copy of said petition shall be served upon him, with a notice of the time when the same will be presented to the said court, at least ten days before such application. In all other cases, the County Court to which such application shall be made, shall, in its discretion, determine whether any notice shall be given, and if any, the mode and manner of giving it.

§6. If it shall satisfactorily appear to such court, upon application, that the husband of such applicant has willfully abandoned his said wife, and lives separate and apart from her, or that he is insane, or imprisoned as a convict in any state prison, or that he is an habitual drunkard, or that he is in any way disabled from making a contract, or that he refuses to give his consent without good cause therefor, then such court shall cause an order to be entered upon its records, authorizing such married woman to sell and convey her real estate, or contract in regard thereto without the assent of her husband, with the same effect as though such conveyance or contract had been made with his assent.

§7. Any married woman may, while married, sue and be sued in all matters having relation to her property, which may be her sole and separate property, or which may hereafter come to her by descent, devise, bequest, or the gift of any person except her husband, in the same manner as if she were sole. And any married woman may bring and maintain an action in her own name, for damages against any person or body corporate, for any injury to her person or character, the same as if she were sole; and the money received upon the settlement of any such action, or recovered upon a judgment, shall be her sole and separate property.

§8. No bargain or contract made by any married woman, in respect to her sole and separate property, or any property which may hereafter come to her by descent, devise, bequest, or gift of any person except her husband, and no bargain or contract entered into by any married woman in or about the carrying on of any trade or business under the statutes of this State, shall be binding upon her husband, or render him or his property in any way liable therefor.

§9. Every married woman is hereby constituted and declared to be the joint guardian of her children, with her husband, with equal powers, rights, and duties in regard to them, with the husband.

§10. At the decease of husband or wife, leaving no minor child or children, the survivor shall hold, possess, and enjoy a life estate in one-third of all the real estate of which the husband or wife died seized.

§11. At the decease of the husband or wife intestate, leaving minor child or children, the survivor shall hold, possess, and enjoy all the real estate of which the husband or wife died seized, and all the rents, issues, and profits thereof during the minority of the youngest child, and one-third thereof during his or her natural life.

Elizabeth Cady Stanton, Susan B. Anthony, and Matilda Joslyn Gage, eds., *History of Woman Suffrage* (New York, 1881), vol. 1, 686–687.

STUDY QUESTIONS

1. How do you imagine the circumstances of a woman in possession of the rights granted to her by the New York law would differ from those of a woman before the law's passage?
2. Of all the rights and privileges granted by the law, which would you argue was the most important? Which was the least important?

Opposition to Reform

The Naiveté of Reform

At first glance, a man like Orestes Brownson would seem an unlikely candidate to complain about the reform impulse in antebellum America. A New England author, minister, and intellectual, as a young man Brownson was a transcendentalist, supported educational improvements, and even founded a newspaper entitled The Herald of Reform. *As a devout individualist, however, Brownson was uneasy with the potentially controlling aspects of many social reforms, and he became generally more conservative as he grew into middle age. One sign of his discomfort and his growing suspicions of the doctrinaire and unduly optimistic nature of reforms and reformers was "Ultraism," an 1838 essay published in the first volume of his own* Boston Quarterly Review.

Orestes Brownson, Ultraism (1838)

Are not our modern Reformers carrying the joke a little too far? They are becoming, it strikes us, a real annoyance. The land is overspread with them, and matters have come to such a pass, that a peaceable man can hardly venture to eat or drink, to go to bed or to get up, to correct his children or kiss his wife, without obtaining the permission and the direction of some moral or other reform society. * * *

Now this in our judgment is to be philanthropic overmuch. It is making philanthropy altogether too great an annoyance. No real good can come to the community from sacrificing the individual. There are things which an individual ought to be allowed to call his own, and over which he shall have the supreme control. Around each individual there should be traced a circle, within which no stranger should presume or be suffered to enter. It is no service to virtue to keep us all forever in leading-strings. If we are to be men and to show forth the virtues of men, we must be permitted to think and act for ourselves. That philanthropy which proposes to do everything for us, and which will permit us to do nothing of our own accord, may indeed keep us out of harm's way, but it is a left-handed philanthropy, and will be found always to diminish our virtues in the same proportion that it does our vices.

It must joy the heart of every benevolent man to see efforts made for the advancement of Humanity. There is room enough for Reform. But we do wish our modern Reformers would enlarge their conception and seek to add knowledge to their zeal. It is well to be zealously affected in a good cause; but zeal in a good cause, if not guided by just knowledge, may work as much evil as good. The world is not to be regenerated by the exertions of reformers who have but one idea, and who fancy that one idea embraces the Universe. Life is a complex affair. The good and the evil it is subject to are so intermixed, and run one so into the other, that it is often no easy matter to say which is which. There is no one sovereign remedy for all the ills of life, no one rule which is applicable at all times to all cases for the production of good. Good and evil both have their source in human nature. The one cannot be greatly increased, or the other essentially diminished, but in proportion as human nature itself is more fully developed; but in proportion to its general culture and growth. The tree of evil is not destroyed by pruning away a branch here, and a branch there. So long as its root remains in the earth, so long will it live, and flourish. All classes of reformers see and deplore its growth. One class thinks all evils come from the breach of the seventh commandment, another class ascribes them all to the eating of flesh or fish, to the drinking of rum, wine, or cider; this class fancies the world would move on as it should, if women were but allowed equal civil and political rights

with men; that class is sure all things will be restored to primitive
innocence, love, and harmony, the moment negroes are declared to
be no longer slaves; and this other class, when nations shall no longer appeal to arms to decide their disputes. Each of these classes of
reformers mounts its hobby and rides away, condemning all as children of the Past, as wedded to old abuses, as the enemies of truth
and virtue, who will not do the same. But not one or another of
these classes shall succeed. All these classes of evils are mutually
connected, and no one of them can be cured separately. The cause
of them all lies deep in human nature, as now developed, and they
must be regarded as inseparable from the present stage of human
progress. The doctors, who are vaunting their skill to cure them, are
merely prescribing for the symptoms, not the disease. War is a melancholy thing. Philanthropy cannot but weep over its doings. But as
long as the passions of the human heart remain as they are, and the
interests of the world continue in their present complicated state, it
is perfectly idle to talk of the cessation of war. Everything manly in
our nature rises indignant at the bare name of slavery; but should
the negroes be declared free, and all other things remain as they
were, slavery would not be abolished. One of its forms would be
slightly changed, but its substance would continue the same. Give
woman equal civil and political rights with man, and if her present
tastes and culture remain, her influence will be just what it now is.
Intemperance is not a mother-evil. It is the symptom, not the disease. Temperance lectures will not cure it. It will remain in spite of
Temperance Societies, in spite of law, in spite of religion, till the
causes producing it are removed, and men are able to find an innocent source of the excitement they crave. Chastity may be commended, but it will not be universal, till the whole community is so
trained that it can find more pleasure in sentiment than in sense.
The object of each class of reformers is, we are willing to admit,
good, and praiseworthy; but it can in no case be insulated and
gained as a separate object.

The work of reforming the world is a noble one. The progress
of Man and society goes on. But it goes on slowly, much more so
than comports with the desires of our one-idea reformers. These
reformers, with one idea, are no doubt worth something. Each class
of them may contribute something to aid on the work. But no one

of them can do much, or run far ahead of the general average of the race. The evils of life rise as lofty mountains in our path. We cannot go over them, nor turn our course around them. They rise alike before all of our race, and form the same barrier to the onward march of all. We must remove them. If we take ourselves to the work with faith and energy, we can remove them. But we can do it only a little by little. Our generation works its brief day at the task, and worn out gives way to another; another comes and removes its portion, and gives way to yet another. Thus do generations labor, and yet centuries elapse before we can perceive that they have made any impression on the mountain. * * * There may be something sad and depressing in this view. Life is full of deep pathos to the wise man. Sorrow springs from experience. He, who knew most of man and his trials, was said to be a "man of sorrows and acquainted with grief." Man's path from the cradle to his union with God, is not of smooth and easy ascent, strewed with flowers, and shaded by groves from which the sweet songsters are ever warbling their wild notes. It is steep and rugged, and we ascend not without labor and difficulty. Yet is there no cause for complaint. Man has some strength; let him use it, and not murmur because he has also some weakness. Something he can do; let him do it, and complain not that there is something he cannot do. * * *

We have no fellowship with the philosophy, that teaches us to regard with indifference the efforts of a single individual, however puny, to advance the cause of humanity. True philosophy teaches us to find a sufficient reason for whatever occurs, and to see good in everything. We ought therefore never to condemn outright any class of reformers, or plan of reform, we may meet; but we cannot refrain from regarding most of the reformers who fill our age and country as extremely short-sighted, and their plans as most wofully defective. We would not make war upon them, nor in our sober moments treat them otherwise than with great tenderness; but we cannot bring ourselves to act with them. Whoever would pass for a man of correct feelings, and of some degree of philosophic wisdom, must see and deplore the ills that afflict himself and brethren; he must labor with all his might to cure them; but he will proceed always calmly, with chastened hopes, and with the conviction that the only way to cure many evils is to bear them. The lesson, To

Bear, though difficult to learn, and one that many of us never do learn, is one of the lessons most essential to man in his earthly pilgrimage. Even these evils, of which we complain, may be made the ministers of our virtues and the means of our spiritual growth.

The human race makes its way through the centuries, step by step, to its destiny. The evils we now see and feel will one day be removed. But new evils we know not of will doubtless spring up, new mountains arise whose highest peaks are not yet seen in the distant horizon. The lessons of the reformer will be ever repeated, and his trials, labors, sufferings, martyrdom, ever renewed. Well, be it so. The brave spirit will not shrink from the prospect. Life is a struggle. Who would that it should not be? It is from this struggle that Humanity derives her strength, obtains possession of her powers; in it she finds her life; in it she lives; by it she fulfills her destiny. Let us accept it as our heritage, and go forth with strong arms and stout hearts,—and yet not with over sanguine expectations of wonders to be achieved,—to the work that lieth nearest us in time and space, and leave the result to Him in whose hands we and all things are, and with whom it rests to grant or withhold success.

Boston Quarterly Review, July 1838, pp. 379–384.

STUDY QUESTIONS

1. Why did Brownson feel that reformers who focused on any one particular cause were doomed to failure? Would you say Brownson was pessimistic about social improvement and human progress more generally?
2. Do you agree with Brownson's assertion that reform posed a threat to individualism?

Reformer "Radicalism" as a Source of Ridicule

If Orestes Brownson admired the spirit of reform but found reformers themselves unduly optimistic and somewhat overbearing, others were far less chari-

table. This cartoon, published in the months leading up to the 1856 presidential election, blasts the new Republican Party as a "reform party" and makes the case that its candidate, John Fremont, would cater to the demands of fanatics if elected. Presenting black abolitionists, women's rights advocates, utopian socialists, and other reformers as ludicrous, intrusive, and dangerous, the artist effectively deployed the sorts of caricatures that simultaneously amused and enraged Americans hostile to reform.

The Great Republican Reform Party, Calling on Their Candidate (illustration, 1856)

(*Wikimedia Commons*)

From left to right:

"The first thing we want is a law making the use of Tobacco, Animal food and Lager-bier a Capital Crime."

"We demand, first of all; the recognition of Woman as the equal of man with a right to Vote and hold Office."

"An equal division of Property, that is what I go in for."

"Col., I wish to invite you to the next meeting of our Free Love association, where the shackles of marriage are not tolerated & perfect freedom exists in love matters and you will be sure to Enjoy yourself, for we are all Freemounters."

"We look to you Sir to place the power of the Pope on a firm footing in this Country."

"De Poppylation ob Color comes in first—arter dat, you may do wot you pleases."

"You shall all have what you desire, and be sure that the glorious Principles of Popery, Fourierism, Free Love, Woman's rights, the Maine Law, & above all the Equality of our Colored brethren, shall be maintained; if I get into the Presidential Chair."

STUDY QUESTIONS

1. What devices and visual techniques does the artist use in this cartoon to ridicule reformers and their proposals?
2. Do you think the message of this cartoon is effective? Do you think it would have persuaded many people not to vote Republican in 1856?

Protests against Religion and Reform

Some opposition to reform activities was rooted in the explicit religiosity of many movements and their supporters. Catholics, for example, not infrequently resented the extent to which reformers infused public school lessons with Protestantism (and sometimes with overt anti-Catholicism) and associated Irish immigrants with drunkenness. Other Americans, particularly those of a more conservative bent, found the evangelical foundations of many reforms inherently suspicious. Still others were hostile to the ways some reformers sought to project their particu-

lar religious morality onto the broader American population. In the first selection below, an evangelical publication describes what it found to be a disturbing tide of anger rising against the religious bent of the temperance movement, particularly in communities that depended economically on manufacturing grain alcohol. In the second selection, meanwhile, a contributor to a Universalist magazine rails against the Sabbatarian movement as a direct assault on the civil liberties of American citizens.

Anti-Temperance Societies (1833)

The proscriptive measures and overweening zeal of many temperance societies are causing a reaction, which, I fear, will be as repugnant to the principles of moderation, and injurious to the *cause* of temperance, as is the extreme which produces it. Created by public opinion, and borne along triumphantly by the enlightened good sense of the reading and reflecting public, the temperance societies have forgotten that they are the *created*, and assume the honor of *creating*. Believing that *they* have formed public opinion, (and not that public opinion has formed *them*,) they proceed as if their resolving any thing, established it—as if their saying a thing *was* so, made up the public opinion that it was *even so*. The thing created has thus endeavored to govern the thing that created it. Oppugnance, reaction and opposition must and will be the result.

* * *

Some months ago, a very large and respectable county meeting was held in Virginia, for the express purpose of putting down temperance societies. They believed them dangerous to the welfare of the commonwealth, and the liberties of the people—not ostensibly, but in reality. In some towns, (in Massachusetts, I believe,) the temperance societies had resolved to deal with, and vote for "temperance men," in preference to any others. Large and respectable meetings were held by persons not members of the societies, and the proscriptive measures retaliated. Resolutions were passed that they would not deal with, or vote for, members of temperance societies, when others could be found suitable, as traders, professional men, or officers. * * *

But the work has not stopped here. I have before me a paper, friendly to temperance societies, which contains the proceedings of a large and respectable anti-temperance society meeting, held on the 12th ult., in Wolf's church, West Manchester township, York county, Pa., in the reports and resolutions of which they contend that the distillation of grain and fruit is, on the whole, productive of more benefit than injury to community—that the use of alcohol in the mechanic arts, and as a medicine, demands the continuance of the practice—that the suppression of this branch of manufactures and commerce would be of incalculable injury to the grain growing districts—and that the measures of proscriptive temperance societies are injurious to the social, pecuniary, political and religious well being of community.

They adopt retaliatory measures, and, as will be seen by the following resolutions, extracted from among several others in their proceedings, roll back the stream on temperance societies. Their measures are *ultra* indeed; as much so as the extreme against which they contend.

Resolved, That we are compelled to consider the members of temperance societies as having arrayed themselves in hostility against the best interests of the farmer and mechanic. We, therefore, will withhold our patronage and support from ministers of the Gospel, who thus impertinently interfere with our secular concerns, in direct opposition to their more sacred and exclusive functions—and also from merchants, mechanics and others—embracing all who have engaged in this unholy crusade against the most productive branch of our agriculture.

Resolved, That in our opinion, the clergy, who generally head, foster and encourage temperance societies, seek to extend priestly influence, to subserve their own selfish purposes, by enslaving the minds of the people, by bringing them under the influence of blind bigotry and narrow superstition. That by such conduct, they become the unworthy servants of that Redeemer who has given us a pure and undefiled religion.

To these proceedings the names of three hundred and twenty persons—two of them clergymen, I believe, the most of them respectable farmers and mechanics, and several of them physicians, respectable as professional men, and all of them respectable as citizens—are attached. Will not all acknowledge that the reaction has commenced at last.

———————

Evangelical Magazine and Gospel Advocate, December 21, 1833.

People of the United States! (1828)

Look to your civil liberties! A large association has recently been formed in New-York, called the "General Union for promoting the observance of the Sabbath." It is composed of clergy and lay-men of high character and influence, and of different denominations of Christians, but principally of Calvinists, from Georgia to Maine. They have formed a constitution, and organized themselves into a grand national establishment.

The 6th article of the constitution is as follows, viz: "Any person may become a member of this 'Union' by subscribing the constitution and signing the following *pledge*:" "We whose names are under-signed, do hereby acknowledge our obligation to keep the Sabbath according to the Scriptures, and we pledge ourselves to each other, and to the Christian public, to refrain from all secular employments on that day—from travelling in Steam Boats, Stages, Canal Boats, or otherwise, except in cases of necessity or mercy, and to aim at dis-charging the duties of that *sacred day*. And also that we will, as circum-stance, will admit, *encourage and give a preference* to those lines of *conveyance, whose owners do not employ them on the Sabbath day*." What is to be the end of these things? Are we determined to assist us in forging the chains which are to enslave us, and fondly to rush into the arms of the specious image whose embrace is death?

The secret moving spring of all this amalgamation of efforts is distinctly seen, and its course will be watched and arrested with all the means which is left us, from this vast monopoly of *piety and intelligence*.

The public must certainly perceive that this proscription does not include only the mass of proprietors of steam boats, stages, canal boats, &c. &c. established for public facility and accommoda-tion, and for the convenience too of these very gentlemen (as it ever has and will be found) when interest or other motives dictate; but that in proscribing men for pursuing their lawful and laudable callings, they at the same time proscribe liberty of conscience and opinion; for all Christians do not think alike in regard to the Sabbath day. Now let me ask of my fellow citizens, and call upon them to think for themselves on this important subject, if such a combination, extending as this does, over the Union, is left to the exercise of a proscriptive power over us, while in the pursuit of those callings to which this country is very largely indebted for its present prosperity—what effect it may have upon our elections, in cases where men, eminently qualified for office, may not happen to concur in opinion with this powerful religious combination, of which very striking examples may be produced? Does not such a combination tend ultimately to the inquiry at the polls as to the religious qualifications of the candidates, and whether they are *strict* observers of the SABBATH, AND WILL PROMOTE THE PASSAGE OF LAWS FOR COMPELLING THE MORE RIGID OBSERVANCE OF THAT DAY? Therefore, fellow citizens, look to your civil liberties. No matter whether they be invaded by a single or combined hierarchy.

Trumpet and Universalist Magazine, August 2, 1828.

STUDY QUESTIONS
1. Why did some Americans oppose temperance societies? How did the author of the article on antitemperance sentiments suggest that temperance reformers were at least partially to blame for the backlash?
2. Why did opponents of Sabbatarianism see that movement as a threat to civil liberties? Were they right?

Female Opposition to Feminism

Although antebellum abolitionists and feminists generally advocated positions with which few modern Americans would quibble, among their contemporaries they aroused perhaps more opposition than any other reformers. In questioning the justice of race and gender hierarchies that many in the antebellum era believed provided stability and were in keeping with God's will, supporters of these movements seemed to threaten the foundations of society and were considered among the most radical people in the United States. Antagonism was especially fierce in the South, where whites believed slavery and a patriarchal family model to be cardinal elements of the region's social order. In her ironically titled poem, "Woman's Progress," South Carolina author and plantation mistress Louisa McCord blasts female supporters of women's rights for stepping so far out of their proper roles as to betray the very essence of what it meant to be a woman.

Louisa McCord, Woman's Progress (1853)

And is this progress!—Are these noisy tongues—
In fierce contention raised and angry war—
Fit boast for womanhood? You shrewish things,
In wordy boisterous debate,—are these
Perfected woman's exponents to show
Her model virtues to a later age?
And shall our daughters cast their woman robes,
A useless cumbrance aside, to seize
Some freer imitation of the man,
Whose lordly strut and dashing stride attract
Their envious love for notoriety?
Shall they, with flashing eye and clanging tongue,
Mount in the rostrum, lecture in the streets,
And, in the arena of election strife,
Claim with shrill voice, and rude dishevelled locks,
"Your votes! your votes!" ye loud-mouthed populace!
Nay;—should that peach-like cheek but feel the breath
Of yonder foul-mouthed crowd, methinks its bloom
Should wither in the contact. God hath made
A woman-nature holier than the man's—
Purer of impulse, and of gentler mould,—
Let her not stain it in the angry strife

Which these, our modern female Reverends,
Learned M.D's, and lecturing damsels, seek
To feed their hungry vanity, and bring
Unnoticed charms before the gaping crowd.
'Tis surely not for this that God hath given
That soothing voice so sweetly taught to whisper
Pity, and hope, and sympathy, and love,
And every holier thought, whose gospel tongue
Can preach its comfort to grief's riven heart!
Here, in the crowd, 'tis harsh and dissonant;
Its softer notes must struggle to a scream
Of impotently shrill, unmeaning effort.

*　*　*

Sweet Sister! stoop not thou to be a man!
Man has his place as woman hers; and she
As made to comfort, minister and help;
Moulded for gentler duties, ill fulfils
His jarring destinies. Her mission is
To labour and to pray; to help, to heal,
To soothe, to bear; patient, with smiles, to suffer;
And with self-abnegation nobly lose
Her private interest in the dearer weal
Of those she loves and lives for. Call not this—
(The all-fulfilling of her destiny;
She the world's soothing mother)—call it not,
With scorn and mocking sneer, a drudgery.
The ribald tongue profanes Heaven's holiest things,
But holy still they are. The lowliest tasks
Are sanctified in nobly acting them.

*　*　*

Sweet Sisters! thus
God wills that we should be; and who profanes
This, the last formed, so the most perfect work
Of His creative will,—this woman nature,—
Who seeks to drag it down, to smirch and blot
Its purer being with the tainting blight
Of passion's license,—doth profane the hope
Of God's creation; doth blot out the light;

Sully the purest beam of reasoning life,
And cast man's nature back upon the beast
To strive and grovel in the lowest lusts
Of passion's vile excess. As God is love,
So reasoning nature lives in him through love;
And Woman in the trueness of her being
Is still the never-ceasing minister
Of love which wearies not, which toils and bears,
And sorrowing for the loved ones, doth forget
Her own life's anguish, soothing others' woes.
Then let our holy task be still to cleanse.
But not to change our natures. Let us strive
To be *more* woman,—never to be man.
These reverend Misses, doctors in mob caps,
And petticoated lecturers, are things
Which make us loathe, like strange unnatural births,
Nature's disordered works. You chirping thing
That with cracked voice, and mincing manners, prates
Of rights and duties, lecturing to the crowd,
And in strange nondescript of dress arrays
Unfettered limbs that modesty should hide;
Thus raising, as it were, rebellion's flag
Against her being's nature—call it not,
Sweet Sisters, call not that unsexed thing
By the pure name of Woman. Let us strive
With silent effort in the Woman's cause,
Perfecting in its destinies, our sex,
And cast aside this foul attempt which clings
To degradation as it were our pride.

* * *

Gentle, pure,
Kind, loving Woman, never can degrade
Her own God-given nature. Only then
When she distorts it to unnatural ends
Doth she degrade her being. Man may rail,
Or mock, or pity her; with tyrant strength
May trample on her weakness, or may sneer
As though his being were of higher mould;

But not for this is she degraded; rather
Ennobled, in the gently bearing it.
There is no degradation which springs not
From our own inmost being. Noble things
Are never trampled into meanness. Low
May be their uses, but vile purposes
Soil not the diamond's hue. Our inmost worth,
At our own heart's tribunal, rights itself,
And e'en midst persecution calmly rests
On its proud consciousness. A noble thing
Is woman's undistorted nature. Let
No taunt, nor jeer, sweet Sisters, shame us from it.
Woman, true Woman, is of larger worth
Than rank or power can fashion. Far above
All that the loud reformer ever dreamed,
Her virtues are no wordy theories,
But sky-born instincts touching on our earth
Still in full flower from Heaven.

Southern Literary Messenger, November 1853.

STUDY QUESTIONS

1 How did Louisa McCord characterize women's rights activists? What sorts of behaviors and beliefs did she think set them apart from women who lived in keeping with their "nature"?
2. Does it surprise you that many women opposed the antebellum feminist movement? How did Louisa McCord's understanding of women and their roles differ from that of her fellow South Carolinian, Sarah Grimké?

Northerners Condemn Abolitionism

Hostility to abolitionism was hardly restricted to the South. Even most white northerners opposed antislavery activism, fearing its consequences for both na-

tional unity and racial order. Throughout the North, abolitionists periodically faced physical assault and sometimes saw their presses destroyed and their meetings disrupted by mobs. Particularly controversial was the postal campaign abolitionists launched in 1835, during which they mailed more than a million pieces of abolitionist propaganda to the South. Terrifying and enraging white southerners, the postal campaign also prompted a wave of protest meetings throughout the North. In dozens of cities and towns, white northerners gathered to express their opposition to abolitionists and their tactics and to show their solidarity with white southerners. At a large meeting hall in Philadelphia in August 1835, for example, an overflow crowd adopted the following resolutions.

Anti-Abolition Meeting at Philadelphia (1835)

Whereas, The indiscreet and improper interference of certain individuals of the north with the domestic relations of the slaveholding states of the south, having endangered the peace of our fellow citizens of that section of our common country, and excited apprehensions and prejudices injurious to the union; and whereas, the citizens of the south having appealed to their brethren of the non-slaveholding states to manifest their disapprobation of the measures referred to, and to rescue them from the incendiary efforts of those who make our territory the seat of a warfare upon the domestic institutions of the south, therefore,

Resolved, That we respond to the call of our brethren of the south, that we *are* their brethren, and, as such, sympathize in their dangers and wrongs, and view with regret and indignation the incendiary measures which have disturbed their tranquillity.

Resolved, That we consider the course of the abolitionists in organizing societies, maintaining agents and disseminating publications intended to operate upon the institutions of the south as unwise, dangerous and deserving the emphatic reprehension and zealous opposition of every friend of peace and the country.

Resolved, That we distinctly disclaim any and all right to interfere, directly or indirectly, with the subject of slavery in the southern states; and that any action upon it by us would be a bold violation of the constitution, and a presumptuous infraction of the rights of the south.

Resolved, That were it our unquestioned right to participate in the regulation of slavery at the south, convinced of the justice and liberality of our southern brethren, and believing that their practical acquaintance with and deep interest in the subject peculiarly qualify them to determine questions arising from it, we would, without fear or hesitation, commit it to their wisdom, justice and humanity.

Resolved, That we regard the union of this country as inseparable from its freedom, greatness and glory; that we consider no sacrifice too great to maintain it, and shrink with horror from all that is calculated in the most remote degree to endanger or impair it.

Resolved, That the course of the abolitionists, by exciting the prejudices of the people of the south, against the communities from which they are assailed, menaces the peace and permanence of this union.

Resolved, That as the people of the south alone have the power to emancipate their slaves, the irritating policy of the incendiaries renders that happy result more remote and difficult of attainment, and rivets, perhaps forever, those chains which they affect a desire to break.

Resolved, That the interference of the abolitionists with the slavery of the south, must inevitably multiply at once the dangers and suspicions of the master, and render necessary a heightened degree of vigilance and security, thus heaping additional restraints upon the bondman, and increasing the afflictions of the object of their misguided efforts.

Resolved, That we regard the dissemination of incendiary publications throughout the slaveholding states with indignation and horror; that measures so directly calculated to involve results at which humanity shudders, cannot fail to meet the hearty and indignant reprobation of the benevolent and patriotic; and that efficient, but legal and moderate measures should be adopted to suppress an evil at once so dangerous and disgraceful.

Resolved, That the obnoxious measures of the abolitionists having produced great and general excitement at the north, have already disturbed the peace of our cities, and threaten consequences still more extended and deplorable.

Resolved, That the efforts of foreign emissaries, paid with foreign money, and sent into the country to assail our institutions, malign our patriots, excite our people and distract our country, are regarded by all who cherish American pride and patriotism, with distrust and contempt.

Resolved, That should the colored population of the south, excited by the causes referred to or by any other, unhappily revolt against the laws and the lives of our southern brethren, (which heaven in its mercy avert), the young men of the north are prepared to meet the danger, shoulder to shoulder with the people of the south, and prove by the ready sacrifice of their blood, their devotion to the peace and rights of all parts of our beloved union.

Resolved, That we recommend to the legislature of Pennsylvania, to enact at the next session, such provisions as will protect our fellow citizens of the south from incendiary movements within our borders, should any such thereafter be made.

Resolved, That the north is sound to the core on the subject of slavery; that the mass of the people of the non-slaveholding states, neither claim nor desire a right to interfere with the institutions of the south; and regard with decided and marked disapprobation the principles and measures of the abolitionists.

Resolved, That we confidently believe the number and influence of those in this state, who are disposed to agitate the subject of slavery in the south, are extremely limited; and that the individuals in this city who are recognised as abolitionists, are, for the most part, wholly disinclined to any and all measures which may tend to excite or endanger the south.

Resolved, That we have reason to believe that there is no abolition press or publication in this city, and that no incendiary measures have been adopted or sanctioned by the friends of emancipation in this state.

Resolved, That we regard those, who, under the pretense of putting down abolition, have violated the laws, and disturbed the peace of the community, as the most efficient auxiliaries of the cause they affect to oppose; that the young men of Philadelphia, opposed to the measures of the abolitionists, pledge themselves, on the first symptoms of disturbance, to lend their hearty and determined aid to arrest and secure the legal punishment of those who degrade their cause by violence and outrage.

Niles' Weekly Register, August 29, 1835.

STUDY QUESTIONS

1. Why did the attendees at the Philadelphia meeting oppose abolitionism? What were their opinions about slavery itself?
2. What did those attending the meeting have to say about the popularity of abolitionism in Philadelphia in particular? Why do you think they felt making that argument was so important?

FURTHER READINGS

Abzug, Robert H. *Cosmos Crumbling: American Reform and the Religious Imagination* (1994).

Barnes, Gilbert H. *The Anti-Slavery Impulse, 1830–1844* (1933).

Boyer, Paul. *Urban Masses and Moral Order in America, 1820–1920* (1992).

Boylan, Anne M. *The Origins of Women's Activism: New York and Boston, 1797–1840* (2001).

Craven, Avery O. *The Coming of the Civil War* (1942).

Dorsey, Bruce. *Reforming Men and Women: Gender in the Antebellum City* (2002).

Fish, Carl Russell. *The Rise of the Common Man, 1830–1850* (1927).

Foster, Charles. *An Errand of Mercy: The Evangelical United Front, 1790–1837* (1960).

Ginzburg, Lori D. *Women in Antebellum Reform* (2000).

Griffin, Clifford S. *The Ferment of Reform, 1830–1860* (1967).

———.*Their Brothers' Keepers: Moral Stewardship in the United States, 1800–1835* (1960).

Harden, Glenn M. *Men and Women of Their Own Kind: Historians and Antebellum Reform* (2003).

Hewitt, Nancy A. *Women's Activism and Social Change: Rochester, New York, 1822–1872* (1984).

Johnson, Paul E. *A Shopkeeper's Millennium: Society and Revivals in Rochester, New York, 1815–1837* (1978).

Mintz, Steven. *Moralists and Modernizers: America's Pre–Civil War Reformers* (1995).

Quist, John W. *Restless Visionaries: The Social Roots of Antebellum Reform in Alabama and Michigan* (1998).

Schlesinger, Arthur M. Sr. *The American as Reformer* (1951).

Tyler, Alice Felt. *Freedom's Ferment: Phases of American Social History to 1860* (1944).

Walters, Ronald G. *American Reformers, 1815–1860* (1978).

INDEX

233